the **KGB BAR** nonfiction reader

D0429791

12/25/04

John —

Thanks for the free
editing & advice.

Merry Christmas!

Mike

the KGB BAR

nonfiction reader

Edited by Mark Jacobson

Series editor: Denis Woychuk

NATION BOOKS

NEW YORK

THE KGB BAR NONFICTION READER

Published by
Nation Books
An Imprint of Avalon Publishing Group
245 West 17th St., 11th Floor
New York, NY 10011

AVALON
publishing group incorporated

Nation Books is a co-publishing venture of the Nation Institute and Avalon
Publishing Group Incorporated.

Library of Congress Cataloging-in-Publication Data

ISBN 1-56025-601-X

The KGB Bar is located at 85 East 4th Street, New York, NY 10003

9 8 7 6 5 4 3 2 1

Book design by Paul Paddock
Printed in the United States of America
Distributed by Publishers Group West

CONTENTS

INTRODUCTION

The nonfiction reading series at the famous KGB Bar did not begin at the KGB. It began, in the winter of 1992, in my living room, in Brooklyn—across the river from Manhattan, for those who don't know. Nowadays, due to the shark-like forward motion of New York City's real estate market, Brooklyn, at least in parts, is considered hip. A place to be. This was not exactly the case in 1992 when I moved out there with my family into a neighborhood which was then called South Brooklyn, a longtime home to firemen, sanitation workers, and other less-than-flush civil servants. Soon after our arrival, however, real estate agents re-nomenclatured the area to fit under the ever expanding rubric of "Park Slope," a label which enables price increases on all items, houses, taxes, and cans of cat food included. This was one more urban irony, as all we wanted was to move somewhere cheap where you got more for your money than living in a crummy one-bedroom apartment with no sink in the bathroom on Manhattan's Lower East Side.

One of the major problems we encountered after moving was getting most of our writer friends to come visit us. Back then, Brooklyn, despite being the birthplace of Joseph Heller, Norman Mailer, and Woody Allen, as well as the one-time home of Walt Whitman, was not considered somewhere writers would want to hang out or be seen, even when researching plots for *Saturday Night Fever*–style movies. This group included journalists, generally among the least toney of people identifying themselves as "writers." Not happy to drink, or write, alone, I decided to take steps. This was the genesis of what became the KGB series: it was a trick to get people to hop on the F train, then regarded as a bad neighborhood on wheels, to visit us at least once a month, always on the first Wednesday.

Many writers did come. Some were friends of mine, people I knew from what is now going on three decades of working primarily for New York City–based magazines and newspapers like *New York*, *The Village Voice*, *Esquire*, *Rolling Stone*, and many others. Some writers we didn't know, but they came, too, far more willingly than I would have imagined. They sat on our couch and read their work.

Besides the (limited) quantity of free beers and the (always) fabulous hospitality, the reason they came became quickly apparent. This was because journalists and nonfiction writers in general, despite their well-honed images as either secretive men or women of streets both foreign and domestic, city-room drones, info hoarders, studious academic types, or semi-elegant essayists, like to hear the sound of their own voices as much as the next egomaniacal, passive-aggressive scrivener. Maybe even more, since until quite recently journalists rarely read aloud.

Throughout recent history it has been no problem to hear deranged, drunken poets of varying abilities screeching their arch and moldy verses on the subway, or in espresso bars backed by atonal jazz. Open mikes for fiction writers have been a purple-prose scourge throughout the land since invention of electricity. But beyond the infernal spin of TV pundits, rarely are newsmen, magazine writers, and essayists heard reading what they've written.

This seemed a something of an injustice, as most of the really good writers I know—most of the writers I know, to be honest—produce nonfiction much of the time. This is almost exclusively work for hire. That is, they get paid to write. This is key. After all, there any number of reasons why someone might want to write: for truth, justice, the American way, etc., etc. Fools have even been known to write "to express themselves," there being nothing (yet) in the First Amendment to prevent it. For me, however, writing for a living—*real* writing, as in not ad copy—has always been the most honorable reason to put pen to paper and/or ham fist to computer keyboard. It shows true commitment, develops a thick skin, and enters the writer into a negotiation with the reader which allows for elitism-smacking give and take that bespeaks of best qualities of this nation.

Writing for a living has its drawbacks, of course. The annals of literature are rife with letters by Mark Twain and Joseph Conrad, written to publishers in attempts to get paid. For working writers, such hectoring letters, e-mails, and phone calls are often a way of life. Sometimes the money in question isn't all that much. Indeed, among the many koans of the free-lance world, it is an unassailable fact that the less they pay you, the worse they treat you. Produce some corporate copy off the top of your head in a taxi, and you will be compensated royally and rapidly. Kill yourself, risk your life to compile something you really care about even if the pay is low, and you will be waiting for that check deep into the next calendar year. But you must get paid. Even if its only a couple of hundred bucks: *It is the principle of the thing!* Writing is not an easy job to do well. So, as a member of this long-suffering, yet truth-seeking crew, it behooved me to give my comrades a voice, a public hearing. If, that is, they were willing to come to Brooklyn.

Four individuals read on the first night of the series. The order is lost in the mists of time, but the people, and the subject matter, remain in memory as clear as an incessantly ringing bell. There was voodooist, cultural explainer/shouter Darius James, who would become a KGB regular (his work appears in this volume), reading from his esteemed, eccentric, phantasmagoric history of 1970s black cinema, *That's Blaxploitation*. Also present was E. Jean Carroll, the now former TV hostess and current psychosocial etiquettist, dipping into her extensive analysis of the life and times of Hunter S. Thompson. Another regular, Michael Taussig (also represented here), Columbia professor and author of books with such deep-dish titles as *Mimesis and Alterity*, read about his extensive, hair-raising anthropological inquiries into the gangster/snake/mysterium-ridden interior of the Putamayan Amazon. I read from a just-finished piece about my trip to India in order to have a one-hour conversation with Dalai Lama, getting a laugh or two when I recalled how His Holiness seemed to take grand delight in calling "Is that right, Jackupson?" across a crowded room of pilgrims.

This was more or less the template for the evenings. While most readings would have one or two authors, we would have five or six, as many as the listeners could stand. We would have no "theme" evenings, no "authors on sports," no "three views on the future of the electoral process." We were against such puerile groupings. The idea was to make it as chaotic and crammed as possible, touching on as many seemingly unrelated mix-and-match topics as we could. We wanted to make it as much like the mythical magazine we wished would arrive through our mail slot every month. The fact that such general magazines were gradually disappearing—either due to finances, over-consolidation in the business, or sheer bad taste—added a kind of urgency to the enterprise.

Overall, however, the notion was that it should be *interesting*. For, the truth be told, although we have presented some of the best prose stylists to emerge in the past several decades (people like Jimmy Breslin, Budd Schulberg, Susan Orlean, David Remnick, and John Berendt, who stopped by one early evening to read parts of his as-yet-unfinished *Midnight in the Garden of Good and Evil*) and played host to numerous "special guests" who felt they had something they wanted read (polymath country singer Steve Earle, jazzman Matthew Shipp, and boxing trainer Teddy Atlas), we have also had a number of readers (thankfully, not too many) who, in the words of some unnamed but laudably cynical city-room desk man, "could not write a suicide note."

The saving grace of such desultory prose was that the pieces were at least about something *interesting*. This is a beauty of a nonfiction reading series. You ask the reader, Well, what's the thing about? and unlike a fiction writer who will start hemming and hawing about tone, color, and the unutterable enigma of it all, the journalist/essayist can say, "Well, its about stealing money in the oil industry in Azerbaijan." Or "the huckster plot to saw Manhattan in half in the nineteenth century." Or "Vietnamese youth gangs." Or "my father's funeral." Or "how Nixon watched George C. Scott in *Patton* every night." Or "how people have holes drilled in the middle of their forehead to open their third eye and it's really popular among rich people in Sedona, Arizona, who have outgrown Botox."

Then you can say, "Well, that sounds *interesting*."

The series met in my living room for a couple of years until some joker from the local *New York Observer* snuck in and wrote a piece about it in a round-up they did on New York "literary salons." Like the mobster chef who reads an unsoliticited review of his small, out-of-the-way restaurant in the *New York Times,* this publicity did not come as welcome news. First, the ceilings in our house are far too low to be thought of as a place to hold a salon. Secondly, we did not want people we didn't know arriving on the first Wednesday of every month and acting as if they had a right to be there, like they were *invited.*

The fact was, they were not invited. We did not want foreign mouths on our beer bottles, or alien cigarette butts crushed into our dinner plates. We did not want to cater to individuals who felt an obligation to raise their hands following a reading to ask idiot questions or make intemperate comments. If a reader wanted to entertain questions he could do that on his own time, but we were not running an open Q-and-A session. In our series people read and then they sat down to make room for the next reader. If there was any further business to be taken up, say a few near-fistfights over the content of an article on the Irish Republican Army, well, let those bozos go out in the street. Besides, I was sick of buying all the beers.

Eventually we went looking for another place to hold the readings. After pit stops at a number of coffee shops, a couple

of bars in Greenwich Village, and a bizarre sojourn at a shut-
tered hair salon (finally, a *real* salon) we arrived at the KGB,
where we have been, every first Wednesday of the month, for
the past seven years.

It has been a copacetic scene here, up the funky marble
stairs, inside the well aged bar, with its black and red painted
walls and its communist memorabilia. As has been noted
before, the building was once the central meeting spot for the
Ukrainian Communist Party. When the current proprietor
and our benefactor, Denis Woychuk, took over he simply put
all the commie-now-perfectly-kitsch stuff up on the walls and
had himself one of the most unassailably ambient bars in New
York. This especially suited one of our readers, Fred Jerome,
the son of V. J. Jerome, once a high-ranking official in the U.S.
Communist Party. "Just like home," he said.

Even for the non-commies among us, the playfully subver-
sive vibe has always seemed normal. It has been a good match,
especially since Denis, who once strode the mighty lectern
himself to read from *Attorney for the Damned,* his memoir
about his former career as a lawyer for the criminally insane
(which describes his defense of Daniel Rakowitz, famous for
making a stew of his murdered girlfriend and feeding it to the
neighborhood homeless people), has always been supportive
of our cause.

"I dig you," said the impresario of the KGB and presenter
of many other somewhat more structured readings, "because
you guys are so *flex.*"

Of course, the readings are now "open to the public," even
if many of the same people show up time after time. A goodly

number of these were present back in the Brooklyn days and their continued attendance is an enduring blessing. Some of them are readers, some are listeners. If you've got readers, you've got to have listeners, or at least people who can fake it. Outside of discouraging readings longer than twenty minutes, we only have one rule: If you read early in the evening, you can't walk out on the other writers without a really, really good excuse. It is a rule somewhat in the manner of Nelson Algren's rules about never playing poker with a man named Doc, never taking the top newspaper, never eating at a place named "Mom's." But it is a rule nonetheless. That, and tip the bartender, the great Dan C.

Along with the fact that now the beers cost money, some things have changed over the years. We have added the yearly Journo-Slam, always on the first Wednesday of May. (One year the date fell on May 1, and "May Day at the KGB" was simply too rich an opportunity not to do something different.) On that day anyone who had appeared previously (we do have some quality control) is invited to read for five minutes or less. Although we champion the long-form nonfictional narrative, a journalist must be able to get his point across fast in this attention-deficient world we live in. A giant gong sounds at the end of every reader's five minutes and no more blather is allowed.

But for the most part the series remains unchanged in both ethos and method from its inception. A couple of months ago we had a fairly representative meeting. Appearing were Elizabeth Royte, who read from her new book detailing the way New York City gets rid of its fourteen tons of solid waste every day—the *tao* of garbage. This was followed by Thomas Goltz, who held forth (Goltz always holds forth, never exactly reads) from his book about war in a small town in Chechnya. Then came Bart Plantenga and his yodelers, who helped illustrate his reading from his recent tome on "Will There Be Yodelling in Heaven?" After him was Blue—just *Blue*—whom we encountered on the subway selling his "observant prose poetry real life tales" and invited to speak his particular truth.

Most people thought the evening pretty good, offering a decent array of topics and points of view. It was, as everyone agreed, *interesting*.

Interesting and *fun*. At least for me, it is always fun. For this let me thank everyone who has shown up over the years. These would include (and forgive me if I've forgotten anyone): J. Hoberman, Elizabeth Royte, Blue, Daniel Racciato, John Berendt, Henry Bean, Wayne Barrett, Marshall Berman, Steve Fishman, Marcelle Clements, David Century, Joan Acocella, Michael Pollan, Natalie Angier, Amy Waldman, Bart Plantenga, Steve Roderick, Julian Dibbell, Fred Jerome, Tom Robbins, Budd Schulberg, Kit Reed, Robert Christgau, Will Hylton, Benjamin De Mott, Richard Goldstein, Neal Medlyn, Teddy Atlas, Tom Perotta, Danny Goldberg, John Berendt, Alan Bergman, Austin Bunn, Lynne Harris, James Hamilton, Jack Newfield, Jimmy Breslin, Michael Daly, Jim Dwyer, Joyce Wadler, Ivan Solotaroff, Paul Solotaroff, Viv Walt, Leslie Savan, Rae Jacobson, Legs McNeil, Josh Max, Peter Noel, Guy Trebay, David Herndon, Jon Langford, Steve Earle, Fab 5 Freddy, Peter Schjeldahl, David Remnick, Antony La Page, Susan Dominas, Kevin Blish, Charlie LeDuff, Scott Malcolmson, Rick Perelstein, Mickey Persson, Antonin Kratochvil, Scott Thode, Elizabeth Kaye, Lucius Shepard, Greg Tate, Neal de Grasse Tyson, Douglas Daly, Peter Rabbit, Irwin

Chusid, Ted Conover, Mary Cory, Luc Sante, Peter Coyote, Chip Brown, Jack Hollins, Bob Reiss, Joel Rose, E. Jean Carroll, Joyce Carol Oates, Cathleen Schine, David Bowman, Guy Martin, Rev. Jen Miller, Erik Davis, Nicholas Dawidoff, Thomas Goltz, Andrew Corasello, Catherine Texier, Vic Ziegel, Charles Pierce, Chuck Young, Tom Disch, John Clute, Alex Kuczinski, Terrance McKenna, T.J. English, Cecilla Farber, Devin Friedman, David Freidman, Tad Friend, Chris Smith, Elizabeth Gilbert, Katha Pollitt, Vanessa Giorgdias, Gerri Hirschy, Mark Zwonitzer, Mark Kurlander, Warren Leight, Cong. Peter King, Ariel Levy, Jennifer Senior, Bill McGowan, Rebecca Mead, Donna Minkowitz, Terry Bisson, Bruce Stutz, Donna Gaines, Susan Orlean, Glenn O'Brien, Elliot Sharpe, David Rakoff, Scott Raab, Mike Sager, Richard Grant, Susan Rosenberg, Sarah Schulman, Mike Golden, Dan Christian, Denis Woychuk, Matthew Shipp, Larry Sloman, Amy Sohn, Susan Terry, Toure, Ted Panken, Bill Tonelli, Mike Wallace, Ian Williams, Armond White.

Special thanks are due to Terry Bisson, a prince of a man, who helped start the series and ran it with me for several years. T.B., who writes mostly science-fiction books that win him all these occult awards and can fix any automobile yet invented except for fuel injection, has always been a most valued friend. Others who at one time or other fulfilled executive roles in this nearly endless procession of word dispensing include Alice K. Turner, Ada Calhoun, Eric Konigsberg, and, presently, the brilliant Bruce Stutz, my longtime collegue, who actually knows how to send out the e-mail list in addition to showing up on time.

—Mark Jacobson, Salonista
New York
May 2004

JOURNALISM
AND
JUSTICE BEGIN
WITH THE
SAME LETTER

A DEATH IN TEXAS

Steve Earle

"Hey, man." Jonathan Wayne Nobles grins at me through inch-thick wire-reinforced glass, hunching over to speak in a deep, resonant voice through the steel grate below. A feeble "What's up?" is the best I can manage. The visiting area in Ellis One Unit is crowded with other folks who have traveled, in some cases thousands of miles, to visit relatives and correspondents on Texas' Death Row. They sit at intervals in wooden chairs surrounding a cinder-block-and-steel cage that dominates the center of the room. There are cages within the cage as well, reserved for inmates under disciplinary action and on "death watch" status. Falling into the latter category, Jon must squeeze his considerable bulk into one of these phone booth–sized enclosures.

It's an awkward moment for both of us. In the ten years we have corresponded we have never met face to face. The occasion is auspicious. Jon and I will spend eight hours a day together for the next three days and then another three days next week. Then, the state of Texas will transport Jon, chained hand and foot, eleven miles to the Walls Unit in downtown Huntsville. There he will be pumped full of chemicals that will collapse his lungs and stop his heart forever. This is not a

3

worst-case scenario. It is a certainty. The only action pending in the courts on Jon's behalf is an unprecedented petition to have Jon's vital organs harvested and donated for transplant before his execution. The supposedly "nonviolent" lethal-injection process literally destroys the lungs and renders all other organs too toxic for transplantation. Neither Jon nor his attorneys have any faith that their motion will prevail. There is no doubt in my mind (or Jon's for that matter) that Jonathan Noble has precisely ten days to live. And I, at Jon's request, will attend the execution as one of his witnesses.

Over the next few days a routine develops. I arrive at Ellis at 8:30 in the morning. We usually spend the first two hours talking about music, politics, religion—subjects that we have covered thoroughly enough in letters over the years to know that we have widely divergent views and tastes. We fill the long awkward silences that seem inevitable in prison visiting areas with trips to the vending machines for soft drinks, candy, and potato chips. I pass Jon's goodies to the guard on duty through a small opening in the steel mesh.

Inevitably, we move on to life behind bars, drugs, and recovery—topics where we share considerably more common ground. We are both recovering addicts who got clean only when we were locked up. Jon began reading about recovery and attending "twelve step" meetings in prison years ago. I can remember a time, back when I was still using drugs, when the "recovery-speak" that filled his letters made me extremely uncomfortable. Now it is a language that we share—sort of a spiritual shorthand that cuts through the testosterone and affords us a convenient, if uncomfortable, segue to the business at hand. There are arrangements to be made. If Jon's body goes unclaimed, as is the case with half of the men executed in Texas, he will be buried in the prison cemetery on the out-skirts of Huntsville. Called "Peckerwood Hill" by the locals, it is lonely space filled with concrete crosses, adorned only with the interred inmates' prison numbers. Those executed by the state are easily identifiable by the X preceding their number. There are, however, no names on the stones. Jon doesn't want to wind up there.

Instead, he wants to be buried in Oxford, England—a place he's never seen. One of his pen pals, a British subject called Pam Thomas, has described it to him in her letters. He likes the picture Pam paints of springtime there, when bluebells are in bloom. Jon says that Pam is working on obtaining permission from the landowner. I, for my part, have a Plan B on the back burner. A Dominican community in Galway, Ireland, has offered Jon a final resting place. At some point it dawns on me that I have spent the last hour helping a living, breathing man plan his own burial.

One thing Jon and I don't talk about much is the movement to abolish the death penalty. In fact, Jon is suspicious of abolitionists. We were "introduced" by a pen pal of his and an acquaintance of mine. She had heard that I sometimes corresponded with inmates and asked if she could give Jon my address. I said "sure." Within a month I received my first letter. It was a page and a half long in a beautiful flowing script that made me more than a little jealous. It contained a lot of the usual tough rhetoric and dark humor I had learned to expect in letters from men and women in prison. After several readings I realized that all of the jailhouse small talk was merely a medium, a vehicle for one pertinent piece of information—that Jonathan Wayne Nobles was guilty of the crimes he was charged with. Jon Nobles was found guilty (almost entirely on the strength of his own confession) of stabbing Kelley Farquar and Mitzi Nalley to death in 1986. He also admitted struggling with and stabbing Ron Ross, Nalley's boyfriend. Ross lost an eye in the attack. Jon never took the stand during his trial. He sat impassively as the guilty verdict was read and, according to newspaper accounts, only flinched slightly when District Judge Bob Jones sentenced him to death.

When Jon arrived at Ellis he quickly alienated all of the guards and most of the inmates. He once broke away from guards while being returned to his cell from the exercise yard and climbed the exposed pipes and bars like an animal, kicking down television arials suspended outside on the bottom tier. Not exactly the way to win friends and influence people in the penitentiary. On another occasion he cut himself with a razor blade, knowing that the guards would have to open his cell to prevent him from bleeding to death. He just wanted to hit one officer before he passed out.

But somehow, somewhere along the line, in what is arguably the most inhumane environment in the "civilized" world, Jonathan Nobles began to change. He became interested in Catholicism and began to attend Mass. He befriended the Catholic clergy who ministered in the prison system, including members of the Dominican Order of Preachers. He admired the Dominicans so much that he set his sights on becoming one of them. He eventually achieved that goal, becoming a lay member of the order and ministering to his fellow inmates, even standing as godfather at inmate Cliff Boguss's baptism. He later helped officiate at the Mass that was celebrated the night before Boguss' execution. When I mentioned in a letter that I had found a bag of pot in my oldest son Justin's laundry, Jon suggested that I bring him to Ellis. He believed his word might carry a little more weight than mine, coming from the other side of the razor wire. I was tempted, but in the final analysis I couldn't bring myself to drag my firstborn through the gates of Hell.

I watched this transformation in the letters that I received. There is no doubt in my mind or my heart that the Jonathan Nobles that sat on the other side of the glass from me in September of 1998 is a different man than the one that the State of Texas sentenced to die almost twelve years earlier. The greatest evidence of this fact is the way that Jon is treated by everyone he encounters, inmates and prison officials alike. A prison clerk, displaying obvious, genuine regret, interrupts our visit. She needs Jon to sign some papers. Jon does so and then informs me that the documents allow me to pick up his personal property and distribute it to a list of people detailed in a note that the clerk will hand me on my way out. He winks and says that he has left something special to me. Inmate Richard Bethard, on his way down the line to visit with a family member, stops to talk and Jon introduces us. Bethard beams, saying that he is one of my biggest fans. The guard patiently waits until the exchange is over before escorting him to his assigned cubicle. Such socialization during inmate transfer is a clear violation of policy at Ellis, but a lot of the rules have relaxed for Jon. He says that it's like the last week of the school year. I believe that it's more likely that he has earned the genuine respect of everyone at Ellis.

The scene is repeated all afternoon. One visitor is a prison employee, who three years earlier went out and bought the *Dead Man Walking* soundtrack CD so that Jon could hear my contribution, a song called "Ellis Unit One," about a corrections officer suffering a crisis of conscience. Another visitor is an elderly woman who has moved to Huntsville from England to be near the twenty-six inmates she corresponds with. She is a recovering alcoholic, and when Jon tells her that I'm in the program she offers to take me to a meeting that night. At this point I could use a meeting so I make a date to meet her at a local church at 7:00. Richard Bethard's codefendant Gene Hathorn stops by. Hathorn, it so happens, is one of my other correspondents at Ellis. "Hey Jon, I hear you got a date. Is it serious?" Jon visibly stiffens. He and Hathorn were friends once but something happened years ago, something Jon is reluctant to talk about.

"Serious enough that they're going to kill me."

Hathorn moves on without another word. I excuse myself to go to the bathroom. The truth is I simply need a break.

On the way back I run into Father Stephen Walsh, a Franciscan friar from Boston who makes regular trips to Ellis to minister to its Catholic inmates. He will serve as Jonathan's spiritual advisor. In that capacity he will wait with Jon in the holding cell over at the Walls until he's escorted into the death chamber itself and will administer the last rights. Fr. Walsh introduces me to Bishop Carmody, of the East Texas Diocese in Tyler, who like me has been asked to witness on Jonathan's behalf. He is a native of County Kerry, Ireland, but has lived in the States for forty years, twenty of them in Texas. Being a sometime resident of County Galway, a little farther up the island's west coast, I find his accent familiar and comforting. He has never witnessed an execution before and admits to being just as scared as I am. "With God's help," he says, "we'll get through this thing together, Stephen."

Every visit ends the same way. A guard gives us a five-minute warning, and Jon hurriedly dictates a list of "things to do" which I must commit to memory, as visitors are not allowed to bring writing instruments and paper into the unit. Then Jon presses his palm against the glass and I mirror his with mine. Jon says, "I love you. I'll see you tomorrow." That is until Wednesday, October 7 rolls around.

It's hot and humid, even at 8:00 a.m. as I thread my rented Lincoln through the drive-thru of a fast-food restaurant near my motel. As I pull up to the window, a pretty Hispanic girl in her early twenties takes my money and hands me my break-fast: an egg and sausage taco and a medium Dr. Pepper. She smiles and says, "You don't recognize me, do you?" Before I can place her myself she volunteers, "I work at Ellis." Of course—behind the reception desk. I received Jon's property from her last night. "I just wanted to say I'm sorry. Jon's a good guy." I glance at her nametag. "Thank you, Delores. I'll tell him you said that. It will mean a lot." I guess that she is prob-ably around the same age as Mitzi Nalley was when she died. Over the last few days the other witnesses have arrived in Huntsville. I had dinner the night before with Dona Hucka, Jon's aunt. She is the only blood relative to make the trip. She has driven all night to be here. Pam Thomas is in from Eng-land, as well. Both are already on the Unit when I arrive. Jon's fifth witness is the director of chaplain's services for the Texas Department of Corrections, Rev. Richard Garza. We take turns leaning close to the glass while a prison employee takes Polaroid snapshots of each of us with Jon. The prison pro-vides this service for the nominal fee of eight dollars each.

10:00. There isn't much time left. At 12:30 we will be asked to leave the Unit and Jon will be transported to the Walls. In the death chamber we will be able to hear Jon over a speaker in the witness room, but this is our last opportunity to speak to him. Jon divides the remaining time between us more or less equally. I go first. Jon looks tired; the stress is showing for the first time. He leans down and motions me closer. I realize he's assessing my condition as well. "You all right, man?" I tell him that I'm okay. Jon is not convinced.

"I'm worried about you. You don't have be Superman or nothin'. This is insane shit that's goin' on here today. You don't have to be strong for the women if that's what you're thinkin'. They're big girls. You need to take care of yourself."

"I know, Jon. I'm all right. I went to a meeting last night and my manager's here now. I've also got a couple of friends up from Houston who have done this before."

"Witnessed?"

"Yeah." That seemed to make him feel better.

"OK, but if you need to cry, it's all right, go ahead and cry."

"When this is all over I'll cry."

"Promise?"

"I promise."

Jon shifts gears suddenly. Back to business. He looks both ways to make sure the guard isn't watching. "Take this." With much effort he pushes a tiny slip of tightly rolled paper, the diameter of a toothpick, through the impossibly tight mesh. Somehow he pulls it off. "That's my daughter's phone number in California. Dona read it to me over the phone last night. They're going to strip-search me and I can't take any-thing to the Walls and I'm afraid I'll forget it. Give it to Father Walsh. Then I'll have it when I make my last phone calls."

I poke the paper in the watch pocket of my Levi's. There were a few other requests. He wants me to call his foster mother and his sister after the execution, and send flowers to two women who worked for the prison who had been kind to him over the years. I promise that I won't forget. "All right, bro. Take care of yourself and your kids. Tell Dona to come back." Hands against the glass one last time.

"I love you, Jonathan."

"I love you too, bro."

Noon. I head back into Huntsville. My manager, Dan Gillis, arrived last night and not a moment too soon. Suddenly, driving has become difficult. It's weird. I'm simply not as coordinated as usual and the world has taken on a kind of surrealistic patina. I need someone to drive for the rest of the day. Also waiting at the hotel are two friends from the abolition movement, Karen Sebung and Ward Larkin. Both have witnessed executions and they have made the trip to support me and assist in any way they can. We talk over arrangements for the transportation and cremation of Jon's body, which, as it turns out, Dan has already taken care of. I make a couple of phone calls and check my messages. Then I shower, shave, and put on a pair of black jeans, a blue short-sleeve shirt, and a black linen sport coat.

4:00. We leave the hotel and Dan drives us to Hospitality House, a guest residence operated by the Baptist Church for the families of inmates. Dona and Pam, as well as Pam's friend Caroline, are staying there. Bishop Carmody and Rev. Garza are already there when we arrive. We are assembled here for an orientation session to be conducted by Rev. Robert Brazile, the chaplain at the Walls Unit. He and the warden will be the only two human beings inside the chamber with Jon when he dies. He goes through the execution process step by step so that "we will know what to expect" and, though it's obvious he speaks with authority, I'm not listening. I can't concentrate so I just nod a lot. It doesn't matter. No matter how well or poorly the witnesses are prepared, they are going to kill Jon anyway.

5:05. Rev. Brazile answers his cell phone and it's Fr. Walsh. He is over at the Walls with Jon and wants the phone number. The one that Jon passed me through the . . . oh my God. I can't find it. I was sure that I transferred the slip from my other jeans into my wallet when I changed clothes but it's simply not there. Dan runs to the hotel and checks my room, but it's hopeless; it was tiny. Rev. Brazil relays the bad news back to Fr. Walsh. I feel awful.

5:30. We arrive at the visitors' center across the street from the Walls Unit. Karen Sebung accompanies me as far as the waiting area where we witnesses are searched, then Dona and Pam are escorted to another room by a female officer. When they return a large man enters the room and introduces himself as an officer of the prison's Internal Affairs Division. He informs us that if we should feel faint, medical attention is available. He also warns us that anyone who in any way attempts to disrupt the "process," as he calls it, will be removed from the witness area immediately. Bishop Carmody sits down next to me and asks when I was last in Ireland. I can't remember. Nothing about my body is working right. My feet and hands are cold and the side of my neck is numb. The bishop is telling me a story about his childhood in Kerry but I can't get the thread of it. I am suddenly fixated on the idea that somewhere nearby Ron Ross and Mitzy Nalley's mother are undergoing a similar process. They are waiting for the clo-sure that the State of Texas promised them twelve years before. I sincerely hope that they get it.

5:55. The corrections officer returns. "Follow me, please."

I haul myself to my feet. We walk across the street and through the front door of the old gothic prison administration building. We turn left as soon as we enter and find ourselves in the waiting area of the governor's office, where we are asked to wait once again. There are two reporters already there. The other three members of the press pool, along with the victims' family members, have already been escorted to the witness area, which is divided by a cinder block wall. The procedure has been carefully planned and rehearsed, so that the two sets of witnesses will never come in contact with each other.

6:00. A corrections officer enters the room. I hear him tell the Internal Affairs officer that "they're ready." We walk through a visiting area similar to the one at Ellis, then out into the bright evening sun for a moment and turn left down a short sidewalk. Another left and we enter the first door of two set side by side in a small brick building built into the side of the perimeter wall. We enter the tiny room in single file. Father Walsh appears from somewhere inside the death chamber to join us. The reporters enter last and the door is locked behind us. I can hear the reporters scratching on their notepads with their pencils. There is only room for three of us on the front row, Dona, myself, and Pam. Dona grabs my left hand and squeezes it hard and then realizing she may be hurting me, she whispers an apology and relaxes her grip a little. She already has tears in her eyes.

Jon is strapped to a hospital gurney with heavy leather straps across his chest, hips, thighs, ankles, and wrists. His arms are extended at his sides on arm boards like you see in the blood bank and they are wrapped in ace bandages. At either wrist clear plastic tubes protrude from the wrappings, snaking back under the gurney and disappearing through a plastic tube set in a bright blue cinder block wall. I think I see movement behind the one-way mirror on the opposite wall— the executioner getting into position. Jon is smiling at us, his great neck twisted uncomfortably sideways. A microphone suspended from the ceiling hangs a few inches above his head. The speaker above our heads crackles to life and Jon speaks, craning his head around to see the victims' witnesses in the room next door.

"I know some of you won't believe me, but I am truly sorry for what I have done. I wish that I could undo what happened back then and bring back your loved ones but I can't." Jon begins to sob as he addresses Mitzi Nalley's mother. "I'm sorry. I'm so sorry. I wish I could bring her back to you. And Ron . . . I took so much from you. I'm sorry. I know you probably don't want my love, but you have it."

Turning to me he seems to regain his composure, some-what. He even manages to smile again. "Steve, I can't believe that I had to go through all this to see you in a suit coat. Hey man, don't worry about the phone number, bro. You've done so much. I love you. Dona, thank you for being here. I know it was hard for you. I love you. Pam, thank you for coming from so far away. Thanks for all you have done. I love you. Bishop Carmody, thank you so much. Reverend Garza and you, Father Walsh, I love you all. I have something I want to say. It comes from I Corinthians. It goes . . ." and Jon recites the lengthy piece of scripture that he agonized over for weeks, afraid he would forget when the time came. He remembers every word.

When he finished reciting he took a deep breath and said, "Father into thy hands I commend my spirit." The warden, recognizing the prearranged signal he and Jon had agreed on, nodded towards the unseen executioner and Jon began to sing. *Silent night / Holy night . . .*

He got as far as "mother and child" and suddenly the air exploded from his lungs, making a loud barking noise, deep and incongruous, like a child with whooping cough— "HUH!!!!" His head pitched forward with such force that his heavy, prison issue glasses flew off his face, bouncing from his chest and falling to the green tile floor below.

And then he didn't move at all—ever again. I actually watched his eyes fix and glaze over, my heart pounding in my chest and Dona squeezing my hand. We could all see that he was gone. Dead men look . . . well, dead. Vacant. No longer human. But there was a protocol to be satisfied. The warden checked his watch several times during the longest five minutes of my life. When time was up, he walked across the room and knocked on the door. The doctor entered, his stethoscope's earpieces already in place. He listened first at Jon's neck, then at his chest, then at his side. He shined a small flashlight into Jon's eyes for an instant and then, glancing up at the clock on his way out, intoned, "Six-eighteen." We were ushered out the same way we came, but I don't think any of us are the same people that crossed the street to the prison that day. I know I'm not. I can't help but wonder what happens to the people that work at the Walls, who see this horrific thing happen as often as four times a week. What do they see when they turn out the lights? I can't imagine.

I do know that Jonathan Nobles changed profoundly while he was in prison. I know that the lives of other people who he came in contact with changed as well, including mine. Our criminal justice system isn't known for rehabilitation. I'm not sure that, as a society, we are even interested in that concept anymore. The problem is that most people who go to prison get out one day and walk among us. Given as many people as we lock up, we better learn to rehabilitate someone. I believe Jon might have been able to teach us how. Now we'll never know.

YOU ARE CORDIALLY INVITED TO MY FUNERAL

Marcelle Clements

As if we didn't have enough problems, now we're supposed to think about our own funerals. It's part of the phenomenon I've come to think of as The New Death: a death that is died with clarity, dignity and a sense of responsibility—in other words, a death you've got to plan for. Instead of finally letting someone else drive for a change, here's one more arena in which we are supposed to become proactive, take charge, use our best time-management skills, express ourselves creatively, get focused, get centered, get real and be special.

Of course, deep, deep down, many of us don't intend to die, but let's say we're trying to go along with the general idea. Just when we imagine we ought to tune in, lie back and, as Timothy Leary once put it, ". . . relax and float downstream," we realize we've got to organize yet another event. Small or large? Somber or whimsical? Catered or austere? Make up your mind: cremation, burial, crypt, vault, mausoleum, sarcophagus. Headstone? How about something in a nice pink laurentian marble?

I read in one of the books now proliferating on planning a funeral, *Death Rehearsal: A Practical Guide for Preparing for the Inevitable* (Octavo Press), that many people buy their caskets

in advance and that, according to author Doug Pokorski, ". . .
it is not uncommon for the owner to put the casket into interim
service as a piece of furniture. . . . Even a plain wooden box for
burial can be stood on end, have temporary shelves installed
and be used as a bookcase." But Pokorski hasn't seen my place.
Where would the extra books go when they are removed to
make way for my corpse? Surely not in the usual piles on the
floor, since Pokorski enjoins us to remember that the
deceased's home should be neatened for visitors before and
after the ceremony. He warns against the increasingly popular
do-it-yourself gig in which no funeral home is involved at all:
"Even when death is peaceful, a dead body can be an untidy
object to have around. Bodily fluids sometimes leak out after
death and should be washed away. . . ." As for what happens
next, he suggests, "You should also be prepared to dress the
body for burial in whatever way you feel appropriate, be that a
simple shroud or the deceased's best dress-up outfit."

The matter of one's own appearance—while one is still
more or less matter—is as perplexing as ever. Formal, casual,
sportive? With or without jewelry? Digital watch or analog?
Ball gown, little black dress or velvet mantle with a cowl? Of
course, I would have to lose a few pounds before I could even
look in my closet.

Which brings up the question of lighting. But never mind.

Personally, I can see myself all too well in my own coffin,
peeking at people's expressions—and what will *they* be
wearing?—from under nearly closed lids, or should I say a
nearly closed lid, since, strictly speaking, Jews are supposed
to lie, unembalmed and unadorned, in plain, closed coffins,
with a big hole at the bottom so that they get to disintegrate
as fast as possible.

But of course that's rather passé. At more cutting edge funerals, people tell stories, show videos, read letters written by and to the deceased. I certainly do not plan to write a letter or anything else for my own funeral. All I need is another deadline. And I can just imagine my editor friends whipping their red pens out of their pocketbooks. "Her sentences were always endless," whispers one. "And my dear—those adjectives!" hisses another. By the same token, I don't think it's fair to ask any of my friends to pen a eulogy. All *they* need is another deadline. And do I have to have an epitaph?

For some reason, all I can think of are the funerals I don't want to star in. I don't want the touchy-feely kind, but I don't want the traditional kind either. I don't want my funeral in a funeral home (too dingy and lugubrious), but I also don't want it to be in a natural setting (too corny), and I don't want it to be at home (I need new slipcovers). Maybe a modest graveside ceremony? Not enough time left to build a pyramid, I suppose. A simple raft floating down a dreamy river, perhaps?

Under no circumstances will I have New Orleans-type music, which has become so banal that there are now Web sites on the Internet providing arrangements. Nix it on the spooky organ music, too. I'd rather hear Metallica. Or maybe something from the French baroque. Or possibly Strauss' "Four Last Songs."

Atmosphere is everything. (And by the way, is it really for your survivors that you are planning or is this yet another "me, me, me" event?) It requires an entirely different set of arrangements depending on whether you're thinking about your family, your lovers or would-be lovers, whether you want to say a last fond farewell to your admirers or get one last chance to demonstrate to your detractors that they've made a big mistake. Who do you see near your coffin? It could be your mother (Heaven help you!); your boss, busy regretting some harsh words; your psychotherapist, weeping at long last; the ultimate unseen audience. . . .

What will your mourners be thinking and feeling? Sorrow, regret, tenderness, relief, triumph, revenge—I suppose those are all things we may feel when someone we care about dies. Of course what we feel is a direct expression of that person's past life, so the best way to ensure a "good" funeral is to live well and fully. But it's a mistake, I find, to think about life when you're trying to think about death. Dwelling on one's almost intolerable fear of dying when one's children are still young can take all the fun out of imagining oneself filling this casket or that urn.

Yes, the more one thinks about it, the clearer it is that the best alternative is simply not to die.

Presuming one has to die, however, in theory it should also be an option to plan to have no ceremony at all, but this is very difficult. Those who grieve for you—if any—will feel betrayed if you opt for what some professionals refer to as "garbage service" (think green plastic bag) or its alternate, "box and burn" (think knotty pine). Traditional funeral versus box and burn is one of those perennial dualities, of course, but lately, there has been a third way, generated by the same mentality that causes otherwise perfectly reasonable people to write their own marriage ceremony. These days there's no end to individualized memorials, interments and cremations and if you're over, say, 30, you can expect to spend a substantial portion of your so-called leisure time slouching at grave sites reciting poetry or sitting in a church of any denomination listening to an organist play "Lucy in the Sky With Diamonds" or standing on a windy bluff holding a hand-kerchief to your nose so as not to breathe in any of the ashes being scattered in this or that memorable location.

Apparently some spots have become too memorable to funeral planners. A recent AP wire story reported that the inhabitants of Venice on the Bay, near Pasadena, Maryland, are complaining that too many people are scattering ashes on the beach. "The remains often don't make it to the eternal home beneath the waves. The ashes instead end up blowing into the faces of unsuspecting swimmers and sunbathers." The residents are not amused. "Who wants to be cooking hamburgers on the grill and have a breeze come and pepper them with someone's ashes?" asked one.

And who, I might ask, wants to end up, after all that trouble, as part of a Maryland resident's hamburger?

There's the rub, and that is why it is so difficult to plan for one's funeral. It's because you have to imagine yourself as dead. How do you arrive at acceptance? Well, if you don't have the benefit of organized religion I guess you take up dis-organized religion. You read *The Tibetan Book of Living and Dying*, or you ask your friends for guidance, or you surf the Internet, or watch other people die on TV and look for hints.

All the frankness of the new death doesn't dispel one's fear of death. In some ways, it intensifies it. Our elders had the luxury of denial, if they needed it. Just think of their euphemisms: At worst they'd "pass away" or go to their "eternal rest." The truth is, one does, indeed, imagine oneself at one's own funeral, but not as dead, perhaps merely sleeping? That's it: You're not dead, you're just lying down. You're lying down, surrounded by people who love you.

(Note to self: Request coffin lid be propped up until very last minute. Just in case.)

Paradoxically, then, trying to be reasonable, responsible and well organized about one's own death leads one to the most vivid fantasies of being buried alive. And suddenly, all those old euphemisms begin to make more sense. That's it! You're not a corpse, you're a loved one. You pass away or you pass on, in your own style, according to your own plans, with your own money, not to your death, but to your eternal rest.

That is, we hope we get to rest. Just in case, though, bury me standing, with my Filofax. No, make that a Palm Pilot III, please. (But . . . you know what? Nix it on the Metallica. Thanks very much. Oh, yes, okay, a little Bach will be all right. Have you got the Passacaglia and Fugue in . . . ? Yes, that's it. That's fine. No, maybe just a little louder, please. A little lower. Yes. That's it. Perfect. Just turn off my cellular, will you, dear? Thank you. And good night.)

IN THE LAND OF THE FISCHER KING

Ivan Solotaroff

The foothills of the Montengrin Alps above the Bay of Kotor are a mottled green-brown, and the rock-strewn mountains rising thousands of feet above sea-level are parched and ugly. In addition to the sounds of shelling from Dubrovnik, 50 kilometers up the Adriatic coast, and the arrival of the U.S. Sixth Fleet, enforcing the worldwide embargo against Serbia and Montenegro, the summer has brought a terrible drought. The olives, wine-grapes, and tomatoes the region is famous for are tiny and shriveling on the vine. The bay, briny from lack of rain, heaves up a thick salt musk that makes the beaches smell like mussels. The rich Italians, fleeing Feragosto, who have saturated this vacation paradise with money, color, and motorcycles for 30 years, failed to show up this season, and everyone from the royal family and mountain warlords to the local Mafia chieftains are cash-poor and nervous.

On the tiny fifteenth-century island of Sveti Stefan, however, 200 feet offshore, imported champagne, Krstac, and the domestic grappa called *loza* are flowing, and a ballet troupe, jugglers, a seven-foot contortionist, belly dancers, and a 32-piece folk orchestra dressed as chess pieces stroll across the flagstone causeway that connects the island to the mainland beaches. In the twilight, the island itself, a former fisherman's

23

and pirate's village, looks like a confabulated chess piece: a maze of ramparts, villas, cathedrals, dark piazzas, tiny, covered passages, and stone stairways spiraling off at extreme angles.

On the westernmost castellation, a Carrera marble terrazo cum three-star hotel restaurant, Bobby Fischer sits like an idiot king with his back to the setting sun. Boris Spassky, who sits alone in his tennis whites two tables over, savors the last of his mineral water as he takes in the pinks and oranges over the Adriatic, impassive but for an occasional suave pass of a hand through his thick silver hair. Fischer, in a newly hand-made aquamarine suit, beige shirt, and a pair of strangely designed, Herman Munster–like black shoes, has every eye in the restaurant but Spassky's on him. Flanked by three bodyguards and a pair of waiters, an elbow on the table and his cheek propped on his fist, he shovels in a second bowl of melon and ice cream, washing it down with full glasses of Krstac. He's gained a good 60 pounds since his last public appearance, and his formerly gaunt and beautiful face, now covered with a scraggly red-brown beard, has filled out so much it's almost unrecognizable. Only the eyes are the same: hazel, wide open, relentlessly shifting, loaded with feeling, confusion, and suspicion.

Throughout his four-course dinner, he's been talking in animated flurries to Eugenio Torre, the serene Philippine grandmaster serving as a second (all-night study partner and researcher) for his World Championship Match against Spassky, the strange comeback that Fischer has decreed to commence 20 years to the day after the conclusion of his famous Reykjavik victory in 1972, 17 years after he forfeited the title. A hot wind blowing off the hills across the bay is taking most of Fischer's words, and I can hear only fragments, but the accent is unmistakably Brooklyn, the Brooklyn of Ebbets Field, Barbra Streisand, and transistor radios: ". . . There's a lot of people without homes now. It's, uh, y'know, like illegal. Like squat-tuhs. They should be arrested or some-thin' . . ." ". . . In America, prisons cost money. In China, they make 'em work. And if they don't work, they beat 'em. Hah. Hah-hah-hah. . . ."

With a thick stench of Havana cigar, a rustle of silk, and the click of alligator leather over marble, Jezdimir Vasiljevic makes his way across the terrazo, trailed by four bodyguards. "Svakako! Svakako!" he's telling one of them: "No shit! No shit!" A small man with a farmer's physique, mutton-chop sideburns, and a wooly haircut that looks like the "After" photo in a Moscow barbershop, c. 1962, he wears a brown, double-breasted gangster suit that's an inch long at the shoulder, wrist, and heel, and carries a rectangular case of expensive brown leather, a mystery accessory that never leaves his side. Referred to as the "paradigm of the new busi-nessman in Serbia-Montenegro" in the Serbian tabloid *Borba*, and as a black-marketeering, arms-dealing Mafioso in the Croatian tabloid *Novi Viesnik,* in a "country" like this there's not much difference. On Sveti Stefan—which he calls "my town"—they simply call him "Mr. BIG," after his bank/holding company, Yugoskandic B.I.G.: Biznis-Informacije-Glamur. Any *informacije* about this man's *biznis* would have to be massively double-checked, but this is impossible. "I am mysterious man," he loves to tell you. "I cannot talk now." Like Fischer, he has a 20-year hole in his c.v. (when he was "abroad") giving rise to various *mon oncle d'Amerique* rumors: that he smuggled Albanian mercury, or fenced South African diamonds in Sweden. Most often cited is that he dealt arms to Israel, and made his fortune during the 1982 invasion of Lebanon.

As for *glamur*, he has pulled off the Serbian publicist's equivalent of raising Lazarus in bringing Fischer here to play this $5 million "Revenge Match of the Century," but he doesn't seem very happy just now. He had planned to found a corporate mini-state in Sveti Stefan—a two-percent tax zone a la Monte Carlo, that would lure foreign business to his bank—but this has been crushed by U.N. sanctions, and he's in serious arrears on the five-year, $570-million lease for this island, three nearby hotels, and 150 acres of adjoining property. Telexes from the U.S. departments of State and the Treasury, threatening huge fines and prison sentences if Fischer breaks the embargo by playing the match, are reportedly coming daily, putting Fischer on edge: Half a mile up the mainland, a pair of high-backed swivel chairs and a huge oak chesstable emblazoned with the match logo sit like corpses at the entrance to the playing site in the Hotel Maestral, the first casualties of Fischer's demands for perfection. (By the start of the match, he will have vetoed 11 more tables and two other pairs of chairs.) Hammering and high-pitched drilling are heard throughout the night from the 75-yard-long playing hall, as workmen construct the floor-to-ceiling concrete barricade that will separate Fischer and Spassky from the audience, leaving a 10-foot aperture in the center through which the players can be seen.

Fischer is standing with his palms open in great drama as Vasiljevic approaches his table, and they leave the restaurant immediately in a phalanx of bodyguards, Vasiljevic swinging his briefcase, Fischer toting a leather pocket chess set and two books. "I got so much to do tonight," he says as he heads up the stairs toward his villa on the other side of the island. His walk is unnatural—left arm and left leg together—and driven-looking. Vosco, the cashier at Under the Olives, an open-air restaurant across the causeway, has been filling me with Nosferatu-ish stories of Fischer's dead-of-night ramblings through the mainland forests, every other night in the month since he's arrived. The other nights, a small motorcade rushes him and Spassky across the causeway to play tennis on an old, dimly lit clay court surrounded by blue spruce and cypress. They say he's phenomenally competitive, and that his agonized screams are heard echoing down the hillside when he loses difficult points.

Spassky gets up to leave a few minutes later and I try to make conversation. "Of course you want to talk to Bobby," he says. "But this is impossible. He does not like the media." Spassky's voice is a comical Bela Lugosi baritone that swells and falls with dry humor and a strangely unctuous self-doubt. Though he's a natural performer, he shares Fischer's contempt for journalists, and tries at all costs to avoid interviews.

I mention the war, and he asks for the latest news about sanctions. A naturalized French citizen for over a decade and a virulent anti-Communist, he seems genuinely mortified to learn of the extent of European condemnation of the match. (The Madrid daily *El Pais,* for example, is running the head-line CHESSBOARD OF BLOOD.) "But you cannot blame only one people," he protests. "In Bosnia and Serbia, both are the same people in power. Bolsheviks. In Bosnia, they get weapons through a special route. And in Serbia"—he raises a pale, beefy index finger professorially—"in Serbia, they have also a lot of weapons. They are bandits. Worse than military. Both sides. It would be nice," he says, filling his lungs with salt air, "if they could make a corridor, like with fire, so that we could get here safely and be here safely."

I ask Spassky if it's true Vasiljevic offered him life insurance as part of his contract. (It's also rumored that a clause in Fischer's 17-page contract stipulates that no noise from the war shall interfere with his concentration during a game.) "Yes, this is a very special question. My safety. We have to look into this. Come," he says, leading me a few steps to the turreted wall facing the mainland. To the left and right, a series of pristine beaches and U-shaped, emerald-green harbors sit perfectly at peace in the gloaming. Two blue cigarette boats with MILICIYA (Police) signs and Browning 50-caliber machine guns on the prow patrol the waters around the island. It's hard to know who they're protecting: Seventy-two of the 100 or so yachts anchored within eyeshot, CNN reported recently, were stolen this summer from the harbors in Dubrovnik.

"Look at this," says Spassky. "A piece of paradise. You know, I used to drive on the coast from Trieste to Bugogno. A beautiful city, but it probably doesn't exist anymore. Do you realize there used to be 700 kilometers of coastline? Now, less than 100."

"Why do you think Bobby has decided to play this match here then?" I ask. "And why now, in the middle of a war, after 20 years of refusing?"

"These of course are the crucial questions," Spassky says portentously. "I can say only, Bobby wants to create the very special atmosphere of Reykjavik. He was the great hero of the West then."

These "crucial questions" feel increasingly moot with each

war-weary photographer, wire stringer, and television crew that checks into the various Sveti Stefan hotels the day before the match's opening ceremonies. When they gather at night, trading war-stories over *lozas* at Dusko's, a dark, Western-style bar with cheap plastic tables along the sea-wall and Dean Martin and Ricky Nelson trading the harmonies on "My Pony, My Rifle, and Me" on the boom-box, it becomes clear that this war—its headlines of 1,000-year racial enmity and "ethnic cleansing" notwithstanding—has, at trench level, become the anarchy of freak individualism run amok, and the total collapse of the marketplace. You get the feeling there's no place in the world that Fischer, who singlehandedly inflated the value of chess and then turned his back on countless millions, belongs more.

"It's like Kipling's 'The Light That Failed' here," says James Mason, a photographer for Black Star who's been covering the war for over a year. "A lot of people who just want to kill people. Americans especially, extremely lost survivalist types going around with headbands, sawed-off shirt-sleeves, and Rambo knives, fighting for either side. They're going crazy in Dubrovnik, firing machine guns and listening to the voices in their heads. They come because there's no daily accounting necessary here."

Ben Hawke, a sometime producer for Australian *60 Minutes*, says he's run into "characters straight out of *Road Warrior*, literally having gun battles off the sides of petrol trucks. There are parts of this country where 10 American dollars won't buy you a litre on the black market, which is where Mr. BIG comes in. Almost every flight in the country's been cancelled because of no fuel, and he has his own filling station across from his little island for the BMWs. He *is* the black market, only he does it legally, through his bank. He's giving 30 to 65 percent interest, monthly, depending on the foreign currency you give him."

Dejan Anastasijevic, a UPI stringer from Belgrade, tells me about the two dozen American mercenaries he met during the leveling of the Croatian city of Vukovar: the Fred Perry Brigade, who "liberated" a lifetime's supply of tennis shoes, T-shirts, camouflage pants, and floppy hats with Fred Perry logos before flattening the boutique with bazooka charges. In Sarajevo, he met a farmer in one of the Serbian strongholds who sold his combine and bought a Russian T-55 tank from the Federal Yugoslav Army, which he drives into the hills after work each evening, so that he can fire on Muslims. "The day I met him it was a ceasefire, but it didn't matter. 'This tank is my private property,' he said. 'No one can tell me how to use it. Communism is over. I'm living in the West now.' While he was talking, I finally understood that Hannah Arendt phrase, *the narcissism of small differences.* That's exactly what this war is."

For 20 years of intractable petty demands, Fischer personified this narcissism exactly. A strange boy with an I.Q. of 181, he grew up in small rooms studying chess with the radio on, refusing to wear anything but corduroy pants and striped sportshirts, developing strange ideas about people—particularly those he loved to call "Commies" and "World Jewry." He shares a "small difference," half-Jewishness, with two "Commie" world champions, Spassky and the current champion, Garry Kasparov (born Garik Weinstein), whom Fischer has accused of "pre-arranging" the games of his matches with Anatoly Karpov. Fischer's father, a German-born physicist who may or may not have worked for the Wehrmacht in the early stages of the war, and his phenomenally strong-willed, Swiss-born Jewish mother, Regina, separated bitterly after news of the Holocaust in 1945, when Bobby was two. The father is said to have moved to South America.

Regina, Bobby, and his older sister Joan lived in various parts of the Southwest before settling in a fourth-floor walk-up in Brooklyn, when he was six. The following year, Joan bought him a cheap chess set at the candy store on the first floor of their apartment building. Though he had a phenomenal knack for puzzles and games, he didn't take to chess immediately; the fascination dates from a year later, when he came upon a dusty old book in the library of a house in Patchogue, Long Island, that the family was visiting. Its pages were filled with pictures and exploits of the nineteenth- and early-twentieth-century masters, and their elegant clothes and austere faces filled Bobby with wonder. He became freakishly singleminded. "All I want to do is play chess," he announced. "Ever."

"Bobby was simply a boy with no relations outside chess," says Viktor Korchnoi, the former challenger for the world championship that Fischer vacated in 1975 to Anatoly Karpov. He met Fischer for the first time in 1960, in Buenos Aires. "Bobby is not crazy, like they say. And believe me I know crazy. He simply failed to keep up normal relations," adds Korchnoi, who recently finished his game (via a psychic) with the 1920s Hungarian grandmaster, Geza Maroczy. "This is a great danger at that age, because chess can take over the mind. Even if you don't want to, you must keep up normal relations, which for a boy that age, of course, is school.

School for Bobby was a blur. A science teacher at Erasmus Hall High School wrote "Not Satisfactory" on a test he got a 65 on. "Tough," wrote Bobby, who felt his teachers were "all mental cases." At 14, already U.S. Champion and a year shy of becoming the youngest grandmaster in history, his notebooks were filled with drawings of grotesque heads and radio-babble: "Hey everybody gather round, c'mon, let's dig these Rockin' Sounds, we got the rugs on the floor . . . Come on now I wanna swim with you." He dropped out at 16. "The stuff they teach you in school," he said, "I can't use." The radio was his source of truth: "I was with Bobby in Yugoslavia in 1968," says the prolific British chess writer and international master Bob Wade, one of the few people Fischer has ever trusted (he once hired Wade to research an opponent's games—something he normally did on his own). "His only real interest was listening to the news on the radio." In Sveti Stefan, Fischer carries a yellow Sports Radio wherever he goes.

He developed a passion for Yugoslavia in 1958, when he came to play his first international tournament, an elimination qualifier to determine the next challenger for the world championship. The Yugoslavs, who are chess-crazy, unconditionally took in the "Corduroy Killer," as he was known in New York, and Bobby played brilliantly, earning a return to Yugoslavia the following year for the final qualifying tournament. Mikhail Tal, the "Magician from Riga" who won the tournament and became the next world champion, defeated Fischer decisively, however, enraging him. Tal, a relentless joker, walked past Fischer on the bridge outside the playing hall, flapping his hands and saying the word "cuckoo" in a high-pitched voice. "Bobby," a journalist here named Miluivka Lazarevic tells me, "ran back to his room in tears, developed a cold, and went to bed. Bent Larsen [the Danish grandmaster who served as his second in the tournament] had to read him Tarzan and Mickey Mouse stories until he got better."

When Fischer returned here in 1961, he got even in a beautiful game in which he sacrificed his queen, not just beating but hoisting Tal, who is often cited as the greatest attacking player of the modern era. The personal element was hardly unintentional. Now 18 years old, Fischer had an understanding of the depths of competition, and could no longer be "psyched out," as he later put it. "It is difficult," said Tal, "to play against Einstein's theory." (Einstein, who submitted to an I.Q. test, scored dozens of points lower than Fischer.) After a long barnstorming in Argentina, Brazil, and Chile (during which Fischer is said to have seen his father for the only time) he also had a new look. In one of two adjustments he would ever make to reality principle, he had given up his corduroys for suits. Seventeen, all handmade in Argentina, England, Trinidad, California, New York, and East and West Germany. "If you get 17 suits," he believed, "you can rotate them. They wear a long time. That's where the poor man gets it coming and going. His suits wear out fast."

Fischer's second adjustment is said to have come a year later, over the radio, when he joined the Worldwide Church of God, after hearing a sermon by Garner Ted Armstrong. It advocated a mixture of Jewish Sabbath and dietary ritual and apocalyptic Christianity: the Second Coming, the end of the world, regenerative baptism (which Fischer apparently abstained from), and, of course, tithing. He did this in a big way—$93,315.35, according to an interview he may or may not have given in 1976. He followed the Church in the late '60s to its headquarters in Pasadena, and has remained there, despite his eventual break. That came, depending on who you ask, after the failure of the world to end in 1972, of Jesus to appear in 1976, or, more credibly, over his disillusionment with the alleged fiduciary and moral profligacy of Church leaders: In 1972, Garner Ted was accused by various members of adultery, and by 1976, the Church's yearly take of $75 million had outstripped Billy Graham's and Oral Roberts' combined.

The break was bitter: There was a flurry of leafleting by Fischer outside the Church's Ambassador College in 1976, a late-night incident of assault on an ex-Church woman he felt had violated his confidence (he later settled out of court with her), and a $3.2 million lawsuit. It left him essentially homeless (he had lived, after his victorious return from Reykjavik, in the basements of the luxury homes of various ministers) and penniless. After 1975, when he resigned his title (because only 43 of his 44 demands for a title-defense match had been met), the rare accounts of his situation all mention cheap rooms in Pasadena and L.A., months of his crashing on former friends, and days spent riding the orange citybus between L.A. and Pasadena, analyzing chess games on his pocket set. At the end of Fischer's one public statement since Reykjavik, a 14-page, Gogolesque pamphlet titled, "I Was Tortured in the Pasadena Jailhouse!" (he had it printed in 1981 after a case of mistaken identity led to his two-day incarceration), he wrote: "When I left home that Tuesday I had nine dollars in cash and well over another dollar in change . . . either a five dollar bill and four ones plus well over a dollar in change or nine ones plus well over a dollar in change (I'm 99% sure it was the former)."

 Other than royalty checks for his 1969 collection, *My 60 Memorable Games* (probably the most cogent chess book ever written), he seems to have depended on the curiosity of strangers. Through back channels, one could place a telephone call to Fischer, for $2,500; $5,000 was the fee for a meeting. One also had to pay him $1,000 to open the letter requesting the meeting, and that letter had to be addressed: Mr. Robert James Fischer, World Chess Champion. Yasser Seirawan, the highest-ranked American grandmaster since Fischer's abdication, knows of at least 20 cases where the money was plunked down, including rabid chess player and fellow religious recluse Bob Dylan, whose tour manager is said to have bought him the meeting as a birthday present.

Most of the other known meetings involved multimillion-dollar offers from various fascists and despots, to play chess in their countries. "Dictatorships," the English grandmaster Raymond Keene tells me, "have an enormous weakness for chess, particularly for Bobby." Ferdinand Marcos' Philippines offered $3 million, the Shah of Iran and Qatar $2 million each, and South Africa, Chile, and Argentina are said to have put up similar amounts. Last year, a Francista millionaire from the south of Spain sent a Basque chess-playing journalist named Leontxo Garcia with a $4 million offer. Garcia spent a few nights walking around Pasadena with Fischer before he was told, "Nah. The figure's too low." "Fischer," Garcia says, "has some very strange ideas, but he is the most brilliant man I ever met. I believe he is more intelligent than Einstein. He didn't seem to care about the money, either."

"Fischer," agrees Bob Wade, "never cared about money. His only desire was to prove that his choices were correct: He wanted chess to be important, because he was a chess player, and he wanted to be important. Bobby knew money was important, but he didn't have a clue why, outside of clothes and status. The only way he could accomplish what he wanted was to fight for a lot of money. Once he got it, he gave it away. He did not know how to spend it. And once he'd become champion, after, essentially, sacrificing his life for it, he didn't know how to spend his time."

Time does seem to be the key to Fischer's return. In 1990, he registered a patent in New York for the Bobby Fischer Anti-Time-Pressure Chess Clock. Unlike standard chess clocks, which tick away remorselessly while a player thinks, this one awards what Fischer calls "bonus minutes" every time a move is made. "It is a gross overstatement," says Korchnoi, "but in chess, it can be said I play against my opponent over the board, and against myself on the clock." With the Fischer Clock, the faster you move, the more time you gain. Only a man who lost 20 years of his life could have conceived it.

Since registering his patent, Fischer has spent much of his time abroad, staying with families outside Brussels, Manila, and, for over a year, in the Bavarian countryside outside Bamberg. Each of the three families had a young child Fischer developed a great affection for. It's said he spent hours teaching each one to play chess.

Janos Kubat, Press Director of the Match, speaks of a "fairy tale motive" behind this match: a series of "It's never too late" letters sent to Fischer, who's about to turn 50, by a Hungarian chess master, Zita Rajcsanyi, occasionally referred to as his fiancée. I spend an afternoon playing chess with Zita—an incredibly patient, mothering 19-year-old with thick glasses, a pony-tail, long, wrinkled skirts, T-shirts, and high-top Converse that she laces all the way up her calf—and find it easy to believe Kubat's "fairy tale." Fischer, in her telling, is an open and very simple book. "He is completely natural. He plays no roles," she says. "He is like a child. Very, very simple."

"We've waited 20 years," says Nebosa Dukelic, the moderator of the match's opening press conference. "It's good we wait some more."

Flanked by Fischer, Spassky, Vasiljevic and a Serbian engineer who has perfected the model of the Fischer Clock that will be used in the match, Dukelic has a huge, helpless smile as Fischer, in a gray business suit, off-yellow shirt, and floral-print tie, keeps some 175 members of the media sweating for 15 minutes under the arc lights while he leafs through the questions he has insisted be put to him in writing. A miniature version of the Serbian-Bosnian war is breaking out in the first few rows between the battle-hardened print and electronic journalists, fighting for space. Swiveling in his chair before them, raking a finger through his beard with bizarre lese-majeste, Fischer smiles, grimaces, and raises an eyebrow: "Hah-hah. That's a good question"; or "Who typed these up anyway? There's a real lot of typos in these questions." Every few minutes he swivels 180 degrees to read the 15-foot sign behind him: THE WORLD CHESS CHAMPIONSHIP. He never looks at the journalists, even when a shoving match breaks out between an AP stringer and an Irish cameraman who's just arrived from Sarajevo.

"Perhaps there is a question for Mr. Spassky?" says Dukelic.

"Nah, I'm first," says Bobby.

"Yes, it's right, the World Champion goes first," Dukelic immediately apologizes. "Perhaps I can help you eliminate some repetitive questions?"

"I wanna choose 'em. That's my agreement," Fischer says, looking over at Vasiljevic. "Alright. We'll start with some typically impudent questions from *The New York Times*." He says *New* so that it sounds like *Jew*. Lest anyone miss the point, he identifies the man as "a Mr. Roger CoHEN." Sitting next to me, Josef Lapid, an elderly Yugoslav who emigrated to Israel in 1948 (he's the editorial writer for the Tel Aviv daily *Ma'a-reev*), starts murmuring: "He can't get away with this. He must answer for this." On Cohen's fourth question: "If you beat Spassky, will you go on to challenge Kasparov for the World Championship?" Bobby brings the house down by swiveling 180 degrees and pointing at the sign. "Can he read what it says behind here?" Roger Cohen is doubled over with laughter. So is Josef Lapid.

The laughter turns to dumbstruck applause when Fischer, looking remarkably like Lenny Bruce reading transcripts of his obscenity trials, answers a question about defying sanctions: "Just one second," he says, rifling through his briefcase until he finds the Treasury Department's August 21, 1992 "Order to Provide Information and Cease and Desist Activities." "So!" he bellows. "This is my reply to their Order not to defend my title here." He hurls a gob of spit on the Order, thick enough to leave a smudge when it's Xeroxed and circulated to the media.

And on he goes: 20 years of private vituperation squeezed into 90 minutes of this and one other press conference a week later. He accuses Kasparov, Korchnoi, and Karpov—"really the lowest dogs around"—of pre-arranging the seven world championship matches they have contested since 1977; World Jewry of blacklisting him for 20 years; the Moscow publisher Physical Culture and Sport (which published a Russian edition of *My 60 Memorable Games*) of owing him royalties of "let's say $100,000, just to open discussions"; and the U.S. government and Time, Inc. of conspiring to defraud him of "tens, maybe hundreds of millions," this dating to his mid-1970s $3.2 million breach-of-contract lawsuit over an exclusive Fischer sold Time, Inc. for Reykjavik. (The suit was thrown out of court when Fischer, representing himself after firing his lawyers, refused to answer questions such as his name and age, on grounds that it was private information.) To understand "why I was singled out for such treatment," he says, "well, you have to understand a lot about the world scene and who controls America . . . what kind of religion they have."

When he begins to analyze communism as "basically a mask for Bolshevism, which is basically a mask for Judaism," Josef Lapid is up on his feet and hollering: "No, we can't leave this anti-Semitic outburst unanswered . . ." Lapid's ejaculation seems to remind the Irish cameraman and AP stringer that they have unfinished business. As another shoving match starts in the first row, Fischer looks up at the audience for the first time and begins to swivel in his chair, a small but extremely satisfied smile playing itself out on his face.

Seven hours later, 45 minutes before the $1 million Opening Spectacle on Sveti Stefan, he still has that smile as he marches ceremoniously across the causeway to the music of a Montenegrin 25-piece brass band, shoulder to shoulder with Vasiljevic, Zita, and Spassky and his wife Marina. I've come early, to talk to Vosco at Under the Olives, and seize the opportunity to try to meet Fischer. Falling in line with the procession, five feet behind him, I pick up his marching beat, a self-conscious lope that from moment to moment looks like a stutter-step at a New Orleans funeral, or a goose-step. Lapid, the Israeli journalist, steps into the procession 20 paces later with a fragile, 82-year-old man, Sadik Danon, the Chief Rabbi of Yugoslavia.

"Bobby was the greatest." Danon is soon whispering to me, unconsciously picking up the goose step as he looks at the back of Fischer's head. He pronounces the name so that it sounds a bit like *Boobala*.

"Are you going to file a protest against his remarks?" I ask.

"No," he says. "I don't want to hurt Bobby. He's just crazy."

Vasiljevic leads the procession to a cafe 200 yards from the causeway. With a flourish of both hands he invites Fischer, Spassky, Zita, and Marina to sit down, and as two dozen bodyguards form a half circle around the table, he instructs a waiter to bring big bottles of mineral water. It's an incredibly hot, still evening.

"I wanted the, uh, you know, individual bottles," Fischer says when the waiter comes out with a tray. "The small kind."

The waiter brings out five small bottles a minute later. Fischer's talking about bug repellent. "It's natural, your stuff?" he asks Marina "Is it natural?" He has a large mosquito bite on his forehead and a crazed look. "I bet it's chemicals, right? I've got a machine that kills them with a beep. You know? They fly in. Bzzzz. Then, beep, pow! Bye-bye bug. Hah-hah. Bzzzz, beep, pow!"

"Mine you put on your skin," Marina tells him.

"Right, the roll-on," Fischer says with great distaste. "See, that's chemical." Sweat is beading up on his forehead, and Spassky offers him a tissue from a packet, which he accepts with great suspicion, then a feeble chess joke as he wipes his whole face: "Usually, I avoid exchanges in the opening. Hah-hah." Spassky offers another two tissues, then the whole packet. Fischer repeats his joke about chess openings as he examines the packet thoroughly. "Ah. Yeah," he finally says approvingly. "German."

Vasiljevic comes to the table with two tall, dark and heavily-bearded men, Milo Djukanovic and Momir Bulatovic, the Prime Minister and President of Montenegro. Fischer looks distrustful as they are introduced—they look like the Smith Brothers, and he clearly doesn't believe Montenegro has a president—and offers the tips of his fingers by way of a handshake. The crown prince fares no better a minute later. Fischer only wants to talk about "those fixed games of those criminals."

"I'm not a specialist on this pre-arranged business," Spassky says with enormous reason. "But I do believe Kasparov and Karpov agreed beforehand to a draw, the 19th game in Lyon, in 1990. This time, I agree, was a fix."

"What you're saying now, Boris," says Fischer, "is just a pinprick. I'm going to demonstrate it all in a book. Proof positive." He has to stop to explain to Spassky what *pinprick* means. "See, the 19th game in Lyon is where it gets really ingenious. They made that one look obvious, so you'd say, 'If'"—he raises an index finger, and a terrible, manic glint comes into his eye—" 'If. Maybe. Just that one.' And you'd forget about all that other injustice."

"It's like the Mafia," says Spassky.

"Nah, Boris, the Mafia's got honor."

"Yes, because they must deal with other Mafia."

"These guys are much worse than the Mafia. So much worse."

Vasiljevic comes over to explain the procession back to the Opening Spectacle. Spassky, who seems for the moment overwhelmed with the absurdity of it all, says something that makes Vasiljevic respond, clearly with some offense taken, "I have no monkeys on my island." Fischer gets confused each time Vasiljevic pronounces the word *spectacle*, a la Française. "We will march back to the bridge, where we drink the Schnapps with the dignitaries. Then, through my town, past the dancers and the circus people, to the Spectock-ck!"

"Through your town?" Fischer asks.

"Yes," says Vasiljevic. "The town on my island."

"Your island." Fischer looks hypnotized. I think about an interview Fischer gave thirty years ago, at the age of 19: "I've got strong ideas about my house," he told the man. "I'm going to hire the best architect and have him build it in the shape of a rook . . . Class. Spiral staircases, parapets, everything. I want to live the rest of my life in a house built exactly like a rook."

"Yes, Bobby," Vasiljevic says, taking a cigar from his pocket and firing it up. "My island."

Fischer stays for only half the Opening Spectacle, which, with its two orchestras, innumerable dance troupes, six-year-old violin prodigy, two sopranos, three folk-singers, six banquet tables, and full fireworks to the tune of the "Hallelujah Chorus," seems to leave him unsated. I follow him to a small, dark piazza in the center of the island, where he watches the contortionist and some rather erotic folk-dancing for half an hour, Zita and Vasiljevic at his side. One of the dancers begins to gyrate a foot in front of him, the guest of honor, and he blushes, vividly, and starts perspiring. "Gotta go," he says, getting up quickly and rushing out of the piazza trailed by a half-dozen bodyguards. At the back of the pack, Zita is looking over her shoulder at the dancers with an enchanted smile.

The match itself is an anti-climax. The question of Fischer's greatness is left unanswered: His play, which through a 16-year career had its own steadily developing logic ("It began to feel," says the international master Walter Shipman, "as though you were playing against chess itself"), now has no signature of its own. The first game is brilliant: "Every move perfect," says Yasser Seirawan. "Terrifying." More to the point, however, is that its perfection and terror are pure Kasparov and Karpov. It has Kasparov's trademark pyrotechnical attack on both sides of the board at once (on bookend pawn pushes—his 19th and 40th moves—you can practically feel Kasparov's hand moving the pieces), and Karpov's patented suffocation technique, in the grip of which the opponent can only watch his pieces slowly rendered useless. In chess terms, it reads like a successful, but extremely didactic attempt to show that the game hasn't passed him by.

His subsequent failures in the next four games, particularly pusillanimous losses in Games Four and Five, have very much the same feeling. It's not that Fischer has lost it, or as Kasparov rather hopefully opines on Finnish television halfway through the match, "The legend of the best chess-player has been destroyed." He's simply playing like one of those well-read but insufferably solipsistic lunch-counter philosophers he sounds like in some of his rants.

His form is outstanding by the time they leave Sveti Stefan at the end of the match's first half, but it just doesn't seem to matter. There's no tension, except for a few comical demands he's laid down: To have the first three rows of seats removed, and to have a sign placed behind the board, reading WORLD CHESS CHAMPIONSHIP, three times, so that no photograph can be taken without that vital information. He has a blue curtain placed over the ten-foot aperture, then has it sealed off with glass. The curtain rises with him and Spassky already seated. They're chatting away happily, as though at the beginning of some domestic comedy, and you quickly get the feeling this is no match at all. When Fischer amiably shrugs his shoulders after his first defeat, saying, "That's what chess is all about. One day you give your opponent a lesson, the next day he gives you one." You get the feeling this simply isn't Fischer either: The old Bobby would have been foaming.

At the airport, heading back to Belgrade, I notice Vasiljevic and four bodyguards entering the police captain's office, and through a crack in the door watch them check in their 9mm pistols. As Vasiljevic reluctantly snaps open his rectangular case and surrenders the Heckler & Koch machine gun inside, he sees me and waves his hand imperiously. "Go way," he says disgustedly.

At the gate, however, he comes over and sits beside me. "Now you know my business secret," he says. "I am no longer mysterious? The *Jerusalem Post* says I am 'of mysterious origins.'"

"Did you sell weapons to Israel?"

"No," he says with a big smile. "Stupid, stupid. I sold medicine to Israel. Printing paper. I saw you at the cafe, before the Spectock-ck. If Bobby knows you are press, he runs 25 meters. And, believe me, if he knows you are Jewish, he runs 50 meters."

"They say that you are a creation of this war. That your money comes entirely from the black market and from all this killing."

Vasiljevic gives me a big grin and tells me that I don't know what war is. "I have seen more wars than this. I grew up with war. Believe me, you don't know war."

"Tell me about yourself."

"No, nothing. I am mysterious. I have two sons, named David and Levy. I invited Sadik Danon to the Spectock-ck. Why don't you ask how I know you are Jewish?"

"Was your sons' mother Jewish?"

"Don't ask. I tell Bobby, 'My two sons are . . . have the Jewish names. You tell me about your chess table. You tell me about your pieces. You can tell me about the light in your chess hall. But my guests, you stay away.' He respects. How can he no. It's my town."

"Do you think he's crazy?"

"No, he's like Hegel."

"Hegel?"

"Yes, everything fascist, and Marx and Hitler follow him. It's like Bobby, a little. You know, Hegel stayed in only one town his whole life. Bobby never goes out either. He hates change."

"Do you mean Kant?"

"No, Hegel. I know philosophy. You don't know."

"Did you get Bobby by promising him his own island?"

"No," he says with an impish smile, "by being mysterious. He is not so difficult. Only for you, you know."

"So you don't agree that Bobby is crazy?"

"No. Not crazy. Irrational judgment. Trauma of the childhood."

"His mother?"

"No, the father. If you mention the father, he will not speak the whole night. Mother, he calls every day. And the sister, crazy sister. I like you," he suddenly says. "I could give you exclusive with Bobby. But it doesn't matter. I talk with him 12 hours, all night, no stopping. It's one word, maybe two. Trauma of the childhood. Bad instruction."

45

Vasiljevic shrugs his shoulders as he gets up to board the plane, where he has the entire first class section booked for himself and his entourage. "Poor Bobby."

SHADOWS OF A ROOM

Teddy Atlas

They wait in line to see the doctor. This makes them nervous, not because of fear of a needle, but the reminder that the moment is growing closer. It is a large room, stripped of makeup, only the essentials, some scattered chairs (the uncomfortable kind), a table, and of course the *scale*. Shirtless men pass the apparatus that checks weight, glancing at it as if too long a look might invoke some sort of retribution. The building is in a forgotten part of the Bronx, where travel can be only for a couple of reasons, none whimsical or touristy in nature. Walking in, your thoughts are of survival—not like the television show, but primitive, instinctual, like this building, the only one on the block still standing. As you climb up the stairs and smell the walls painted in urine, those words *still standing* stick in your head.

Finished with the doctor, they moved to the scale. Each approached it carefully, as if it were something they did not like yet needed to respect. Some would get on with a cocky arrogance. Others would step on cautiously as if they were crossing a field of mines and this was the last yard. Many would take a deep breath like they were about to dive into a pool, breathing again only when the head behind nodded that the weight was okay. With those rituals out of the way, everyone separated into small groups.

If these were young enlisted men, this would be the battlefield and the groups would be small troops. Like the Army, each packet of people had a strong young male and an older man who seemed to be in charge, the soldier and an officer. As the younger man sat, he stared at the older man as though orders would be coming, or as if they'd done this before. The young man looked as if what was about to be said was the most important thing he would ever hear.

The atmosphere of the room had changed. It was like the climate at a wake, relaxed talk in the lounge area but stricter and less conversation inside. People knew why they were here.

These men were here to fight. Twenty or so young amateurs would be paired off in boxing matches. They were all here for different reasons. Some to become world champions and to claim the rewards that come with that, others wanted to better armor themselves for the private wars they were facing in their neighborhoods or their homes. Some were looking for help, and the one-on-one attention and demands that came from their trainers. Still others came on dares from their peers, and some, well, they weren't sure; they seemed to be lured by a primal calling to arms, a need to know what they could do and what they actually would do when put into a threatened position with no guarantees.

The process now was to match the fighters according to weight and experience. Officials from the Amateur Boxing Federation would do this. It is not an exact science. Although the weight categories are controlled by the scale, properly matching the experience of each contestant depends on the honesty of the trainer and boxer and the accuracy of the boxer's passport. The passport is a license that theoretically records all of his bouts. This way you can evenly and fairly match fighters. In reality not all bouts get recorded. Some kids fight in places where passports are not needed, and here people do not interpret honesty as moral truth but instead as the Holy Grail of Survival. It is not measured in volume but in physical moves, and, like a war, whatever it takes to ensure survival becomes acceptable—within, of course, the boundaries of enforcement.

As the aspiring warriors wait to be matched, the first enemy shows his face—fear. The weapon of choice is imagination, and the bullet time. There will be a wait of a couple of hours before a punch can be landed, and it is during this period that many a casualty can take place. Some are lost before leaving their foxholes. Now is a time to think, and that battle can be larger than anything real, simply because it is not. There are no parameters, no fences to keep the mind from going. Only experience and discipline can keep the soldiers of the imagination from storming the walls. You are alone. For some it's the first time. Without alcohol to fuel them or numbers to secure them. Without hate and anger to propel them or weapons to insure them. Like a person at the end of life's travels, you have only yourself—and, for some, they don't even know who or what that is, not yet.

As the bouts are being made, time is like a destroyer storming through the sea, using minutes like depth charges. While you wait you can only think, and that can be a bayonet to the belly. They say a drowning man will grab for a razor blade—well, an inexperienced fighter will look for hope and reassurance anyplace available as he sits waiting in that war room called a dressing room. He will size up potential opponents as they walk about the room. He'll look at one who seems to be his size and start to analyze his strengths and weaknesses. But being new to this battlefield, he does not recognize the sniper who has come disguised in imagination, the sniper whose only order is to exaggerate so as to avoid a battle by scaring his adversary away.

Now, as he peeks at his potential opponent, he notices every move he makes. How he walks with confidence or without. He watches as the other man shadow-boxes, looking for any flaw he can find and noticing anything that he can recognize as talent, matching it against his video memory of past greats and remembering the things he'd heard his trainer emphasize—shoulder snap, combinations, leverage, control—and sure enough, this guy has all of it! Yes, if there was reincarnation, this was Sugar Ray Robinson, back again. As he watches the reborn Sugar Man snap off brilliant combination after combination, he realizes the room has gotten warmer and most of the air has been removed.

He remembers one of the older fighters from the gym had told him to take deep breaths. As he steadies his respiratory system, the nervous system acts up. His left leg begins to jump. He tries to hold it still with his closest arm, so as not to bring attention. But now his whole left side is bumping up and down, arm and leg. Aware that his opponent or his opponent's camp may see this, he immediately begins mouthing words to the involuntary beat he is keeping. Running out of words, he remembers advice from a trainer: "Motion relieves tension." The trainer told him that is why waiting fathers pace up and down the hallways in the maternity wards—"It is nature's way of relieving the tension."

Immediately he gets to his feet and begins to bounce up

and down. He walks, mimicking fighters he'd seen, now understanding it was not a traditional dance but a Heimlich maneuver for fighters. It seems to work; his body begins to idle at a slower pace. His heart jumps a couple of beats as his trainer yells to him: Time to wrap up. He moves to the corner of the room, where the trainer has two chairs, one turned backwards facing the other. The one turned around has a folded towel on the top of the wooden back. Sitting on the forward-facing chair, the boxer places his arm on top of the chair with the towel. His trainer stands in front of him and tells him to open his hand and extend his fingers wide and stiff. The trainer takes a roll of gauze and begins to wrap it around the boxer's wrist. After several loops he brings it up in a crisscross motion around the hand. After several layers the trainer carefully curves it around the thumb before going up top, where he goes back and forth, creating a pad over the knuckles. As the gauze moves in and out, disappearing each time it goes under the hand, the fighter begins to fall into a trance, broken only when the trainer tells him to make a fist. Now his teacher takes thin strips of adhesive tape that had been cut and placed on the wall and places each one on the fighter's wrist and runs them one at a time between his fingers, pulling the padding on the knuckles tight, creating an almost castlike wrapping.

"How does it feel?" the soldier's asked by the general after each strip is secured. Now more white tape is put over the gauze and around the wrist. Once both hands are done the trainer smiles at his work and barks, "Now use them!"

Understanding that he is another step closer to what lies beyond that door, the boxer tries to block out the vision of a long-ago story he'd read about Captain Hook and his practice of walking men off the plank of a ship. But as hard as he tries, he can't shut off his mind's projector of eight-millimeter-riddled bodies dropping into a dark sea. He suddenly feels a deep coldness that seems to spiral down his body. The ground feels almost loose as he orders himself to swim for the surface. He shakes his head to the side, noticing the light in the room, for a moment happy to be there. Then he sees the boxer he had sized up as his opponent. Instinctively, he moves his eyes down to the other's feet. What kind of shoes was he wearing? If they were the expensive yellow ones, the choice of top amateurs, that would probably mean he was an experienced fighter. But if he only wore sneakers, what a reprieve that would be: the tools of a beginner. As he directed his eyes down, he turned his head slightly so as not to make it obvious. Before he fixed onto his target he stopped for a moment, acting as though he were looking at a crack in the wall, how reasonable he thought it would seem to anyone watching him that he would be staring at this; also it bought him time, time to think if he wanted to know what were on those feet. He turned like a man half looking at the roulette wheel as his last hope for a win bounced through the slots. With a sudden quick glance he saw what he had hoped not to: *yellow shoes.* The feeling in his lower chest reminded him of a day as a young boy when his mother drove away as he stumbled into the concrete block called school. He reminded himself of how that must not have turned out too bad since he didn't have any other thoughts of it.

With that hope he remembered there was another piece of equipment that could offer information on the caliber of his opponent: the mouthpiece. If it were the white rubber one that could be bought in the store for two dollars, there would still be hope that he was dealing with a novice. What he did not want to see was the form-fitted piece made by a dentist, usually in bright colors. Only a fighter of merit with people backing him could afford such protection. As he looked up he saw his opponent smile, and there was nothing white, just a perfect piece of hard red rubber.

All sound seemed to leave the room. Only a familiar light tone remained. It was the same sound he'd heard as a kid when his father put that horn-shaped seashell to his ear. Only this was in both ears. As he swung between shades of black and gray, he tried to remember how he'd gotten here. Why had he allowed himself to get into this situation? His mind traced a map of the subway system. Never clear on which trains led to where. Now he realized that the No. 5 or 6 train would take him into Lower Manhattan, far from here. The temporary shaking in the building reminded him how close the station was. How easy it would be to say he had to go to the bathroom. Once outside, he could rip the hand wraps off and he could buy other clothes or go home in his trunks.

Everything seemed reasonable, perfect, except when word would get out about how he ran, how he had punked out. There was no escape from that.

There was still time. It was an old building—reckless, even dangerous people lived there. How many times had a fire begun in places like this? That would not be an impossibility. He thought about it almost as if his thoughts could make it happen, like gathering kindling for the flame. He was bro-kering a deal with whatever powers that controlled such things, a thought not completely selfish; after all, he clearly said in his mind that he would not want anyone hurt. Just a pass, a temporary obstruction of time and place, a postponement.

What he didn't realize he had gotten was a bridge, a passage of time, a distraction to carry him forward. The moment was here, the clerk in charge of handing out the gloves yelled his name: "You're up!"

His trainer walked toward him with one glove tucked under his arm and the other extended forward. He noticed how his trainer had already spread the laces wide so he could fit his hand inside. As his man held the glove low with his arms stiff, he sunk his left hand into the first glove. As his trainer's voice mingled with the other sounds in the room, he heard, "Left hand first." His trainer was reminding him that they had always done that in the gym, so he wouldn't forget that the jab started everything.

He tried to concentrate now, squeeze out the things that were crowding him. Try to leave only what he thought of when the fight was still in the distance. Remember how proud he felt when he envisioned his hand being raised and his father hugging him, as he did his roadwork in the dark of morning. His hand hit the bottom of the glove as he moved his fingers, grabbing at the soft leather for something to hold. The trainer told him to hold the glove against his stomach as he pulled the laces together. "Push," the trainer said, so he could keep the hand set firmly in the glove. The trainer pulled at the laces, putting a thumb over the drawn string so it wouldn't escape. The fighter noticed that, and tried to knot his own resolve; he was not going back, and for a second he felt stronger than ever before. His trainer tied the knot, then turned tape over it. One of the other fighters from his gym brought over the robe; the tournament supplies them for any boxers who don't have their own. Earlier he had frowned at the colors now they had no meaning. As he was told to loosen up, he wondered why his arms were so heavy. Like when you have gum stuck to your shoe and you try to walk. He pushed his arms forward, but they seemed to pull back toward his body. The locker-room door was now open. He looked down the hallway and was surprised at how long it seemed. As his trainer rubbed the back of his neck, another official from the Federation came over to the trainer. As they talked he felt his breathing come easier, but at the same time he thought this could be another trick played by his body.

He asked his trainer what had happened. The opponent had pulled out, he was sick, there would be no fight today.

It took him some time to realize how easily his arms slid up and down as he threw a punch against the wall. He felt very strong. "I was ready to go!" he yelled to his team, surprised at how firm his voice was. He said he was disappointed; after all, he'd worked so hard in the gym, all for nothing. As his people removed the gloves he marveled at how quickly they came off. As he returned the robe he looked at how faded and worn it was. When he turned to walk toward the front of the room, he saw the fighter that he had thought was his opponent. The man was just getting his gloves on. That wasn't even the guy I was going to fight, he laughed to himself. He waited until the boxer was finished being gloved. He watched the fighter warm up. He was shocked at how much slower his punches were now. There were no combinations. The sharp snappy jab looked rubbery. The footwork looked awkward. Just what his trainer had told him not to do. The confident smile that the reborn Sugar Ray Robinson wore earlier seemed to have been replaced by a nervous, almost sickly, look.

It was like when he went to the movies and someone gave him 3-D glasses, he suddenly saw things he'd missed before.

He whistled a tune as he dressed. While he was packing his gear he thought about his opponent and wondered if he was really sick. For the first time, he realized he had not been alone. That guy felt the same as him. As he headed down the hallway he wondered if he'd come back next week. As he got to the end of the hall he stopped, dropped his bag, and looked back, shaking his head at how short that walk was.

THE SINGLE-MOM MURDER —FEBRUARY 4, 2002

Vanessa Grigoriadis

"Is this New York?"

It was a question that Ava had asked her mother as they passed through towns along I-95 on the drive from Cape Cod to Manhattan over the Christmas holidays. It was a long haul, one that Christa Worthington, a forty-six-year-old free-lance journalist, single mother, and resident of New York on and off for twenty years, had rarely undertaken in the few years since she had made the difficult choice to leave the city. But at age two and a half, Ava seemed capable of taking the trip without a total meltdown, and Worthington wanted a bit of time out of the drear of the wintertime Cape, so they packed toys and snacks into the Honda Civic and hit the road. Worthington had been invited to a party to be thrown later in the week by *New York Times* theater critic Ben Brantley, a close friend and former colleague. It seemed like the perfect excuse.

"Is this New York?"

When they reached Manhattan, it was a great home-coming. Worthington's friends were in town for the holidays, and Brantley's party, a big, boozy gathering at an East Village theater, was full of the old gang from her time at fashion magazines in Paris and New York. People remarked how terrific she looked. Though it had meant doing calisthenics to tapes in her living room at night and going to Weight Watchers meetings in nearby Provincetown through the fall, Worthington had finally lost the twenty-odd pounds she'd put on during pregnancy—what she called her "mother pudge." Woody Allen and Soon Yi were at the party—that alone was worth the trip.

Then, on January 6, weeks after she had headed home, Worthington's friends received shocking news. Back at her cottage in Truro, a "down-cape" town just ten minutes away from the curling sand-and-shrub end of Cape Cod, Worthington had been beaten savagely and stabbed in the chest. She'd bled to death on her kitchen floor. She was there more than twenty-four hours before she was found. Ava had been with her.

Detectives found Ava's bloody hand prints all over the house—on a Disney videotape Ava had tried to stick into the VCR, on her own sippy cup (from which she had apparently tried to feed her mother), on a box of Cheerios she'd managed to pull from the counter. She needed her diaper changed, badly; she'd explained to the man who found her that "Mommy fell down." A precociously talkative child, Ava was nevertheless still nursing, though she made endless promises to her mother that she would stop. On that terrible night, she'd pulled aside the V of Worthington's nightgown.

For Christa Worthington, Ava was the latest, happiest chapter in what had sometimes been a turbulent life. Told for years by doctors that she would not be able to have a child, she conceived at forty-three. From the outside, her life could seem idyllic. Her family had deep roots in Truro—around the corner from her house there's a road called Worthington

Way—and the first EMT on the scene was a cousin. Part of a clique of relocated parents who were struggling to bring up sophisticated kids in a rural environment, Worthington played French cartoons so Ava could pick up some of the language, and even sent her to a playgroup with a Spanish-speaking nanny in the hope that she might become trilingual. Ava had a real memory for songs, and Worthington had started to play classical music around the house to help develop her ear.

But in the days following Christa's death, it became apparent that the drama and complications that often characterized Christa Worthington's life had by no means ended with Ava's birth. "Everyone always thought Christa played the victim," laments a friend, "and now it turns out that she wasn't exaggerating at all."

In no time, police assembled a roster of possible suspects out of Agatha Christie—the married ex-lover, a local "shellfish constable," who was Ava's father; the aristocratic father with a twenty-nine-year-old heroin-addict girlfriend; an old boyfriend with an angry streak, known to her friends simply as "the magician"; and the neighbor and former boyfriend with a rare brain condition who found her body—he told police he was "returning a flashlight."

Worthington had complained to friends in the weeks before she died that she was a "pariah" in her family and among other townspeople in Truro. She was angry at her father. She'd talked about moving back to the city, restarting her career, getting back in the game. It might have been safer.

Outside the clapboard funeral home in Worthington's hometown of Hingham, Massachusetts, a hard-bitten female cop dispatched by Christopher "Toppy" Worthington, Christa's father, was trying to keep order over the scrum of media: video teams from CNN and Fox News, *People* photographers brandishing telephoto lenses, large delegations from the Boston papers.

"I told yaa before," the cop kept shouting, "not one foot of yaas on the property."

Inside, the scene was far more sedate; continually arriving Worthingtons bent over Christa's flower-laden casket and tried not to weep while viewing the cardboard collages of snapshots Worthington's cousins had assembled. There were sixty or so photos: Christa leaning back on a veranda overlooking the Italian seashore, Christa with three friends in HAPPY BIRTHDAY tiaras, Christa pensive on the windswept Vineyard ferry. "She looks just like Greta Garbo," sighed one of the Worthington aunts, gazing at a black-and-white shot of her niece in Paris.

Toppy himself remained in one corner of the home for nearly the entire four hours of visitation, looking as though he wished he could disappear into the garish floral wallpaper. Soft-spoken and rail-thin from riding his mountain bike nearly every day, he was offered condolences by a continual round of family and friends. He avoided the wake's main attraction, Ava.

Parading about in a green velvet dress topped by a Peter Pan collar, Ava smiled a wide Worthington smile as she navigated the crowd. Ava is now living with Cliff and Amyra Chase, the Cohasset couple designated as her guardians in Worthington's will, which bequeaths $700,000 to the child.

"Yesterday," whispered one of her old baby-sitters, watching her, "Ava went into the corner of the room and said six times, loud and clear, 'Get out of my house, I'm not afraid of you.' Six times she said it."

Ava was there because a child psychologist had advised relatives it was in her future best interest. She held court in a circle of adults—"No more monkeys jumping on the bed!"—until one of her teenage cousins scooped her up and took her to see the collages.

They stopped first in front of a photo of Worthington in her mother's old studio—Gloria Worthington had painted until her death, from cancer, three years ago.

"Where's Ava?" asked Ava.

"I don't know, honey," said the cousin, hiking her up on her hip. "Maybe you weren't born yet."

The next photo was of Ava. It was a summer day on the beach and she was squinting up into the camera, knee-deep in the water, alone.

Ava extended a chubby finger at it. "Where's Mommy?" she asked.

Even at forty-six, Worthington had the lineaments of an appealing girlishness, with pillowy lips, perpetually pink cheeks, and bright, frank eyes. The part of her personality she showed most people was reserved and maybe even a bit shy. "Christa had the innocence of a girl from a small town who thought the world was just such a sweet place," says Knight Landesman, publisher of *Artforum*. "But she was far too sophisticated for that, so you knew it had to be slightly faux."

Christa was like that, layered. "She was such an odd combination of personality traits," says a friend. "She never drank and had long ago quit smoking, wasn't a party girl at all, and was so protective of her daughter you almost wanted to tell her to back off. Yet she would do things to hurt herself. She could really fly to the flame."

If there was one aspect of Worthington's character that commanded the respect of her peers and in which she herself took the most pride, it was that she was brave enough to take the road less traveled.

By moving to Truro, Worthington chose solidity, family, and rootedness over the glitz and excitement of Manhattan. In addition to tracing her roots to the one of the most prominent old families in the Hamptons, the Halseys, Christa Halsey Worthington was granddaughter to perhaps the most respected couple in Truro history: John and Elizabeth "Tiny" Worthington (so named because she stood nearly six feet and wore a size-ten combat shoe when driving ambulances in World War I) are credited with saving the area from the ravages of the Depression. John employed the male half of the town at his fish-processing plant, and Tiny the female at her fishnet-making business; in fact, she invented the fashion of fishnet.

"Christa was very connected to Truro," says a friend. "In a good—and bad—way."

Though Worthington cultivated a deep connection with the stark beachscape—"However fancy the Hamptons become, there is still God in this country, a Puritan God of straight and narrow instincts who demands a degree of awe," she wrote in *Hamptons Country* magazine in 1998—there was much about Truro that upset her. She had long had a difficult relationship with Toppy, a former Massachusetts assistant D.A., who later practiced private law. He, in turn, had problems with the rest of the family, a land-poor clan that lived in Worthington ancestral homes in Truro. There were arguments about whose land was whose; most recently, Worthington felt slighted by an aunt in Florida who sold two parcels she believed to be half hers. In a drastic move, Worthington had even hired a private investigator to look into the situation.

There were other issues, less financial in nature. Toppy had a girlfriend. He was seventy-two. She was twenty-nine. Toppy said he was in love, but let it slip at some point that the woman had been in jail. Worthington hit the roof. She told friends she thought her dad had been "hypnotized."

"Toppy's girlfriend was Christa's obsession of the moment," says a friend. "We told her to forget it: Write a book. Go to Paris. Do anything but sit in Truro and bite your nails over this woman."

She'd moved to Truro to live a simpler life, but from the beginning, Christa being Christa, there was plenty of drama. The first year, she lived in Tiny's unheated, two-room cottage on Truro's town harbor—which the family called "Tiny's hut." She met a guy, Tony Jackett, a married commercial fisherman who now holds the job of local "shellfish constable"—people sometimes joke that he has the last job in the fishing business on the famously over-fished Cape these days. Back then, Jackett had been fishing for flounder every day on his forty-five-foot dragger *Josephine,* anchored in Provincetown. But he'd taken refuge in Truro's Pamet Harbor during a storm and the *Jo* had sunk. He'd raised her, but it was going to take some time to get her back into fighting shape, so the harbormaster was helping him out with part-time work.

Jackett and Worthington began a torrid two-summer-long affair. She told him she was unable to have a child. They didn't use protection. She got pregnant. She informed him that she was definitely having the baby, but he didn't need to be part of the family unit.

"Let's put it this way: Christa had me by the nuts," Jackett says in his thick Massachusetts accent. He pantomimes grabbing something the size of a nectarine. "But she didn't squeeze hard."

As dramatic as Worthington's personal life could be, she was realistic about her once promising career. "Christa would have laughed at the headline about her death in the *Times*: A MURDER IN CAPE COD jolts the fashion world," says a friend. "She had no illusions that the fashion world would be jolted by anything she did at this point." Adds her best friend, Melik Kaylan: "She was . . . disgusted over the feral New York media scene and its interest in trashy culture and celebrity and so on. She was trying to point her life in a more serious intellectual direction in a personal and professional way."

After graduating from Vassar in 1977, Worthington worked briefly as a paralegal before rising through the magazine ranks at *Cosmopolitan* and then Fairchild Publishing, where she landed a job as *Womens Wear Daily*'s accessories editor— "Getting showered with invitations to the best parties and, of course, free fancy sunglasses," recalls a friend. "She was doing a lot better than the rest of us from Vassar at that time," says *Brides* managing editor Sally Kilbridge, who remembers brown-bagging with Worthington at the World Trade Center fountain during their premagazine days. "I could tell she was proud of herself, and we all thought it was incredibly cool— and were incredibly jealous."

In 1983, Worthington made her friends more jealous when at the age of twenty-six she was sent to Paris by Fairchild. "Working at the Paris *W* bureau was a kind of baptism by fire, a sort of graduate school for fashion," says Kate Betts, former editor of *Harper's Bazaar*. "In writing, you learn by mimicking others, and even before I met Christa I knew her byline. She was the perfect Joan Buck-style writer that I tried to emulate."

Worthington interviewed legends like Yves Saint Laurent and Thierry Mugler and went to her share of polo matches and grand balls, though she felt the glamour factor was overrated. She was once assigned to a party given by Baroness Hélène de Rothschild for the engagement of her son to a Belgian princess; Worthington wasn't allowed into the party itself—only the W photographer was invited—but was summoned to the baroness's home afterward for photo captions. She described it to a friend who wrote a profile of her for the *Cape Cod Times*: "There she is, in bed with lace-embroidered pillows around her tapestry-draped bed overlooking the Seine with her dachshund at her feet and a pink ribbon in her hair matching her pink-and-white nightie. It's three in the afternoon and she's still in bed; and she works very, very hard at giving me the right names, and she's eating champagne truffles. . . ."

"Christa had this great, wry bemusement about that whole world, a kind of 'Isn't it odd that all these people find fashion and money so important?' " says author and friend Jay Mulvaney, who visited her often at her tiny "but fabulous" apartment on the Left Bank and remembers, not without some glee, that she had a discount at Chanel. "But she wasn't taken in by that world—she had that Waspy disconnect: She was already *there,* so she didn't understand why people had to try so hard."

"When it comes down to it, I know that none of this matters," Worthington remarked in the Cape Cod *Times* interview. "The Yankee no-nonsense approach to life is in my blood. The idea of fashion to most Bostonians is very silly, and they're quick to assess what is silly and what is important, especially in my family."

In 1988, Worthington, who by that point had worked her way up to the prominent position of W's acting bureau chief, was passed over for the job in favor of Dennis Thim, a promotions executive at Fairchild's now-defunct men's magazine M. "Christa was devastated, but that was just the way it was at W," says a colleague. "It's always been a boys' club." Counters Fairchild chairman and editorial director Patrick McCarthy: "Christa didn't like being bureau chief—there were too many administrative duties. She just didn't want anyone else to be bureau chief." Though it's unclear exactly how Worthington came to leave the company, it is part of Fairchild lore that she was fired by John Fairchild most unceremoniously: In the elevator on the way to lunch with Worthington and Thim, Fairchild simply remarked, "Christa, you know Dennis, right? He's replacing you."

January in Truro holds a special kind of cold. There's nothing to stop the wind blowing off the ocean, and the memory of summer somehow sharpens the chill. The population, 20,000 in August, shrinks to less than 1,600, and with that the taffy shops close down and restaurants with names like Terra Luna cover their windows with plywood. At the local deli, the only customers are handymen renovating summer cottages for their seasonal owners, which gives the blonde behind the counter more time to read. Today she's immersed in Leo Damore's *In His Garden,* a chronicle of the last murder to occur in Truro, back in 1968, when carpenter Tony "Chop Chop" Costa killed four young vacationing women and buried their dismembered remains in graves only three feet deep, in a patch of the Truro woods where he used to grow marijuana. The graves were found less than a mile from Worthington's house.

"I'm reading this so I can understand the way people are acting now," says the blonde, closing the book. "The fear. The panic. It's nuts." This is her second job; she's also a night police officer. "Tim Arnold. Questioned him myself that night. He didn't do it. Don't know who did it. Don't have a clue."

Arnold found Worthington. He's the ex-boyfriend with the unusual brain problem, cavernous malformation (the blood vessels in his brain are abnormally enlarged). A children's-book illustrator, he lived literally in Worthington's backyard for a year without meeting her. One of Ava's nannies set them up on a date: He joined Worthington and Ava on their daily walk. He lived at her house for four months; after a breakup, he moved back home, or, rather, into the home of his aging father, who has just sat down to the newspaper and some breakfast. The newspaper with an article about his son as a possible murder suspect.

A mug of coffee in his hand, Arnold slowly makes his way over to join his father at the kitchen table. He is a big man, but his tiny voice makes him smaller. He keeps pushing his horn-rimmed glasses up and down the bridge of his nose, but they don't seem to serve much purpose. Since an operation in the early summer on his brain stem, Arnold has had double vision, and he keeps his left eye closed for long periods—the effect is slightly spooky.

Arnold has said that he cannot speak about the night that he found Christa on the advice of his lawyer, who would probably rather that we didn't get into the intricacies of why he drove over to her house to return the flashlight when she lives so close by, and why he didn't have a flashlight himself on the Cape in the wintertime, and in any case he doesn't want to relive the experience of telling his father (who had driven over with him) that he thought Christa was "d-e-a-d" so as not to upset Ava, and then walking back through the woods to call 911 from his phone since he couldn't find Worthington's. So we talk about his relationship with Christa.

"I think Ava's presence had a lot to do with it, in retrospect," says Arnold. "Ava is beautiful. She's so sensitive. She can be very sensitive to what people's agenda is, for good or ill. She can get easily hurt." His eye flicks open. "That's what I can tell you most about Christa—about her relationship with her daughter."

In recent months, Arnold says, he'd visit Worthington with the sole purpose of seeing Ava. And Worthington? "She was very . . . complicated," Arnold says. "We had lots of quarrels, just low-level quarrels. She could be very caustic, and her comments had a destructive quality to them. Angry. I used to chide her for being a Dorothy Parker wannabe. She'd laugh."

He sips the coffee. "You know, I just saw Ava yesterday," he says. "And when I left, she really didn't want me to go. It was heartbreaking." If they were so close, maybe Arnold should be her new dad. His eye snaps closed, and he rubs it with a knuckle. "Well," he says finally, "I can't make that argument to anybody."

Shell-shocked after losing out on one of the best jobs in Paris, Worthington decided to follow a British "painter-slash-librarian" boyfriend to London, where she began to freelance in earnest. Some of her writing seems rushed ("The world's top fashion designers make fantastic clothes; for most of us, reality bites painfully at the cash register") but most is well researched and vibrant. Worthington turned her passion for antiques and flea markets into a niche, writing on such topics as antique snuffboxes, modern book collectors, and refurbished ship's compasses.

Then there was another typical "Christa drama," as one friend describes it. In the summer of 1989, a Con Edison steam pipe blew up outside the apartment she owned on Gramercy Park and was renting out to one of her editors, Deborah Kirk. It killed two workers and a building resident, injured twenty-four others, and seriously damaged her apartment. Soon Worthington became involved in a suit against Con Ed; when things fizzled out with her man in London, she decided to go back to New York and deal with the legal hassle. She was surprised at how happy she was to be back in the city, and once she moved back into her apartment, she made it a real home, decorating it with a mix of funky tapestries and flea-market knickknacks as well as a huge antique mirror that she had shipped over from Paris—"the only thing of any value Christa ever owned," says a friend.

While Worthington did get steady work at *Elle* and later *Elle Décor* during the tenure of friend and confidante Marian McEvoy, she found it hard to establish herself as a writer outside the fashion world, and even there she was seen as someone who was talented but out of the game. Most of her income came from a commission to write copy for three "Chic Simple" books—on scarves, accessories, and clothes. "Flirtatious or functional, gloves are the hats of the hand," she wrote in the accessories guide's hand-wear chapter. "They dramatize instantly: they can't help it. They're all about movement, so they tend to provoke. The dropped glove is a mating cry; the gauntlet, the call to combat."

Not particularly challenged by these haiku, Worthington began an obsessive romance with a quiet, moody, yet handsome guy whom friends remember only as "the magician." Their stormy relationship was par for the course. "There was always this or that drama with this or that guy, and they seemed to reach the soap opera stage very quickly," says friend and television producer Billy Kimball. "Christa liked to see herself as the heroine of her own nineteenth-century novel."

Worthington herself wrote on the topic. "Pain addicts are perhaps the real fans of *Wuthering Heights*, preferring the fix of unrequited love. For it is about a love that prefers the bell jar of bliss, the cocoon of torment to the inglorious reality of 'he's just a guy with a mother problem.' "

"The magician" was in fact really a magician, who did the occasional children's party and nightclub gig, but mostly he hung out at a Third Avenue dive near Worthington's house, where he would "do his card-floating-in-the-air-level tricks and then sucker people into buying him beers," according to the bar's owner. "Problem was that when he was done, watches and wallets would sometimes be missing." The magician lived with Worthington in her studio apartment for a while, though friends say she eventually got sick of his unpredictability and temper tantrums. When she called it quits, friends say, he smashed in her front door. She talked about getting a restraining order.

Among the locals in the outer Cape, Tony Jackett is a legend. Born and bred in Provincetown, grandson of a Portuguese harpooner, the fifty-one-year-old Jackett has the looks of an aging George Clooney and the sex appeal to go with them. A fixture at selectmen meetings and weekly art openings, he's fished with Sebastian Junger and is a main character in Peter Manso's *Ptown: Art, Sex, and Money on the Outer Cape*. With a wife who wears her heart on her sleeve, and four grown kids who've always been the most popular in town, Jackett is the local good old boy, everyone's best friend. But he had a secret.

"There I am working a second job cleaning cottages so we can pay the car insurance," says his wife, Susan, an upbeat blonde with luminous blue eyes behind long bangs. "I'm pressing his shirts before he goes up to Pamet, and little do I know what he's doing when he gets there."

It's the week after Worthington was murdered, and the couple are sipping tea at the kitchen counter of their Sunshine home in a less affluent corner of Truro. Every bit of wall space is covered with family photos and oil portraits of their kids when they were young; their Persians, Fang and Emerson, nap at their feet, and three candles burn near the stove. "One is for my Native American adopted son, who died of AIDS," explains Susan. "Another is for my mother, who also passed away. And this one—this one is for Christa."

Unlike members of Worthington's family, who have refused to speak to any member of the press, the Jacketts were initially open after Worthington's death, until their lawyer turned off the spigot. Part of it was because they're trying to win custody of Ava and seem to think that the media might help them do so, although all the tabloids have done is point out the discrepancy between Jackett's shellfish-constable salary and Ava's substantial inheritance, and part of it was because they've been through therapy over Jackett's affair with Christa—a lot of therapy.

"I never wanted to be a fisherman," explains Jackett, who has a tough, deliberate way of moving and speaking that's bit De Niro-esque. "My dad was a fisherman. I hated fishing! But Susan got pregnant when I was twenty-two. I was fucked. I think I felt like my life had passed me by. I think that's why I had this affair."

"You think," sighs Susan, "after thirty years, you know a person. But I guess we had just drifted in separate directions."

"I was having a midlife crisis," protests Jackett.

Possibly as a result of all this therapy, the Jacketts were able to forge a relationship with Worthington, who had asked Jackett to tell his wife about Ava by the time Ava turned two—she wanted to be ready with an answer when Ava asked who her dad was. "I guess in Europe or somewhere, that kind of request would be normal," says Jackett. "For me, it took some getting used to. But somehow my wife, an amazing woman, was able to transcend the emotions of hurt and betrayal, and take her feelings in a direction of focusing on the child." He says this often, like a mantra: "The child is innocent."

Worthington asked Jackett to put Ava on his health insurance, and he complied; Jackett, at the urging of his very understanding daughter, had Worthington over for tortillas and baby-sat once in a while when she ran errands. Worthington had given the Jacketts a car seat so they could take Ava to their home in their car. Ava was supposed to come for a visit the day Worthington was murdered, but at the last minute, Worthington heard about a play group that had invited a music teacher to tutor the kids, so she asked to reschedule. "Yeah," says Jackett, smirking a little, "Christa was always trying to introduce Ava to *cult-cha*."

"Well, we were disappointed, because we wanted to see the baby," says Susan, and then, much more emotionally: "Honestly, we were becoming friends! Christa just loved that child so much, it was infectious." The Jacketts insist they are ready for the challenge of raising this citified woman's daughter, but first, of course, they have to break the news to Ava that Jackett is her father. Ava had yet to ask, so Worthington never had the chance.

In the last year of her life, Worthington added another complaint to her long list of woes: money. Though she cared little about what money could buy her, she became obsessed with the freedom it would afford both her and Ava in the future. How was she supposed to write fiction, she complained to friends, if she always had to worry about the next paycheck? "It wasn't that Christa felt that the world owed her a living," says friend Steve Radlauer, "but she did feel that there was enough money around with her name on it that she didn't need to struggle with stupid articles that she didn't want to write."

Though Worthington reportedly received $1,700 from her trust each month, the big money was still controlled by Toppy (Worthington had no siblings, so presumably it was all to pass to her upon his death). She didn't quite know how much there was, but she did know that he had cash on hand. After her mother died, he'd sold their waterfront Hingham home and moved into a small two-bedroom near a busy intersection in Weymouth—the difference between the two properties was almost half a million. "I don't know if it was because Christa felt her dad didn't pay enough attention to Ava," says a friend, "or because she had some lingering anger at him for withholding love from her when she was a child, but all I can say is that she became consumed with figuring out what he was doing with that money."

After much browbeating by Worthington, Toppy finally confessed that some of the money was going to pay for an apartment he had rented for his girlfriend in a Boston suburb, Quincy, and to pay her "medical bills," he explained cryptically. As it turns out, Elizabeth Porter is a heroin addict with arrests dating back to 1992. A beat-up brunette with her curly hair dyed red, she has at times been a prostitute; oddly enough, she was involved in another high-profile murder case in 2001, as she once "escorted" Dr. Dirk Greineder, the Boston allergist convicted of killing his wife. She's also HIV-positive.

This was too much. On Worthington's recent trip to New York, for Brantley's party, Worthington said that she was looking into having Toppy declared legally incompetent, effectively putting herself in charge of his finances. "Porter," says a friend of Christa's, "was about to get her oil well unhooked."

The story has moved quickly since Worthington died. That week, Porter was hauled into the police station for a lie-detector test, along with Ed Hall, the man who lived with her in the apartment where Toppy paid the bills. Hall passed; Porter's results were reportedly inconclusive, possibly affected by heroin. Two mornings later, Porter and Hall were arrested on a stoop in nearby Roxbury while shooting up, and the Quincy landlord took advantage of this arrest to evict them. Hall remains in custody, perhaps because he's unable to come up with the $500 bail; Porter was last seen at a Boston emergency room, with Toppy. He had taken her because he was afraid she had pneumonia.

Toppy is also being asked to take a lie-detector test. And there is no indication that the police have stopped entertaining alternative scenarios: They were working the phones again, asking Worthington's New York friends to "rack their brains" about anyone who might've wanted to do such a horrific thing to their friend. "We're working around the clock, and we're optimistic—this is in no way a cold case," says Jim Plath, the supervising detective on the case at the Yarmouth State Police barracks. "But this is a tough one. It's a really, really tough one."

They're not talking about what Ava might have seen.

The yellow police tape at the end of Christa Worthington's driveway is garlanded with bouquets. Candles in glass jars, left by well-wishers in the days following Christa's death, are still stuck in the muddy dirt.

The yard is a chaotic jumble of stoves and refrigerators, wheelbarrows and baby carriages—they're toys. Inside the gray-shingled bungalow, every available surface is covered with toys or boxes of cereal or pastel-colored pacifiers; children's books are stacked on each step of the main stairway, a stairway whose banister is covered over with fishnet, perhaps one use for the material that Tiny Worthington never considered. Even the Christmas tree is still up. This was Ava's place, the world Christa made for Ava.

A few days before Christmas, Worthington went to a dinner at a friend's in Greenwich Village. The adults chatted as Ava frolicked. Christa's friend Terry Reed remembers Christa stopping in mid-sentence. "I can't stand it, she's too adorable," Worthington said. "I was supposed to wait for Christmas, but I can't." She brought out a shopping bag and presented Ava with her present, a pink tulle tutu, in which Ava continued her happy dance. "Isn't she amazing?" said Christa. In her life, Ava was the one relationship that stayed perfect.

Susan Jackett, the woman who may well end up acting as mother to Ava, couldn't be more different from Christa. "Since my mom died," she said, sitting in her kitchen, "I've been on this spiritual path, reading books about life after life, and I think that Christa's spirit didn't leave the house till the police got there: I think she just stayed there that night, to look over her baby. She just hovered."

For Ava, no doubt, she'll hover for a lifetime.

MY COCAINE MUSEUM

Michael Taussig

Y ou can find it when you face the sun, close your eyes,
and watch the colored lines dance. Follow them,
follow the heat, and you'll get there like I did, all the
way to *My Cocaine Museum*. Not that there wasn't what you
might call a prototype, a most clear and definite and beautiful
prototype, spooky in its own way too, the famous, the world-
famous, the extraordinary Gold Museum itself. Not that it
needs that sort of hype. No way. For this is no vulgar carnival
sideshow. This has science behind it and a lot of soft lighting
as well, not to mention big money and something even bigger
than money: the image of money, which, as you know, was
there in gold all along. And still is—as you see when you go
downtown Bogotá, Colombia, and climb to the second floor
of the Banco de la República off Carrera Séptima and there
enter the glittering residues of the time before time when only
the Indians were here, happy, so it seems, happy with their
gold and happy with their coca too. Only later did it become
cocaine.

Surrounded by slums on three sides, beggars and street performers in the park opposite, the museum provides a closed-
off space, dark and solemn, in which pre-Colombian gold

artifacts are displayed in spotlit cases. Said to possess 38,500 pieces of gold work, the museum, like gold itself, is an ornament adding dignity and art to the money-grubbing reality of the bank—not just any old bank, of course, but the Banco de la República, the bank of the nation-state, same as the Federal Reserve Bank in the U.S.A.

But what, then, is an ornament?

One block away on the Carrera Séptima stands the beautiful colonial church of San Francisco, which, like the museum, is stuffed full of gold shimmering in the dark. Country people and slum dwellers come and caress the foot of one of the saints, which as a consequence glows even more than the gold behind the altar. Hustlers working their way along the sidewalk outside are likely to be wearing gold chains in imitation of the guys who make it big in the drug trade. Like any book worth writing, *My Cocaine Museum* belongs to this sense of the ornament as something base like the foot of a saint or a hustler with a golden wrist, something that allows the thingness of things to glow in the dark.

To walk through the Gold Museum is to become vaguely conscious of how for millennia the mystery of gold has through myth and stories sustained the basis of money worldwide. But one story is missing. The museum is silent as to the fact that for more than three centuries of Spanish occupation what the colony stood for and depended upon was the labor of slaves from Africa in the gold mines. Indeed, this gold, along with the silver from Mexico and Peru, was what primed the pump of the capitalist takeoff in Europe, its primitive accumulation. Surely this concerns the bank, its birthright, after all?

It seems so monstrously unjust, this denial, so limited and

mean a vision incapable of imagining what it was like diving for gold in the wild coastal rivers, moving boulders with your bare hands, standing barefoot in mud and rain day after day, so unable to even tip your hat to the brutal labor people still perform today alongside the spirits of their parents and grand-parents and of all the generations that before them had dug out the country's wealth. It seemed such a rip-off of my work as an anthropologist too, using anthropology and archaeology to dignify the bank with the bittersweet spoils of genocide and looting.

The Gold Museum is also silent about the fact that if it was gold that determined the political economy of the colony, it is *cocaine*—or rather the U.S. prohibition of it—that shapes the country today. Not to talk about cocaine, not to display it, is to continue with the same denial of reality that the museum practices in relation to slavery. Like gold, cocaine is imbued with violence and greed, glitter that reeks of transgression. What's more, cocaine has roots deep in prehistory too.

Like gold, coca was of great interest to the Indians long before the arrival of Europeans. Indeed, among the most significant objects in the Gold Museum are its golden *poporos*, curvaceous containers shaped like a Coke bottle and used by Indians to contain the lime made from burnt and crushed seashells that, added to toasted coca leaves, facilitates the release of cocaine into the gut and bloodstream. You insert a stick into the spout of the *poporo* and then withdraw it so as to put gobs of lime in your mouth while chewing coca leaves. I say "your mouth" but I must mean "their mouths," plural, as with the men seated all night around a fire, like the Indians

79

of the Sierra Nevada de Santa Marta, as I was informed by María del Rosario Ferro just yesterday. Gathered together like this, they are discussing a communal problem—whether to allow her to stay with them, and why the heck is she there, anyway? When they take the end of the stick out of their mouth and reinsert it back into the *poporo*, they spend several minutes rotating the stick around the lips of the spout, making a soft suffusion of sound that spreads like wind stirring in the forests of time. Actually, they do not so much rotate the end of the stick around the lip of the spout of the *poporo* as they seem to be writing in curves and dashes punctuated by little stabbings. There are maybe as many as a hundred men doing this simultaneously, each with his own *poporo* and his own woven cotton shoulder bag containing toasted coca leaves. It is dark. It is loud, this softer-than-soft sound, she tells me, the sound thus magnified, maybe like the sound of the Caribbean Sea from which the shells come as far as this high mountain.

As I understand this phenomenon, the speed and rhythm of the jerky rotating movement around the spout of the *poporo,* and hence of the soft suffusing of scratching sounds, correspond to the movement of speech and thought, the Arahuaco word for thinking being the same as breathing in the spirit (*kun-samunu*). But of course these are not the squeaky-clean *golden poporos* we see resplendent in the Gold Museum in Bogotá that stand naked and exposed, bereft of any sign of human use, let alone of any sign of this exceedingly strange crust of coca-saturated saliva around the mouth of the *poporo*. Rightly, the museum is fixated on the object, which puts an end to speaking, let alone the relation between breathing and thinking. Here, gold freezes breath no less than thought as we gaze absentmindedly at the auratic glow, completely uninformed as to the wonders of what these *poporos* might mean. Too bad.

But then would dried spittle last long in the rarefied atmosphere of a museum? A museum abhors clutter. There can be little sympathy for Walter Benjamin's enthusiasm when unpacking his library, that "from the start, the great collector is struck by the confusion, by the scatter, in which the things of the world are found." For what this scatter implies for him is its fantastic otherworldly character, as when he says: "Every passion borders on the chaotic, but the collector's passion borders on the chaos of memories. More than that: the chance, the fate, that suffuses before my eyes are conspicuously present in the accustomed confusion of these books." To impose order on such chaos is to render tribute to chance, such that the final arrangement adds up to what he calls a "magic encyclopedia," which in itself serves to interpret fate. This corresponds nicely with the Indians in the Sierra Nevada, writing their thoughts onto the crust of dried spit around the mouth of their *poporos*. Something like this also underlies William Burroughs's attitude to the disorder we call order, as when he notes that the chapters he is writing of what will become *Naked Lunch*, "Form a mosaic with the cryptic significance of juxtaposition, like objects abandoned in a hotel drawer, a form of still life." And the aim of that? To make people aware of what they already know but didn't know they knew.

For all its nastiness, spit is vulnerable to both time and good taste. Spit is hardly the sort of thing—if thing it be—that would serve the needs of a bank's claim to culture. Spit is the very opposite of gold in Western economics, such that it lends itself to the evacuation of equations many of us live by, those equations connecting beauty with goodness and goodness with making sense by finding or imposing forms on the welter of experience that is the universe. Spit is anarchic as regards form. What other philosophy might therefore be at stake here, "just around the corner"? A philosophy not of form but of substance and force—such as gold, such as cocaine—*transgressive substances*, I call them, aswarm with all manner of peril that may not provide much by way of stable form to the world but certainly much by way of exuberance and perturbation. Indeed, spit did find its Western philosopher in 1929 in Georges Bataille, who, for one of his cranky dictionary entries in his magazine, *Documents* (that lasted only two years but still manages to amaze), wrote this:

> A dictionary begins when it no longer gives the meaning of words, but their tasks. Thus *formless* is not only an adjective having a given meaning, but a term that serves to bring things down in the world, generally requiring that each thing has its form. What it designates has no rights in any sense and gets itself squashed everywhere, like a spider or an earthworm. In fact for academic men to be happy, the universe would have to take shape. All of philosophy has no other goal: it is a matter of giving a frock coat to what is, a mathematical frock coat. On the other hand, affirming that the universe resembles nothing and is only *formless* amounts to saying that the universe is something like a spider or spit.

Not so much *My Cocaine Museum* as *My Spit Museum*?

As for the Indians of the sierra, this dried crust of spit around the mouth of the *poporo* grows over time and is shaped carefully to form a cylinder, says Gerardo Reichel-Dolmatoff in his celebrated study of the Kogi, among whom he lived between 1946 and 1950. It is absolutely forbidden for Kogi women to chew coca, and Reichel-Dolmatoff sees the *poporo* as in fact a sexual rival of the women. When a young man is initiated, he is given his first *poporo* filled with lime. He thus "marries" his "woman" in this ceremony and perforates the *poporo* at this time in imitation of a ritual defloration. "All the necessities of life," concludes Reichel-Dolmatoff, "are concentrated in this small instrument that for the Kogi comes to mean food, woman, and memory. No wonder the Kogi man and his poporo are inseparable."

Petted and patted over time by incessant scribbling with the tip of the stick, the crust of dried coca-and-lime-thickened saliva is as likely to be a flat disc as a cylinder, an object of beauty far exceeding any gold work in the museum. It is perfectly symmetrical. Faint greenish lines like a spider's web wander around its sides; while viewed from above, the disc contains faint rings like that of a cut tree trunk. In his nine months camped out in the mountains of Boyacá, the crust, or *kalamutsa* (in Kogi speech), thus created by Mamo Luca, a Kogi priest I met in 2003, was roughly three-quarters of an inch thick and two and half inches in diameter. When asked, he referred to his obsessive petting and patting as "writing thoughts," the crust itself being his "document." More like a magic encyclopedia, I thought, it being the Mamo's task to continuously exert his thoughts while chewing coca to figuring out for the sake of his community what costs Mother

Earth has incurred due to the wrongdoings of human beings. "Pretty much what I aspire to do with *My Cocaine Museum*," I said to myself.

The ruddy brown body of his poporo was only six inches high, fitting snugly in his left hand, which it never once seemed to leave, night or day. Indeed, the *poporo* is more like a living extension of the body, or should I say of the mind, than it is a mechanical artifact. The crust of the *poporo* of Ramón Gil, in the foothills of the Sierra Nevada near Santa Marta, was even more impressive, being about six inches wide, like a pie, and two and half inches thick.

Invited for a consultation in 2003 to the Gold Museum in Bogotá, and then asked as to the possibility of his carrying out a "cleansing" of the museum's 38,500 gold artifacts, Ramón Gil said he would need the menstrual blood of the museum's female staff, plus the semen of the men, including that of the board of directors of the Banco de la República. Needless to say, his demand was not met and the gold work remains in its polluted state. According to Mamo Luca—who dares not enter the museum on account of that pollution—gold is valuable because it is the menstrual blood of Mother Earth in which is concentrated all her power and that can only be extracted through appropriate ritual ensuring that all is in harmony at the site of extraction—e.g., "that the river is good, the animals are good, the plants and the woods are good." Essential to such purifying ritual, paying Mother Earth for the defilement of gold extraction, is thinking—yes! thinking— and such thought is achieved through imbibing coca and "writing thoughts" onto the previous thoughts embodied in the yellow crust of dried spittle around the mouth of the *poporo*. And according to Mamo Luca, before the birth of the sun, people used gold instead of crushed seashells in their *poporos*.

The centerpiece of the museum's display is a *poporo* with four golden balls around its orifice. In a darkened room, placed against black felt without the slightest hint of irony or self-consciousness, this spotlit *poporo* has the following text beneath it:

> This poporo from Quimbaya, which began the collection of the Gold Museum in 1939, identifies Colombians with their nationality and history.

Another poporo, thinner than most, is shaped like an erect penis. Others take the form of a jaguar, full-bellied fruit, or a person that is half-alligator. There is one *poporo* shaped as a golden woman, naked, with birds hanging from her wrists, and we are informed that burnt human bones were the source of the lime it contained. Gold and cocaine are firmly connected since ancient times, before even the birth of the sun, by art, sex, magic, and mythology, no less than by chemistry.

The Gold Museum is already *My Cocaine Museum*. But it is only when we know of these connections that we can, as Antonin Artaud put it, "awaken the gods that sleep in museums," not to mention the ghosts of African slaves, who with their bare hands dug out the gold that kept the colony and Spain itself afloat for more than three hundred years. However, unlike the Indians, destroyed by Europe and centuries later "awakened" by the aesthetic and stupendous monetary values accorded pre-Colombian gold work, these other ghosts are truly invisible and their polluting power—their miasma—all the more disturbing.

And that is why I have undertaken to create this, *My Cocaine Museum.*

Unlike the Gold Museum located plumb in the center of the nation's capital, my museum lies at the furthermost extremity of the nation where the Pacific Ocean seeps into four hundred miles of mangrove swamps and trackless forest, where the air barely moves and the rain never stops. This is where slaves from Africa were brought to mine gold in the headwaters of the rivers flowing fast down the Andes, which run north to south but a few miles from the sea. This is where I have visited a few weeks at a time every summer in the 1990s through to 2002, and before that in 1971 and in 1976, intending to write a book about the gold-mining village of Santa María located at the headwaters of the Río Timbiquí.

During those years, as gold dwindled to little more than memories, cocaine appeared on the horizon. It had spread west over the Andes from the Amazon basin, where U.S. government–enforced spraying with defoliants drove coca cultivation into these forests of the Pacific Coast. By 1999 cocaine traffickers were coming to Guapí, the largest river port in the region and merely one river south of the Timbiquí, buying cocaine tons at a time several rivers south. Living it up in the Hotel del Rio Guapí, these traffickers would take off in fast launches in the morning and return at nightfall to carouse with the local police. The excitement was palpable, and along the middle reaches of the Saija, but one river north of the Timbiquí, the largest guerrilla army in Latin America—the FARC—had coca fields as well.

In other areas of Colombia, cocaine draws not only the guerrilla but behind them come the paramilitaries with the thinly concealed support of the state's military apparatus. Dependent on cocaine trafficking, the paramilitaries torture and kill peasants they claim are collaborating with the guerrilla. Other than in the north near Panamá in the Chocó region, the Pacific Coast knew none of this spectacular paramilitary violence till the massacre of peasants in April 2001 in coca-growing areas at the headwaters of the Rço Naya, several rivers north of the Timbiquç. To the south of the Timbiquç in that same year, paramilitaries had assassinated human rights workers in the port of Tumaco, on the border with Ecuador, and were edging in on coca fields in the Patç a drainage. In October they took up temporary residence in the lower Timbiquç too, causing waves of anxiety if not a general hysteria. Since then, fears have abated but the nightmare of imminent paramilitary bloodshed can never, ever be discounted. It is in this sense that *My Cocaine Museum* stands with its door ajar on the impending apocalypse.

Is the danger proportionate to the value of these gorgeous "flowers of evil," gold and cocaine? With gold we see perhaps the irony more than the danger, the irony of poverty-stricken miners at the end of the world up to their waists in water and mud, searching, at times for years, for the stuff of dreams and legends, before throwing in the towel. Likewise with cocaine, the drama is intense, so intense that what this drama opens your eyes and heart to is a weird but invigorating place where words and elemental forces of nature form hybrid entities, neither natural nor human, more like the foot of a saint or the golden wrist of a hustler that glows in the dark. It is here, philosophically speaking, where *My Cocaine Museum* begins, where transgressive substances make you want to reach out for a new language of nature, lost to memories of prehistorical time that the present state of emergency recalls.

It goes like this: gold and cocaine are *fetishes,* which is to say substances that seem to be a good deal more than mineral or vegetable matter. They come across more like people than things, spiritual entities that are neither, and this is what gives them their strange beauty. As fetishes, gold and cocaine play subtle tricks upon human understanding. For it is precisely as mineral or as vegetable matter that they appear to speak for themselves and carry the weight of human history in the guise of natural history. And this is how I want *My Cocaine Museum* to speak as well—as a fetish.

This is the language I want, a substantial language, aroused through prolonged engagement with gold and cocaine, reeking in its stammering intensity of delirium and failure. Why failure? Because unwinding the fetish is not yet given on the horizon of human possibility. Would that we could strip these fetishes of their mythology and thus expose the true and real substances themselves, naked and alone in their primal state of natural being. Yet even if we could, we would thereby destroy that which animates us, those subtle tricks played on human understanding by substances that appear to speak for themselves. The language I want is just that language that runs along the seam where matter and myth connect and disconnect continuously. Thus, *My Cocaine Museum* does not—I repeat, does not—try to tease apart nature from culture, real stuff from the made-up stuff, but instead accepts the life-and-death play of nature with second nature as an irreducible reality so as to let that curious play express itself all the more eloquently.

As a museum dedicated to natural history, *My Cocaine Museum* follows the flow of the river from the headwater village of Santa Marça deep in the forest, past the provincial capital of Santa Bárbara lying downstream just above salt water, across the still waters of the river mouth to the swamps that form the puffy edges of the coast itself. Some ten miles out at sea as its terminal exhibit, *My Cocaine Museum* disappears into itself on an ex-prison island that is now a national park, a museum island of natural history that early on in the Spanish conquest of the New World was given the name of Gorgona after she whose face turned those who looked at her to stone. The Gorgon haunts *My Cocaine Museum*. No doubt about it. She comes before the gods, before nature was separated out from culture. She comes before time, they said, living at the end of the known world near the night where time is space. She petrifies. She is the patron saint of museums. Yet my site moves. There is more to the Gorgon than at first appears.

But I am not that interested in museums. I find them dead and even hostile places, created for a bored bourgeoisie bereft of life and experience. What I am interested in is the life of gold and the life of cocaine where one is dying and the other taking off, although cocaine has more than its fair share of death too. What interests me and I hope you, too, about the end of the earth where the rain never stops and the trees reach the sky is an ambition as old as the hills, namely, to combine a history of things with a history of people forced by slavery to find their way through these things. What sort of things? Heat and rain, forests and rivers, stones and swamps, color and islands—those sort of things—and especially the miasma emanating from the swamp. And why? So that along with the ghosts of slavery haunting the museum, nature itself is released along with the rush of the time-compacted magic of gold and cocaine.

UP THE RIVER

Patrick Symmes

For four decades, Colombia's civil war has spiraled down-ward into a maelstrom of purposeless violence, a cruel conflict sustained by drug money, political ambition, and fantasies of revenge. Several guerrilla groups of nearly mythological status attach and retreat across a landscape of hidden jungle camps, cold passes, and sudden road blocks. To put a face to these anonymous fighters, I flew into one typical town, called "Sandbanks" here, which had been besieged and surrounded for days. One dawn, I was invited to place my trust in strangers, and cross the front lines toward places unknown, in search of parties unidentified.

My phone rings at 7:01 a.m. two mornings later. "There is someone at the front desk for you," the receptionist tells me. I throw on some clothes and go out. It is a man I can only call The Contact. We have had several frustrating conversations in recent days, vague chats about "political actors" and "persons with knowledge of the situation." I think we are maybe going to have a cup of coffee and another pointless talk, but he looks at me and just says, "Get your cameras."

I do, and then we march out the front door, around the

block and behind the hotel, where I am introduced to a man in a white shirt. We shake hands. "You are late," he says, and sets off into a slum.

The Contact and I follow, trailing thirty feet behind. A disused path leads down to the river. The man in the white shirt clambers down to the waterline, whistles, and then comes back up. I buy a thimble of coffee with The Contact's money—I've forgotten my wallet—and then a canoe pulls up. It is made of brightly painted planks, twenty-three feet long and three feet wide, with no seats. This is the classic *yonsin,* misnamed long ago for the Johnson brand of outboard motors that powered the first of these fast canoes.

As I climb in, the man in the white shirt says, "You may have to spend the night." I've been awake for fifteen minutes, so all I can think to ask is, "With whom?"

"La guerrilla," he replies, and the canoe pulls away, leaving the man in the white shirt on the bank.

The Boatman shakes my hand and gestures for me to sit in front. We shoot down the Magdalena River at twenty miles an hour, spray flying, the skinny boat dashing behind vast islands and then rejoining the main channel. After an hour we turn up a broad *quebrada,* or side branch, and then race through an endless series of sweeping bends, leaning into the turns and accelerating in the straightaways.

The early-morning sun lights us for five minutes just as we approach a riverside checkpoint sometimes—sometimes—manned by Colombian marines. The Boatman tells me that we are on a bird-watching expedition. Do I understand that? I do. I turn the phrase *expedicion ornotoligical* around in my mouth, but the government post is abandoned, and we roar past. Then the sun rises behind the clouds again, and we turn into yet another side branch. We swing steadily through an ever tighter series of horseshoe bends, the river folding back on itself. We slow and get quiet. There are more agonizing hidden bends, muddy banks that look like ambush posts, and an endless wall of green. It is already hot, and impossible to see much in any direction.

I am let off at a dent in the bank. A little path leads up to a clearing ringed by a high green wall of trees and vines. As instructed, I walk into the clearing, sit down, and then the *yonsin* leaves.

I swat at insects for half an hour and finally build a tiny grass fire for the smoke. This doesn't scare off a single mosquito. There is a lot of time to think about bad movies set in the jungle, and then about Gabriel García Márquez, lingering in his cancer ward, composing lists of all the things Fidel Castro absolutely never told him. In *The General in His Labyrinth,* García Márquez warned against loitering like this, on the banks of this very river, the Magdalena: "There were men roaming that desolate place," he cautioned, "who were as big as ceiba trees and had the crests and claws of roosters."

Fifteen more minutes and I hear a rustle, and then look over to see a forehead. It turns into a head, and then a camouflage uniform, and then five more uniforms. The six men step out of the brush. They aren't as tall as ceiba trees, and their claws are Galil and AK-47 rifles. They come right over to me, pretending to be relaxed. The first thing they do is shake my hand, one by one, and then stamp out the grass fire.

The guerrillas are in camouflage, with worn webbing that holds radios, rifle grenades, and spare clips. Some of them have shoulder boards in the red and black of the National Liberation Army (ELN), which is a relief: I wouldn't want to run into the wrong set of armed men out here. They are all wearing battered leather combat boots and have small green towels draped over one shoulder, which they use to swat at bugs. They leave one man to watch me, and then vanish into the jungle again. For the next two hours the mosquitoes are on me like NATO on Belgrade, and the guerrillas have clearly picked their dumbest soldier to guard me, fully aware that I will not get one single word out of him. Finally, the other five guerrillas reappear.

One of them—a vaguely amused twenty-eight-year-old, tall by local standards—searches my camera bag. He has two radios and a codebook, and I finally realize he is the leader. I explain that I am a journalist, that he may have received a message I was coming, that I want to ask about American poli—

"Yes," he interrupts. "We had a very nice woman from the *Washington Peest* one time."

"*Post*," I blurt out. I can't stop myself. "*The Washington Post.*"

"*Pist?*" he asks.

"*Post.*"

"Yes," he says. "*The Post.* She never sent me the article she wrote. Why do you suppose *that* is?"

He pats me down carefully, then tells me his real name, but later insists that I forget it. I have to refer to him by his war name, which is Commandante Diego. He is the commander of the ELN's southeast front, one of four in the Middle Magdalena region, and is currently orchestrating the siege of Sandbanks.

We get in another *yonsin*, sitting on the gunwales and packed tightly together, knees interlocked for stability in the tippy canoe. I look down, avoiding their eyes, and study the interspersed pattern of legs: camo, denim, camo, denim, camo. The canoe motors upriver, through smaller bends, and we pick up a second *yonsin* with two more guerrillas. All the men are silent. I'm thinking about the extremely small possibility (the *im*possibility, really, if you consider odds and chances and geography) that a new Black Hawk helicopter gunship is patrolling over this area. Six choppers—state-of-the-art machines, bristling with rocket pods, miniguns, and other tools for fighting drugs—have been delivered to the army back in Sandbanks.

Maybe one of these lethal machines is going to stumble overhead, by chance, and the pilot is going to look down and see two canoes filled with guerrillas. Despite the U.S. pretense of getting involved "only" in fighting drugs, there is only one battlefield in Colombia, and the pilot is not going to pause to see if we are ELN guerrillas or FARC guerrillas, or to inquire whether we take drug money, or to ask if that is a civilian on board. He's just going to lean over the cyclo, drop the ship down fast, and press a button. Sooner or later, in one spot or another, a piece of the American drug war will come hurtling out of the sky looking for these men.

Around noon, we pull into the bank, camouflage the two *yonsins,* and hike in single file through the forest.

The secret jungle hideout is first betrayed, as are all guerrillas camps, by the amount of laundry hanging around. After spotting a T-shirt and then a pair of socks, I walk on a bit and notice a pic and a few chickens. Finally we come to a grove of wild plantain trees, with a handful of people loitering in the cool yellow shade. The guerrillas have assembled a few crude stools from logs, but this isn't the summer-camp lifestyle I saw in the camps of their FARC rivals. FARC tents have mosquito netting; the ELN tents are just black plastic sheets draped over ropes. The ELN kitchen tent looks deadly; FARC has brick ovens for baking fresh bread.

And instead of FARC's guerrilla girls splashing about in a river in wet panties, I find a few men in sweat-soaked camouflage uniforms, somebody's girlfriend with a miniskirt and a baby, and another 500,000 mosquitoes. There are only a half-dozen fighters waiting in the camp. Each of them comes over and shakes the hand of the *commandante,* and his men, and then my hand, too.

Diego fetches a thermos of coffee, and we settle into the command tent and light two mosquito coils. I rest on a log; he sits on a battered camp chair. There are a couple of plywood tables holding the laptop, printer, TV, and VCR without which no guerrilla encampment is complete. Everything is run off a big truck battery, but later I hear a small generator rumbling the in the bushes. We sip the piping-hot coffee.

"The worst enemy of the Colombian people is the oligarchy," Commandante Diego announces, *sip,* "and then the second worst is the *burguesía* of the United States, which tries to keep them in power."

He tells me about the founding of the ELN in July 1964—a few days before I was born—and how four decades without victory have actually helped them, allowing the ELN to become "well consolidated, politically—this is a very consolidated project."

Diego talks for an hour about the oligarchy and about Colombia's grave crisis of inequality; about the need for schools, health clinics, employment, crop-substitution programs, and infrastructure of all kinds; about the lack of "space" within Colombian politics, the way reformers have been subject to assassination ever since Bolívar was chased up the Street of Sighs in Bogotá; about the need for a new justice system, a new economy, a new military, a new social order, a grand political discussion involving all sectors of the society, and land redistribution in all parts of the country, not just some. Despite what the media says, they don't much care for Cuba. ("You have to respect Fidel, though," Diego offers at one point. "That *hijo de puta* can work. He's like Yimmy Carter.") They are Colombian nationalists and Colombian patriots seeking a Colombian socialism. They view the drug war as a thin cover for a U.S. takeover of Colombia, and will fight us every way possible.

This all sounds a little familiar. FARC had said the same things, in the same language. I ask him how the ELN differs from FARC. "We are not very different," he immediately replies. "Not ideologically. The plans are really similar. It is more a difference in style."

By "style" he is referring to the fact that FARC protects coca plantations and taxes cocaine-processing plants. The ELN has mostly left the drug business, but for now they fund their war with "detentions," or what most Colombians call kidnapping. The ELN took 695 of the 2,945 people kidnapped in Colombia in 1999, including a seventy-three-year-old peasant they kept in a hole in the ground for thirty days. They'd hoped to make $150 from him. "We are the most accused of kidnapping," Diego acknowledges, "but we don't kidnap. We detain people within the political-economic context of the war." I confess that I can't see the difference. "The difference," he replies, a touch angry, "is who makes a profit. We just detain people. If they pay voluntarily then we don't detain them!"

Outside the tent, there is a maze of paths through a cloudy quagmire dotted with self-sustaining encampments of rage. There will be no peace here either. Diego doesn't even pretend this will end soon. They support a peace process, he says, but in the next breath he admits that he feels a "military-political" victory for the ELN is certain. They look forward to a confrontation with the United States, to drawing Americans into a disastrous battle. "We call it the final war," he says. "It could last five, ten, or twenty years."

TRAINTIME

Lucius Shepard

The man who calls himself Missoula Mike has passed out again, slumped onto his side, still clutching a nearly empty quart bottle of vodka. His face is haggard, masked by grime and a prophet's beard gone mostly to gray; his clothes—jeans and a flannel shirt—are filthy. He appears to be in his sixties, but just as likely he's an ill-used forty-five. He coughs, launching a wad of phlegm that lands in his beard. Then, waking, he props himself on an elbow and stares wildly out at me from his lean-to. The glow from our dying campfire fills his wrinkles with shadow, flares in his eyes, exposes stained, gapped teeth, and for a moment his features, ghoulishly underlit, resemble those of a Halloween mask, a red-eyed hobo from hell.

"Punk-ass camp thieves!" he says, veering off in a conversational direction that bears no relation to what we've been discussing. "Them bastards don't fuck with me no more."

Six or seven inches of vodka ago, when Mike was capable of rational speech, he promised to reveal the secrets of FTRA (Freight Train Riders of America), a gang of transients that have been characterized by the press as the hobo mob. In return, he extracted my promise not to use his real name—if I did, he said, he would be subject to reprisals from his

99

brothers in the gang. But since we began to talk, no secrets have been forthcoming, and he has instead engaged in a lengthy bout of chest-beating, threatening other gang members who have wronged him and his friends. Now he's on to camp thieves.

"They know Ol' Double M's got something for 'em." He grabs the ax handle he keeps by his side, and takes a feeble swipe at the air to emphasize his displeasure. "Cocksuckers!"

This drunken stream of invective and threat more or less corresponds to the course of interviews I've done with other FTRA members, and with those who pretend to be FTRA. Now that a certain amount of heat has been generated by television pieces and newspaper articles, many legitimate FTRA members have put aside their colors—bandannas ritually urinated upon by the participants in the wearer's initiation—so as not to attract attention from police. On the other hand, a number of independent hobos, seeking a dubious celebrity, have taken to wearing them. Mike has earned a degree of credence with me because he keeps his colors in his pack.

We're in a hobo jungle outside the enormous Union Pacific switchyard at Roseville, California. Here and there the darkness is picked out by cooking fires tended by shadowy figures. Shouts and laughter punctuate the sizzling of crickets, and every so often the moan of a freight train achieves a ghostly dominance. By day, the jungle had the appearance of a seedy campground, lean-tos and sleeping bag nests scattered among dry-leaved shrubs; but now, colored by my paranoia, it looks like the bottom of the world, a smoky, reeking, Dantean place inhabited by men and women who have let some personal failure or defining moment—most often an addiction or a war—turn them away from society, people whose identities have become blurred by years of telling tall tales, by lying and showing false IDs, and in the process creating a new legend for themselves out the mean fabric of their existence. Many are working behind fortified wine and crank, and few appear capable of the organized villainy attributed to them by the press. It's as one rider said to me: "Two tramps can't even agree on which kind of beer to buy, so how're they going to do that kind of crime?"

A gangly hobo, much younger than Mike, comes over to bum a cigarette. He peers at Mike and says, "Hey, man! You fucked up?" He glances at me, as if seeking confirmation, and I allow that, yeah, ol' Mike is pretty severely fucked up.

Mike sits up, unsteady, but manages to maintain a sort of tilted half-lotus. He mumbles something I can't quite catch.

"You the guy's been askin' 'bout FTRA?" The gangly hobo says this as he stoops to light his cigarette from an ember.

"Yeah." I wait for him to get the smoke going, then say: "You FTRA?"

"Hell, no! Couple those motherfuckers lookin' to kill my ass."

"Oh, yeah? FTRA guys? What happened?"

The gangly hobo eyes me with suspicion. "Nothin' happened. Just these pitiful fuckers decided they's goin' to kill me for somethin' they thought I done." He makes a gesture of disdain. "They been goin' round three months sayin' I better keep the hell off the rails. But"—he spreads his arms, offering a target to whoever cares to take a shot—"here I am. You know? Here I fuckin' am."

I question him further, but he's said all he wants, and soon he stumps off back to his camp. Mike's eyes are half-closed, his head begins to droop. But then a long plaintive blast of train sadness issues from the switchyard, and he stiffens, his eyes snap open. I get the idea he's listening to a fey signal from the back of beyond, a sound only he can interpret, one ordering him to some cosmic duty. His features are composed in harsh, attentive lines, and with his ax handle held sceptre-style, his beard decorated with bits of vegetation, in the instant before he loses consciousness, he looks dressed in a kind of pagan dignity, the image of a mad, primitive king.

My initial impression of FTRA, informed by sensationalized TV coverage and a handful of newspaper articles, was of a murderous tribe who preyed upon the weak and innocent, and held barbaric initiation ceremonies that—along with ritual urination—involved rape and beating. Hardcore felons armed with weighted ax handles called Goon Sticks, who utilized the rails and switchyards to facilitate their criminal enterprises, which included drug-running and contract murder. But facts that might substantiate this impression are difficult to establish. Railriders have told me horrifying tales about the FTRA; yet they've subsequently admitted that their information comes secondhand. The rails constitute an enormous grapevine, conveying information about where to get the best Dumpster pizza in Denver, how to find water near the Rio Grande yard in Pueblo, and so on. If you were to believe a tenth of the FTRA stories that come your way, you'd think the rails more dangerous than Baghdad during the blitz.

Estimates regarding the size of FTRA membership range from seven or eight hundred to upwards of two thousand—most riders would subscribe to the lower figure. The general perception of the gang by law enforcement is more of an annoyance than a serious threat. Several police officers have put forward the idea that on occasion FTRA members serve as mules for biker gangs, bringing in heroin from Mexico, but none have gone so far as to say that this is endemic. The crimes with which FTRA hobos are most frequently charged are trespassing and petty thievery, and these incidents are handled by railroad bulls, who usually let the offenders off with a ticket. Local cops don't spend much time in the railyards, and according to one detective, the average hobo's hygiene is so bad that most officers don't want them in their patrol cars. It's difficult to imagine a cop turning down an important bust because the perpetrator has body lice.

There's little consensus on any subject among FTRA members themselves, not even concerning the origin of the group. The most believable story has it that a group of thirteen hobos, Vietnam vets all, were hanging in a Kalispell, Montana, bar in 1985, watching a freight train roll past. When an X-TRA container came into view, a hobo whose train name is Daniel Boone said jokingly, "We oughta call ourselves the FTRA—Fuck the Reagan Administration." Thus Daniel Boone is acknowledged to be the founder of the gang, an honor he reportedly now considers an embarrassment; he has given up his life on the rails and has become an itinerant preacher in the Bitterroot Mountains of Montana, living out of a camper van. Other stories vary from the Kalispell scenario only in degree, imbuing the gathering with a more serious purpose. But Mississippi Bones (aka Marvin Moore, a gang member currently serving a sentence for first-degree murder) claims that the organization was founded in the 1940s by a black hobo named Coal Train, who died some thirty years later in a lean-to next to an abandoned Texaco station in Desert Center, California. Bones says that he "carried the old man some wine" and sat with him for a while, and has no doubt that he was the actual founding father.

The matter of its origin aside, the question remains as to why FTRA was formed. Was it intended as a joke? Was it born from a need for mutual protection? Or was it, as some journalists maintain, a handful of White Power advocates with mean things on their minds that has grown into a tabloid-style phenomenon, a homegrown American nightmare that poses a significant cultural threat? If you're to believe Officer Robert Grandinetti, the answer to this last question is a resounding yes.

Grandinetti is a heavyset, affable man closing in on retirement age, who works out of the Office of Special Police Problems in Spokane, Washington. He has made FTRA his special project, not only pursuing and arresting its members, but devoting considerable time to raising the national consciousness as regards their particular menace. He's appeared on *America's Most Wanted* and makes presentations on the subject to federal commissions and law enforcement groups. Days, he patrols beneath the city's railroad bridges, areas where riders gather to "catch out" (the hobo term for hopping a freight). He carries a Polaroid camera with which he takes a picture of anyone he suspects of associating with or belonging to FTRA, and these pictures are then mounted in hefty scrapbooks, along with mug shots and photgraphs of FTRA graffiti. His files are voluminous, he has compiled an extensive database on the gang membership, and has a collection of FTRA artifacts, the most impressive exhibit being a Goon Stick (he calls it a Gooney Stick), an ax handle to one end of which has been welded a softball-sized lump of lead. He speaks with such relish about the subject, expressing a gruff fondness for certain gang members, I can't help thinking that there's something in play here more than the usual proprietary close-ness that cops display toward the criminals they pursue. It's as if he has not merely set himself up as the FTRA's nemesis, but is also their most avid connoisseur.

As we sit in his office, a fluorescent-lit cube with several desks and a prominently displayed employee award, Grandinetti's words sound practiced, and he utilizes visual aids—photographs, FTRA bandanas, and so forth—with the facile air of someone who has given the same show many times before (this due in part, I assume, to the fact that over the years he has lectured on police matters in the Spokane school system). He tells me that there were more than 450 trespass deaths on railroad property during the past year, and he believes that a significant percentage of these were homi-cides perpetrated by FTRA. To support this assumption, he cites a number of cases in which the victim was struck by a train in a switchyard, but there is very little blood at the scene, suggesting that the victim was killed elsewhere, and the body subsequently placed on the tracks so the impact of the train would cover up the actual cause of death: blunt force trauma. But Grandinetti admits that in most of these cases it's impos-sible to determine whether the crimes were committed by FTRA members or unaffiliated hobos . . . or by anyone else, for that matter. Switchyards are often situated in or near dan-gerous neighborhoods, and the idea that an indigent may have murdered a hobo is far from unthinkable.

Over the course of an hour, Grandinetti sketches his vision of the gang. He explains "double-clutching"—the FTRA prac-tice of getting emergency food stamps in one town, then hop-ping a freight to the next, getting more food stamps there, and continuing the process until they have six or seven hundred dollars worth, which they sell to a grocery store for 50 cents on the dollar, thereby supplying themselves with money for drugs and alcohol. He describes how FTRA hobos will "hustle junk" (pick up scrap metal) and steal wire from freight yards, strip the copper and sell it in bulk to recycling businesses. Otherwise, he says, they "work the sign" (Will Work for Food) in order to get cash. He talks about the "home guard," hobos who have taken to staying for long periods of time in a town and serve as procurers of drugs for transient members. Little of what he says would be denied by FTRA (though several members told me that they would never steal from the railroads, because you don't shit where you live), and none of it seems consequential enough to fall under the umbrella of the Rico statutes.

In order to believe that FTRA is a menace to society to the extent Grandinetti posits, it's necessary to believe that there must be some order to the gang's apparent disorder. Officers charged with obtaining revenue and determining goals. Chapters that communicate one with the other. Some sort of structure. When I broach the subject, Grandinetti tells me at first that he knows of no such hierarchy. But when I press the issue, he says he's heard of a group within FTRA called "the Death Squad" whose function is to carry out hits. He claims that this group run by Daniel Boone. It's at this juncture that Grandinetti begins to preface his statements with the phrase "I can't prove it, but . . ." and tells me he's learned from informants that two gang members were hired by right-wingers to derail an Amtrak train in Arizona a few years back. He's also heard that a White Power group is attempting to organize FTRA into a hobo army. In light of the physical condition and mental disposition of the hardcore hobos I've met,

I find these propositions absurd. If I needed a train derailed, I could think of better prospects for the job, and if I intended to raise an army, I'd seek out recruits who still had liver function. And if I'm to give credence to Grandinetti's assertion that Daniel Boone is ordering hits from his camper van in Montana, I would be forced to assume that Boone maintained some type of instantaneous communication with his minions scattered nationwide. In all my travels, I haven't run into any hardcore hobos with cell phones.

Under pewter skies, we drive out into the industrial wastes of the Spokane Valley and stop by the railroad tracks beneath the Freya Street bridge, its cement pillars and abutments spangled with FTRA grafitti—cartoon train tracks, swastikas, lightning bolts, along with messages and dates and train names. Among them is a section of wall devoted to a memorial for Horizontal John, an FTRA member who died of liver failure underneath the bridge the previous summer. Two hobos are camped here today, warming themselves by a small fire. Sheets of cardboard lie on the packed dirt nearby, and there are signs of past encampments: a worn-out shoe; a wadded pink cloth that might be a piece of blanket; empty cans; soggy newspapers. Neither of the two men are FTRA, but Grandinetti takes their pictures and checks them for warrants. One has a minor charge outstanding against him. Grandinetti's associate applies handcuffs and calls for a patrol car to take him to jail. Once this has been handled, Grandinetti strolls about, commenting on the graffiti. He's amused by one that warns AVOID JABBERJAW. Jabberjaw is a transient hooker rumored to have contracted AIDS, and Grandinetti says that this might be the ultimate cure for FTRA.

I come across a series of messages left by a rider named Big Ed that insult and taunt the gang, and I comment that Big Ed must be pretty damn big to risk FTRA retribution. Grandinetti doesn't appear to have heard me, and I'm starting to think there's a lot more relating to the gang he's not hearing, that he's disposed to hear only what paints them in the most baleful light. During our initial phone conversation, I mentioned that someone had told me he thought FTRA was nothing more than an urban legend; Grandinetti became angry and said he didn't want to talk to anyone who held that view. It's important to him, I realize, that FTRA pose a menace worthy of national attention, more of a menace than it perhaps is. I doubt he's trying to sell me anything—not consciously, anyway. He's a true believer, an evangel of the cause, and this work will be his legacy, his mark. I ask if he's going to miss all this when he retires, or if he's looking forward to going fishing. He looks offended, and tells me he's going to be kept very busy, thank you, traveling and lecturing about the FTRA.

After Grandinetti drives away, I wander about for a few minutes. These open spaces under modern bridges, enclosed by sweeping arches and pillars, have something of the feel of a church, as if they're cathedrals upon which construction was suddenly halted, now standing unused except by those who deface them, who have adapted them to some less grandiose form of worship, This one, with its memorial wall and solitary pilgrim—a sole remaining hobo sitting head down and silent by his guttering fire, a slight bearded man in a shabby brown coat—has that atmosphere more than most. The hobo turns his head to me, and it seems he's about to speak. But maybe there's too much authority in the air, too much of a police vibe. Without a word, he picks up the cloth sack containing his possessions and hurries off along the tracks.

The maximum security unit of the U.S. Penitentiary at Florence, Colorado, a red-brick-and-glass chunk of modern penology that sits atop a subterranean high-tech Kafkaville of sanitized tile and electronic gates, seems way too much prison for Mississippi Bones. He's a diminutive, frail-looking man of late middle age with a lined face, dressed in chinos and walking this day with a cane due to an injured foot. I meet him in a mid-size auditorium ranged by rows of black vinyl-covered chairs, all bolted to the floor, where vistors and inmates can mingle under the watchful eyes of guards. This morning, except for a guard and a prison official, who converse at a distance beside a desk, we're the only two people in the room. Every surface glistens. Dust is not permitted. I imagine there are secret angles involved in the room's design that will convey our slightest whisper to the area of the desk. Bones sits on the edge of his chair, hands on the head of his cane, and nods at the two men watching us. "I hate those sons-of-bitches," he says. "They're trying to listen to us, so we got to keep it down."

Bones is serving a twenty-five-year stretch for killing a fellow FTRA member named F-Trooper, a crime for which he does not apologize; he claims that if he hadn't done the deed, F-Trooper would have killed him—he had already tried it once, going after Bones when he was camped by Rattlesnake Creek in Missoula, Montana, attacking him with a skinning knife, twisting it in his side until he had more or less removed three of Bones's ribs. The attack was provoked, Bones says, by F-Trooper's lust for his wife Jane.

109

It took Bones nearly a year to recover from his injuries. He underwent five operations, was stricken by a lung infection, and his weight dropped below 100 pounds. He was living on Percodans, and he expected to die. When he got back on his feet and went out again onto the rails, he ran into F-Trooper in the railyard in Missoula. F-Trooper, Bones says, had been planning on going to Helena to get his food stamps, but he changed his plans and decided to ride to Portland with Bones and his wife. Bones realized then that he was in danger from the man, and he says that he acted in self-defense.

At this juncture, Bones gets to his feet and demonstrates how he shot F-Trooper. He makes his right fist into a gun, places his forefinger against the top of my head and pretends to fire down through my skull. It's an interesting moment. He no longer seems quite so frail.

"If I hadn't been drunk," Bones continues, "I'da never been charged. See, the boxcar we was in had a big red *X* marked on the side. That means they was goin' to break the car off and send it to the repair yard. But I was so drunk I didn't notice the mark. I figured F-Trooper would just go on off to Portland with the rest of the train."

Bones's relationship with FTRA points up something that I'm coming to believe, that petty squabbles proliferate throughout the membership, and that ultimately the gang is more a danger to itself than to anyone else. During the interview, Bones voices bitterness toward a number of his FTRA brothers whom he says took money from the police to testify against him; he expresses particular loathing for one Moose, whom he says had no knowledge of the crime and lied about it to the authorities. "I kept to the code," he says. "I didn't give up nothin' on nobody. And that's a lot more than some of those sons-of-bitches did for me."

Bones speaks of his affection for various gang members, but his attitude toward the rituals of FTRA is less respectful. For one thing, nobody jumped him into the gang, he participated in no intiation; he started wearing the bandana and silver concho on his own authority. "I wore the red out of Arizona," he says, referring to the color of the bandanas worn by gang members who ride the old Southern Pacific routes. "Nobody would gainsay me." He scoffs at the notion that there is any sort of hierarchy in the gang. "You get six or seven together," he tells me, "and somebody'll call the shots. But that's all." He disputes the idea that rape and beating are part and parcel of FTRA initiations. "Once in a while some punk'll want to get in, and then there'll be a fight, but it ain't a regular thing. I never heard 'bout nobody getting raped." He's equally dismissive of the idea that the gang poses a serious menace.

"They're saying we're a threat to society, but the truth is, society is more a threat to us. Tramps get murdered all the time." He tells me about the time he was sleeping with his wife in a lean-to in the hobo jungle near Pasco, Washington, when a local opened fire on them from the bushes with a rifle.

"The thing you got to understand," he says, "hobos don't want much. FTRA or independent, it don't matter. They want a piece of dirt in the shade, they want their food stamps, they want something to drink, something to smoke, and something to screw."

Bones is scarcely what the law would consider a credible witness, certainly not as credible as Officer Grandinetti. He has an extensive arrest record, and he goes on at some length about "utilizing personal magnetism to subdue ruthless people," which speaks both to a measure of craftiness and a healthy streak of arrogance. He lies effortlessly; he's lied to me and subsequently admitted it. Like anyone in prison, he's working every angle he can, and I suspect he's working some angle with me. Not that I can fault him for it—he's alone, he has no idea where his wife is, no one writes him, and except for his lawyer, I'm the only person from outside the walls with whom he's had contact. But despite this, and while I'm hesitant to make an informed judgment about his character based on a single interview, I find what he tells me if not credible, then at least genuine in its essence. My acceptance of what he says probably has something to do with his enthusiasm for hoboing, for trains, for animals—especially his German shepherd, Star—and the outdoors. This enthusiasm seems an irreducible distillate of the man, and the longer we talk, the more what he says seems funded by that portion of his sensibility; and the more frequently he goes back to what we've previously discussed in order to clarify some point, or to reshape a story so it better reflects the truth. It's as if he's gone past his natural suspicion of me, and is having a good time talking to someone from the world.

Our conversation turns to the trains, and when I tell Bones about my infant experiences on the rails, he lifts an eyebrow and says, "You've ridden?"

"Yeah, a little."

Bones continues looking at me for a long moment, his expression neutral, and I think he's trying to fit the information into his understanding of me, reassessing my potentials. Or could be he's merely surprised. Then he grins, and I can see the face of the boy emerge from all those lines and wrinkles.

It's a look of unalloyed pleasure, as if everything around us—walls and razor wire and guards—had vanished, and we were sitting on a patch of dirt somewhere warm, passing a bottle.

"Man, ain't it fun!" he says.

Madcat's a veteran of Desert Storm, and he's got pictures to prove it. Shots of him and his buddies dressed in camo and standing around in the sand. He keeps them wrapped in a small American flag, and uses them like ID. Breaks them out, explains the meaning and circumstances of each, then packs them up, never to be shown again. I've tried to get him talking about the war, thinking that the reason he's on the rails, homeless, must have some relation to his tour of duty. He hasn't told me much. He describes the enormous encampment in the desert where he was billeted, a medium-sized town of lion-colored tents and roaring machinery. Once, he says, he was driving a truck through the desert and came upon a crate of Stinger missles lying in the middle of nowhere. He thought this was pretty funny until he was ordered to transport them to them to an arsenal and learned that they were unstable, that a sudden jolt might launch one straight at the back of the his head—at least that's what he was told. He drove at three mph all the way, and was disciplined for his tardiness.

"Don't matter you got smart bombs," he says, "when all there is, is idiots to drop 'em."

There's no mention, however, of any specific trauma.

Madcat doesn't talk much about anything in his past. From his accent, I'd guess he's from the South, maybe Texas; the way he pronounces *forward* ("fao-wud") puts me in mind of people I know in Houston. He's of average height, skinny, got a touch of gray in his ragged beard. Early thirties, I figure. A sharp, wary face dominated by large grayish blue eyes, the kind of face one sees staring glumly at the camera in Matthew Brady's Civil War photographs. Whenever we've ridden together, he rarely speaks unless I ask him a question. For the most part he stays quietly drunk and plays with dogs belonging to other hobos. Since many FTRA hobos travel with dogs, he's gotten to know quite a few of them.

"They're all right," he says. "Now, you mess with 'em, they'll stand up to you. And there's some you want to be careful around. But you can say the same about a lot of bars you walk into, the people there."

This particular afternoon I'm supposed to meet an FTRA member known as the Erie Flash at Madcat's "office," a Seattle tavern that caters to transients. Ranks of pint and half-pint bottles of Thunderbird stand in front of a clouded mirror behind the bar, and the chewed-up leatherette booths are occupied by an assortment of damaged-looking people: an elderly Santa-shaped gentleman with a lumpish, mauve nose; a pair of down-at-heels Afro-Americans; a disheveled middle-aged couple who're having an argument. A chubby Aleut woman in a torn man's shirt and jeans sits at the bar, holding her head in her hands. Madcat's not in terrific shape himself. He's nursing a glass of wine, pressing the heel of his hand against his brow; he's been in a fight, and sports a bloody nose and a discolored lump over one eye. Fighting is the most prominent symptom of Madcat's problem. When he's staying in the cities, he'll get in a fight a day, sometimes more, and he's done jail time as a result. He claims that fighting is the only way he "can get the devil out." But when he's riding or jungled up near a switch-yard, it seems that the closeness of the trains soothes his particular devil. Maybe, I think, the trains have a similar effect on others; maybe that explains at least in part why there's so much sadness out on the rails; maybe some hobos are attracted to the trains because the potency of those 2-million-ton presences and their metal voices act to subsume their pain.

We've been waiting almost an hour when the Flash makes his appearance. He's tall, physically imposing, and has a biker intensity that's in line with his reputation as a dangerous person, a man who—according to the grapevine—has no compunction about murder. Under a denim jacket, he's wearing his FTRA colors, a black bandanna held in place by two silver conchos. Thick dark brown hair falls to his shoulders, threads of gray here and there. His hands are large, with prominent knuckles, and his well-defined features. He's been staying with a local woman in her home, and looks healthier than other gang members I've encountered. Like most hobos, he doesn't offer a handshake to someone he's just met.

I tell him I'd like to hear his angle on the FTRA story, and he says fiercely, "I ain't got no damn story. Not one I want you to hear." But after I buy him a pint of Thunderbird, he seems mollified and takes the stool beside me. I ask him if there's any statement he'd like to make about the gang in general.

"Sure, I got a statement for you." When he talks, he has the habit of starting out looking down at his glass, or some other object close at hand, then slowly turning his head sideways toward me, a tight movement, finishing the turn as he finishes his thought—he might be tracking the carriage of an invisible typewriter. "None of you gave a shit about us before. We could all dry up and blow away, you wouldn't care. Now this nut case kills a few people, this poor son-of-a-bitch goes around hearing voices . . . Fuck! How'd you like it I come in your house and go to asking a bunch of dumb-ass questions?

How 'bout I barge into your living room and say, 'Scuse me, buddy. You always drink two martinis 'fore you screw your girlfriend, or is that just 'cause it's Tuesday?' "

I start to speak, but he cuts me off.

"You got your own nuts you can write about. Ted Bundy and all the other freaks. Sidetrack [Robert Silveria's train name] don't have a damn thing to do with the FTRA." He holds up the empty pint, which he's drained in three gulps, and I signal the bartender.

"Sooner or later," the Flash goes on, "one of you shitbrains is gonna piss somebody off and get yourself killed. Then you'll have a fucking story. The rails ain't no place to be asking questions. It's dangerous out there. Hobos want to be left the fuck alone. That's why we're out there. You keep pestering us, we'll let you know about it."

By the time he's started in on his third pint, the Flash has completely abandoned his intention of not talking to me, and is taking it upon himself to smarten me up, chump that I am. He's mellowed; his gestures are not so tightly controlled, and his voice has acquired a lazy, gassed quality, all of which causes me to think that his original hostility might have been chemically enhanced.

"People are setting up Eddie Bauer tents in the jungles," he says. "Walking around with scanners and hiking boots. You take a stroll through a place where everybody's starving, and you're packing a bag of groceries, what you expect's gonna happen? The rails is where we live, man. It ain't a fucking theme park. All this shit you're stirring up"—he taps me on the chest—"one of you's gonna wind up eating it. And it ain't because the FTRA is the fucking mafia, y'know. 'Cause it ain't. We take care of our own, but that's as far as it goes."

I ask him if there's a hierarchy in the gang, any structure, and he lets out a scornful laugh.

"You think I kill people?" he asks.

The question catches me off guard. "I don't know. Do you?"

He gives me a steady look. "I do what I have to. We all do what we have to, right?"

"I suppose so."

"Well, that's exactly what I do . . . what I have to. That's your structure. That's all the structure there is."

"So you're saying it's the survival of the fittest?"

"I'm saying that right here, the three of us"—his gesture includes me and Madcat—"if we're out riding, one of us is president, one's vice president." He grins. "Then there's you."

"If that's all it is, why join a gang?"

"Brotherhood, man. You need me to explain brotherhood to you?"

The Aleut woman a few seats down makes a low keening noise, and the Flash eyes her with disfavor.

"I got no reason to tell you shit," he says, coming back to me. "I told you some of the things I done, you wouldn't understand 'em anyhow. The world you live in, the only excuse there is for killing is self-defense. But where I live there might be a thousand good reasons for killing somebody any given moment. That don't mean you got to enjoy it. But you better be up to it."

I think of men accustomed to killing whom I've spoken to in prison, who've handed me similar bullshit. All of them maintained an outlaw stance until they felt they were in a circumstance in which they had nothing to prove, no one to impress; then they revealed a more bouyant side of their natures, brimmimg over with cheerfulness, their talk rife with homily, as if bloodshed had done wonders for their spirits, as if, having crossed over the border of acceptable human conduct, they had been delighted to discover that they had retained their basic sensibilities and not been transformed into a depraved subspecies by the resonance of their crimes, and now were inspired to offer counsel to those less advanced along the road to wisdom. I sense this potential in the Flash; though he hasn't dropped his badass pose, I believe that in another environment, he'd loosen up and get anecdotal about his crimes and analyze himself in terms of a woeful past.

'You and me should take a ride sometime," he says. "If you want to get to know somebody, best way is to take a ride with 'em."

He's mocking me, and the only thing I can think to say is, "Yeah, maybe."

"Well, you let me know, huh?" He gets to his feet, digs for his wallet, then remembers that I'm the one paying. He nods to Madcat and says, "Safe rails, brother." And then he's gone.

Madcat is holding his head to one side, a hand still pressed to his brow to alleviate the throbbing of the lump above his eye. I ask if he's okay, and he says, "Pissed off is all."

"Why's that?" I ask, and he says, "The guy who whipped me, he wasn't that big a deal. Guess I ain't as much a man as I used to be."

He seems unreasonably distressed—he's lost fights before. I can't think how to restore his spirits.

"You still up for riding?"

"Oh, yeah. I'll be fine."

But he looks utterly dejected.

I ask if he wants some more wine before we head out, and he says, "Naw, fuck. Wine don't do no good for me."

He stares down into his glass, swirls the liquid around; then lifts his head and turns his gaze to the street, watching the passers-by with a forlorn expression, as if seeing in their brisk movements yet another condemnation of his weakness.

"Wish't I'd had me a bottle of whiskey," he says. "I'd been drinking whiskey, I'da kicked his ass."

We're riding in a boxcar south along the Columbia River, which must be nearly a mile wide at this point, and it's hard to tell which is the reflecting medium and which the source of light—the river, every eddy bearing a captive glint, or the starry sky above. The towering hills that follow the watercourse show dark and nearly featureless, all but their lowermost reaches in shadow, making it appear that the curtain of night has been gathered into great black folds at the edge of the bright stage it delimits. Though it's incredibly loud in the car, too loud for speech, something about the solitude and immensity of the scene, and perhaps the sense I have of the peculiarly American tradition of which I'm now a small part— the rail riders of the Civil War era, the hobos of the Depression, the FTRA—all this serves to describe a silence inside me, to shut me off from the rattling and the cold iron smells of the train, even from the noise of ambient thought, and after a while, emerging from an almost meditative state, I wonder if this is what Adman means by "the Drift".

Adman is the train name of Todd Waters, a brisk, fiftyish man with a neat gray beard who runs a successful Minneapolis advertising agency. He's been riding for more than twenty years, and admits to being what is called a "yuppie rider" or a "yuppie hobo." Most tramps use shoestrings to tie off their trouser cuffs when they're boarding a freight, to prevent the fabric from catching on something and causing them to fall. Adman uses velcro fasteners. When I met him he was a wearing a sporty cap, and a denim jacket and trousers that appeared to be matching, and I thought he would look more natural steering a yacht than hopping a freight. He's given to comparing the quintessential hobo to a Hermann Hesse character whose purpose in life was "to make men homesick for their freedom," and he asserts that the experience of riding elevates him into a state he calls "the Drift," wherein it seems that his dreams and thoughts are colored not by his own past, but by the stars he's passing beneath and the places he's passing through.

I can't quite go there with Adman—I haven't yet found anyone on the rails who's made me homesick for my freedom. But you have to respect Adman, because he's done something with his romantic zeal. Back in 1983 he created the Penny Route, encouraging people to contribute a penny for every mile he rode; he wound up raising more than a hundred thousand dollars for the National Coalition for the Homeless. Since then he's established himself as a respected figure in the hobo community, someone who can speak both to and for the transient rail population. What's troublesome about yuppie hobos in general, however, are the increasing numbers of sport riders and scenery freaks who sally forth onto the rails without regard for the risks involved. Should someone with a little fame—a minor rock star, or a peripheral Kennedy relative—decide to hop a freight in order to research a part or just to feel that Jack Kerouac thing, and then fall under the wheels of a boxcar, Officer Grandinetti will be turning up on every television program from *Nightline* to *American Journal,* wagging his finger and putting the bogeyman face of FTRA on the tragedy, whether it applies or not, and the media frenzy will begin.

From the standpoint of the railroad companies, one might think that an intensified law enforcement focus on the subject of FTRA, wrongheaded or not, would be a good thing, since it would probably result in even more security and fewer criminal incidents involving transients. But Ed Trandahl, a spokesman for Union Pacific, laughed when I mentioned Grandinetti and said, "Oh, yeah. We know about him." He went on to say that "The FTRA is a totally overblown deal. Union Pacific has thoroughly explored this with our railroad police, and there's no massive organization at work here. Our investigators have gone over hundreds of cases and we can't find any correlation to what Mr. Grandinetti is saying."

The poster boy for those who adhere to the Grandinetti view of FTRA is Robert Joseph Silveria, a thirty-nine-year-old hobo known as Sidetrack, who recently pled guilty to two counts of first-degree murder in Salem, Oregon, and is scheduled to be tried in Kansas and Florida on similar charges. Detective Mike Quakenbush, who arrested Silveria and extracted his confession, believes that Silveria "is good for a lot more murders" than those with which he's been charged, an opinion shared by quite a few others, both in law enforcement and among the transient population; he described Silveria as being cordial, amiable, having a pleasant manner typical of serial killers, which allowed him to get close to his victims, who were killed by blunt force trauma. He reminds him, Quakenbush said, of Eddie Haskell from *Leave It to Beaver*. But Silveria is not a member of FTRA. In fact, he made a point during his confession that his crimes had nothing to do with FTRA. There's no doubt that Silveria rode and jungled up with FTRA hobos, but such loose associations are common on the rails and hardly constitute evidence of collusion.

Quakenbush's take on FTRA is more restrained than that of Grandinetti. In his view, its members have the profile of a fifties or sixties biker gang, and though they have no set hierarchy, he suspects there may be powerbrokers among them, "people who can get things done." But he told me it's impossible to get a handle on them because of the anonymous nature of their lifestyle, which enables them to slide through the system, to move two states down the road in a matter of hours without going through easily surveilled areas such as airports and bus stations. Maybe, he said, there's a pecking order based on seniority, on how long an FTRA member has been riding; but again, it's hard to be sure. My impression of Quakenbush's attitude toward FTRA was that it's interesting to him from a law enforcement standpoint, but that he has more pressing matters on his desk.

The freight I'm riding gains elevation, and the Columbia comes to look unreal, like a big swath of sequined dark blue cloth stretched between two trembling hands that are causing it to ripple, lending it the illusion of fluidity. It's very cold, and the cold is damping thought. I recall stories I've heard about frozen bodies found in cars, and I wish I had a warmer sleeping bag. I wonder if I should try to stay awake, but fatigue overtakes me. As I drift off, I have a little flash dream. I'm floating outside the boxcar, moving along with the train, and I have a strange fisheye perspective that lets me see many of the cars at once—gondolas, grainers, 48s. Hobos are riding every one, slung beneath them, atop them, peering out the windows of a slave engine unit, visible as shadows. Each is occupied with some task, doing something with their hands, and it seems that taken all together, their separate, simple actions comprise a single intricate action. I float closer to the train, hoping to see what they're up to; but when I get too close, when they notice me, they disappear.

The day after New Year's, 1998, and I'm at a hobo gathering in New Mexico, maybe a hundred people jungled up on a patch of desert figured by saguaro and mesquite and sage and a big, dark lizardback tumble of rock that sticks up beside a section of Southern Pacific track. Atop the rock, several flags are flying—U.S., Confederate, MIA, Anarchist. The raising of the Anarchist banner caused a minor dust-up earlier in the day, when one of the encamped riders, said to be a KKK member, objected to its presence; but he's been appeased. He and his family spend a good deal of their time zooming around on motorized all-terrain bikes, making an aggressive show of having fun, and don't mix with the rest of us.

I'm perched on a ledge close to the flags, gazing down on the place. Beneath and to my left, some elderly hobos are sitting beneath two small shade trees, occupying chairs arranged in a circle around the remains of the previous night's campfire; beyond them, a communal kitchen has been erected, and people are busy cooking hash for breakfast. Farther off, there's a trailer on which helium tanks are mounted; they're used to fill balloons, which now and again can be seen floating off into a clouded pewter sky. Children scoot about, playing and squabbling in the dirt. Tents scattered here and there; vehicles of every description—pickups, campers, old shitboxes. The whole thing calls to mind a scene from a low-budget film about life after some civilization-destroying disaster, the peaceful settlement of the good guys in the moment before the motorized barbarians come swooping down to rape and steal gas. Trains pass with regularity, and when this happens, rockets are set off and people move close to the tracks and wave. The engineers sound their whistles, wave back, and on occasion toss freight schedules from the engine window.

The King of the Hobos, Frog Fortin, an FTRA member whose coronation took place last summer at the hobo convention in Britt, Iowa, was supposed to put in an appearance here, but to my dismay, he's a no-show. The majority of the attendees are railfans, people who've done some hoboing but who now have day jobs and families and can't be classified as hobos—they simply love trains. There are also, as mentioned, some old-time hobos, men in their sixties and seventies; and there are staff members of the *Hobo Times,* "America's Journal of Wanderlust," a publication that in my view has an overly sentimental take on the transient lifestyle, and is given to printing treacly hobo poetry.

Most of these folks don't feel like talking about FTRA. Some disparage them, passing them off as drunks who're more likely to harm themselves than anyone else. Others are hostile when I mention the subject. They feel that FTRA has brought down the heat on all riders, and don't want to contribute to more bad publicity. Most of those who are willing to talk don't have much to add to what I already know, but I meet a photographer who's ridden with FTRA, who tells me about black FTRA members— New York Slim, the Bushman, et al—and attributes FTRA racism to the enforced racism inherent in the prison system. It's more habitual, he says, than real. Another rider, Lee, agrees with him, and says that although the FTRA use racist iconography in their tattoos and graffiti, they are "oddly egalitarian racists."

Lee is a forty-two-year-old wilderness squatter who was

involved with the Earth First movement until he became fed
up of the group's internal politics. He lives in a tiny house he
built himself in the midst of a redwood forest in Northern
California's so carefully camouflaged it's almost impossible to
spot it from a distance of fifteen feet. There he publishes
Hobos from Hell/There's Something about a Train, a zine in
which you can find stories about the rails written by a variety
of hobos. He's dressed, as is his custom, all in black. Black
sweats, black raincoat, black baseball hat. Makes him harder
to spot in the yards at night. Though he's no hermit, his face
has the sort of mild openness I associate with someone who's
spent time in solitude. His features are a bit weathered, but his
energy and humor make him seem younger than his years. He
says he looks forward "to the collapse of the Industrial State,"
but when that happens, he'll miss the trains. It strikes me that
for Lee a perfect world would be one in which man has
become extinct, the planet has reverted to a natural state, and
the only reminders of its human past are the trains, evolved to
an inorganic form of life, traveling endlessly across the wild
and making their eerie music.

I ask Lee a question I've asked almost every hobo I've met:
"Twenty, thirty years from now, given improvements in the
technology, railroad security systems are likely to be pretty
daunting. You think people will still be able to ride?"

Lee's answer is the same as those of all the rest, an unequiv-
ocal no. But it seems an answer based more on a romantic
attachment than on reality. If the railroads can cost-effectively
rid themselves of the liability risks and logistical problems
caused by riders, I have no doubt that they will do so, and this
entire subculture may be done in—as have many others—by
the the mealy blight of the ordinary.

Because I want to talk about FTRA, Lee decides to take our conversation up to the flags, where no one else will hear. But we wind up talking less about FTRA than about "the next generation of hobos," one that includes the "crusty punks" and young eco-activist riders. Lee places the latter in the tradition of the Wobblies, who used the rails to spread their political message back in the 1930s; he describes them as "goal-oriented, self-educated wanderers." The crusty punks are pierced, tattooed, homeless youths who come out of hardcore squat scenes in urban areas, and are "apolitical, non-racist white trash." A subgroup, the "gutter punks," he likens to the untouchable caste of India. He expresses concern that these younger riders haven't been accepted by the old hobos, mainly because their rowdy behavior has attracted the attention of the police and thus brought down even more heat. He seems to like them all, has ridden with them, but he's frustrated by the crusties' self-destructiveness. I wonder if his attitude toward them, his compassion, may echo a similar attitude that caused him frustration when he was involved with the Earth Firsters.

That night people gather around the campfire, drinking beer and swapping rail stories. There's SLC, a hobo out of Salt Lake City who once owned a mail-order computer company which he lost to the IRS, and has just spent a month working on a hog farm; there's Dante Faqwa, an old-time hobo; there's Buzz Potter, editor of the *Hobo Times*; there's a lady hobo, Connecticut Shorty; there's a short, truculent guy in his late twenties who calls himself Bad Bob. Lee is there with a couple of friends. Adman is there. Along with many, many others I haven't met. Listening to scraps of conversation, it's possible to believe that I'm in a hobo jungle back during the Depression:

"Is the Sacramento Kid around the fire?"

". . . wasn't a bull for a thousand miles . . ."

". . . it's always been a motherfucker to catch out of . . ."

". . . they closed the mission in Atlanta . . ."

". . . the train didn't go til sundown . . ."

". . . best chicken I ever ate came from that alley . . ."

Whenever a train draws close, fireworks are set off; star-bursts flower overhead as the engine approaches the camp, roaring and moaning, flattening the brush with the wind of its passage. Night is the best time to watch trains; they seem grander and more magical. There's a gravity about them you can't feel as strongly in daylight. They are, I think, kind of like the giant sandworms in *Dune* . . . of course, it's possible this and all my previous perceptions are colored by the fact that I'm seriously baked. Two monster joints and a bunch of beer. Whatever, I realize that I'm being seduced by all the happy-wanderer, freedom's-just-another-word-for-freighthopping, hash-cooking, Dumpster-diving *esprit de* poverty that's rising up from these sons and daughters of the iron horse like heat from Mother Nature's steaming yoni. Which is okay, I suppose. I'll have to turn in my cynic's card, but hey, maybe I've migrated to a better world. Maybe the stars are actually spelling out song lyrics, and the pile of stones shadowing us has turned into the Big Rock Candy Mountain.

Then the singing starts for real. Old broadwater ballads such as "Barbara Allen," delivered by a friend of Lee's whose sweet tenor exhibits signs of academic training. A rider in a bush hat and desert camo hauls out a guitar. In a brief conversation ear-lier that day, he made violently homophobic comments; but now, with no appreciable acknowledgment of irony, he pro-ceeds to deliver a thoroughly professional rendition of "City of

New Orleans," concluding with the reverential statement, "That song was written by Mister Steven Goodman." More train songs follow. The mystical union of the rails is dissolving into a hootenanny. I sense that once all the railroad songs have been exhausted, a few verses of "Where Have All the Flowers Gone" may not be deemed inappropriate.

Adman drops into a chair close by, and says something about "the bluehairs in their RVs," contrasting these conservative seniors and their feeble journeyings with "the wisdom in the eyes of old hobos." His delivery grows increasingly rhapsodic, peaking as he describes how during one series of rides, his cassette recorder broke and he was forced to scavenge for batteries. "I hooked it up with batteries from a *Dumpster,* and I'm listening to *opera.*" His voice full of wonderment, as if recounting, not long after the event, how the young Arthur Pendragon pulled Excalibur from its imprisoning stone. He's probably as blitzed as I am, but even knowing this, it's hard to bear. The whole scene has become an enormous sugar rush, and I have to get away. I like these people. No matter how dippy this part of their fantasy, the rest of it's way cooler than most. They don't need me making "ribbit . . . ribbit" noises from the back row, something I'm tempted to do. I move out into the darkness, where other refugees from the fire are drinking cups of beer and looking off into the blue shadows of the desert.

Tonight I'm drinking more heavily, sitting on a grassy embankment next to a Portland strip mall with half-dozen crusty punks. They're happy to drink up my money, but only one wants to talk. Her name, she tells me, is Jailbait. She could pass for thirteen, says she's seventeen—if you split the difference, you'd probably be right. Dirty blond hair hangs into her eyes, accentuating her waifish quality. Clean her up, dress her in something besides baggy jeans and a hooded sweatshirt, she'd be breaking ninth-grade hearts. As things stand, a crop of inflamed blemishes straggles across her forehead, so distinct against the pale skin it makes me think I could connect the dots and come up with a clown's face or a crude map of Rhode Island; and maybe it's only a combination of the malt liquor and the neon sign on the roof behind us, but her teeth look kind of green.

Jailbait's been living in a squat with her friends for six weeks, but now it's getting cold, they're thinking about LA or maybe San Diego. She tells me she comes from LA, but I hear the great Midwest in her speech. I ask why she left home, and she looks off into the sky, where stars are sailing clear of a patchy mist, and says without inflection, "It was just fucked up." She's been riding for a year, she says, and she's never had any trouble with FTRA.

"They yell sex stuff at us sometimes, y'know. But that's about it." She rubs at a freshly inked homemade tat that spreads from the soft area between thumb and forefinger to cover the back of her left hand. I can't make out what it's supposed to be—a blurred network of blue-black lines—but I'm fairly certain the tiny scabs at the center are tracks.

"We don't hang out with them much," she goes on. "Some of them are cool, I guess. There's one I met last summer played the harmonica. He was nice. But most of 'em, they're these old fucked up guys, y'know."

"They never gotten aggressive with you?"

"Carter got chased by them once." She glances up at her friends, who are sitting above us on the slope, and addresses a sullen, muscular kid with the basic Road Warrior look: stubbly scalp, heavy designwork on his neck and arms, and enough cheap facial jewelry to set off an airport detector. "Wasn't those guys chased you back in Pasco FTRA?"

Carter shrugs, takes a hit off his forty.

"He stole some of their shit," Jailbait says. "But they couldn't catch him."

"I didn't steal nothin'," says Carter. "I was just walkin' past and this ol' fuck started waving a knife."

"If you didn't steal nothin', you were thinkin' about it." This from a chunky blond girl in a tight turtleneck and a stained black mini and torn stockings. Her makeup's so thick it reminds me of Kabuki.

"Fuck you!" says Carter.

The girl's voice grows querulous. "You know you were! You said you were gonna see if they had any wine!"

Carter jumps to his feet and makes as if to backhand her. He goes off on her, shouting, his face contorted with anger, using the C-word with frequency. He's sick of her skanky hole, why doesn't she just fucking die.

The girl turns her head away, holds up an arm to ward off a blow; she's crying, cursing him softly.

The other three boys—less accessorized versions of the Carter doll—laugh and do some high-fiving.

"C'mon, Carter," says Jailbait. "Don't be an asshole."

A switch might have been triggered in Carter's brain, releasing an icy fluid. He grows calm, mutters a final word of warning, and sits back down. The chunky girl lifts her head a bit and glares at Jailbait.

It doesn't matter what sort of question I ask the crusties, I realize. I could ask about their favorite TV show and tap into the same group dynamic, the same pattern of sullenness evolving into fury, then lapsing into drunken silence. I'm curious about them, but they're impervious to curiosity. They're floating on some terminal wavelength that's beaming the length and breadth of the country, controlling them as they slide from exotic chemical peaks to troughs of low self-esteem. Another tragic cliché being woven into the decaying electric tapestry of the End Times.

I tell them I have to go; I'm hoping to catch out from the switchyard across the river in Vancouver, Washington, in a couple of hours; the guy I'm riding with says they're putting together an eastbound.

"That's a pussy yard," Carter says, giving me a challenging stare; it's the first time he's spoken directly to me for an hour. "Fuckin' old lady could catch out of Vancouver."

A babble erupts from the other boys, they're throwing out the names of various yards, ranking them according to degree of difficulty. Vidalia's no problem. Likewise Dilworth. The bulls at Klamath Falls have gotten nasty. Salt Lake City's not too bad, except for all the pedophiles.

"You think you know something, don't you?" Carter says. "You got it all figured out."

This confuses me. I can't decide if Carter's smarter than he looks, if he has a sense of what I'm thinking, or if this is just another bellicose twitch. I'd prefer to believe the former—it would be nice to be surprised.

"Figured what out?"

Carter comes up into a half-crouch, balanced on one hand; he's trying to look menacing, doing a decent job of it. "Fuck you," he says.

I'm almost drunk enough to respond. Carter doesn't really want to fight, though I'm sure he could get into it; he just wants to win the moment—it's all he's got worth risking a fight over. Could be he's a rotten kid and deserves his crummy life. But I don't need to make things worse for him. Nor am I eager to have my head danced on by him and his pals.

The six of them straggle up the embankment, away from me, and against the backdrop of the convenience store,

I think we're in somewhere in Montana, one of those small towns on the eastern prairie that at night show like a minor cluster of stars too disorganized to suggest a clever shape. The train has stopped, but I can't see any signs from where we are, just low, unlit buildings and a scrap yard. I'd ask Madcat, but he's asleep. We're sitting on the rear porchlike section of a grain car, bundled up against the early morning chill, and I worry about whether we should get off, hide in the weeds in case they check they cars. Then the train lurches forward, and we're rolling again. As we gather speed I see two men jogging along the tracks behind us, trying for another car. In the electric blue of the predawn darkness, they're barely more than shadows, but I have an impression of raggedness, and I'm pretty sure one has a bushy beard. FTRA, I think. Officer Grandinetti is right, he just hasn't taken his vision of the gang far enough. FTRA is everywhere. And nowhere. Mystical, interpenetrating, sinister. I've asked one too many questions, and from his fastness deep in the Bitterroots, Daniel Boone has focused his monstrous intellect upon me, sent thought like a beam of fire from a crystal to sting the minds of his assassins and direct them to me.

A cold-looking, egg-yolk-yellow smear of light spills up over the eastern horizon, the gunmetal blue of the sky begins to pale, and the day reveals rolling wheatfields and a tiny

reservation town of trailers and rusted pickups standing a half-mile or so from the tracks. It's an ordinary sight made extraordinary by my vantage, tired and dirty, sitting inside the roar of the train, in the midst of solitude, seeing a moment no one else will see, the shimmer of the wheat, clouds with silver edges and blue-gray weather heavy in their bellies pushing in low from the north, and the abandoned look of the trailers, discolored siding and sprung doors, one pitched at an angle, come off its blocks, and watchful crows perched on a fence-line-like punctuation—it's all infused with a sense of urgent newness, the mealy blight of the ordinary washed away. Maybe this is something I should be homesick for. But . . . I remember Mississippi Bones walking away at the end of our interview in the prison at Florence, leaning on his cane, a guard at his side. Halfway across the room he turned back, stared at me for a second. In retrospect, I think he might have been making a judgment as to whether it was worthwhile to offer me advice. When he did speak, his tone was friendly yet cautionary, like that of someone telling a child not to play in the street.

"Stay off the trains," he said.

LO, CULTURELAND!

YODELING: VELVET THROATS AND LEATHER PANTS FROM GERMAN PROTO-HIPPIES TO JUGEND SS

Bart Plantenga

"The Tyroleans are here again: I will have them perform those songs for me, even though I can only tolerate the popular yodeling outdoors or in big rooms."—Goethe, 1829

Tim Burton's over-the-top 1996 film *Mars Attacks!*, about menacing Martians conquering a globe of naïve earthlings, features the yodel as the vocal equivalent of a secret Psy-Ops weapon that ultimately saves the earth from alien domination. At a climactic instant, the headphones of an eccentric old lady fan of yodeler Slim Whitman suddenly slip off her head, exposing the Martians to Whitman's histrionic yodeling-crooning "When I'm calling you-oo-oo . . ." The yodeler's high notes shatter the Martians' helmets and their heads explode in great bursts of green cerebral goo. Forget the power of love, this is the power of yodeling.

Farfetched? Well, yes *and* no. Manfred Bukofzer, in his 1936 "Magic and Technique in Alpine Music," described the magical powers of various Alpine tones when combined with certain mystical words (usually cow names). Meanwhile, seventeenth-century tales describe Swiss mercenaries suffering from *Heimweh* (homesickness) who, upon hearing certain Alpine songs, would go AWOL, berserk, or even die. Laws were passed forbidding hysteria-arousing yodeling in the presence of Swiss soldiers.

But what *is* this vocal dynamite? Greeting? Warning? Joyous outburst? Pious ululation? A cowherd's hootchy-cootchy come-on to his most udder-endowed? Or just some irritating "variation upon the tones of a jackass," as Sir Walter Scott opined in 1830? Probably a bit of all of the above.

Simply put, yodeling is unlike other vocalizations because it emphasizes that jolt of air that occurs as the voice passes from bass (low chest voice) to high head voice (falsetto)—and vice versa. No glottal jolt, no yodel. A genuine yodel (*juutz*) is wordless and not "music" per se, but an acoustical signal associated with cowherds communicating with each other and with their herds. Ed Sanders of the Fugs calls it "a kind of homemade Morse code for people in the mountains." Yodeling's unique ability to project over great distances stems from its abrupt changes in pitch.

In addition to Switzerland, two countries whose histories are entangled in yodeling are Austria and Germany. The word *jodeln* first appeared in a song in 1796 in "Der Tyroler Wastl." *Mildheimisches Lieder Buch* (1799), a book of art songs and folk songs, included Alpine yodels, that some-time inspiration for composers of the Romantic era such as Beethoven (1770–1827) who wrote numerous Tyrolean *lieder*. His *Symphonie Pastorale* (1809) includes a "triple pedal at the opening with its horn yodel" where the *ranz des vaches* serves as leitmotif with horns replying to an oboe's calls. *Symphonie Fantastique* (1830), by Hector Berlioz also includes a *ranz des vaches*.

The Romantic Movement was "neither precisely the choice of subject matter," as Charles Baudelaire noted, "nor the exact truth, but rather a way of sensing things . . ." and saw yodels finding their way into *lieder* as embellishments and refrains.

Romanticism, largely an artistic-intellectual movement, spotlighted the yodel as a pure expression of a prior folk culture, marking it as a key to Alpine-Germanic identity. French philosopher Jean-Jacques Rousseau (1712–1778), in his Romantic pursuit of the inherently pure and natural in nature, discovered the simple yodel. In his *Dictionnaire* under *"Musique,"* he presented the notation for a *ranz de vaches.*

Romanticism's notion of the dissolution of the individual in the collective ambience of culture was developed by philosopher Johann Gottfried von Herder. Herder saw individuals as valuable only insofar as they could integrate into the greater collective *volk*. Herder transformed *volk* from something provincial into something national with his collection of folksongs, *Alte Volklieder* (1779), which included many *Betruf, Juchzer, Kuhreihen,* and *Jodellieder,* all yodel-related songs that galvanized German uniqueness.

Swiss, Austrian, and German national songbooks like *Des Knaben Wunderhorn* (Youths' Magic Horn) served as effective editing tools for removing blemishes from the national character. The Swiss *ranz des vaches* and German *kuhreihen* were deemed authentic folk expressions because they portrayed the idyllic herder's lifestyle. There's no shortage of these distinctive herder songs.

Beethoven, Mozart, and Schubert listened attentively to folk music and borrowed its themes and sounds, fusing their individual visions with those of folk culture until their own music became synonymous with pride of place. Smetana and Dvorák celebrated native Bohemian landscapes and folk rhythms. Austria's Johann Strauss and Johann Straus, Jr.

exploited the waltz and infused it with yodel-like leaps and phrasing, particularly in Strauss the younger's 1874 operetta *Die Fledermaus*. In Richard Strauss's opera *Arabella* (1932) the pretty hostess, Fiakermilli, yodels as she hands a bouquet to Arabella.

As the 19th century droned on, the fusion of music with nationalism became not only seamless, but natural and obligatory. But was yodeling employed for nefarious national interests? Let's close the nineteenth century, with the Wandervogels: cowlicks and dimples; rosy cheeks and ideals; bare legs and guitars. How did this Romantic youth protest movement, situated somewhere between boy scout and hippie, devolve from its lofty goals into something so conformist, phalangist, and viciously enthusiastic as the *Hitlerjugend*?

> I'm a Wandervogel too
> I'm breathing life's fresh air
> And to sing my song
> Is my greatest desire
>
> —Otto Roquette (1824–1896),
> "Das Lied der Wandervogel"

The movement, founded in 1896 outside Berlin, was basically a back-to-nature, search-for-value youth movement trying to escape a cynical materialistic society, that rehabilitated abandoned traditions by singing nineteenth-century folksongs around open campfires.

In 1913, the Wandervogels gathered at Hohe Meissner, a mountain south of Kassel steeped in German folklore. At this "Festival of Youth," a Woodstock of its day, they managed to hammer out proclamations against "unfruitful patriotism"

and their war-mongering materialistic elders while declaring their allegiance to Romanticism's virtues: truth, beauty, individualism, and principle over nation.

World War I destroyed a generation of German youth, casting a gruesome shadow over Romantic idealism. The Wandervogel psyche began to change shape; while some continued to pursue nature and mysticism, others turned to political extremes—both Left and Right.

Various bowdlerized and mangled standard songs (including yodels) sung by Wandervogels were considered perfect echoes of the fatherland. They helped rouse the Germanic people beyond pride, to an enthusiastic defense of their peasant heritage (as increasingly defined by the state) and ultimately beguiled an entire people toward the cause of Nazism. According to author Pamela Potter, "The growth of the *Jugendmusikbewegung* [youth music movement] . . . in the 1920s and 1930s fueled the interest in folk melodies." These melodies contained "certain national traits which, although difficult to describe, are clearly felt to represent the general character of the people."

The *Hitlerjugend* was officially founded in July 1926 and would emerge as the sole legitimate German youth organization after the Nazis came to power in 1933. They managed to funnel the myriad ideals of innumerable early-twentieth-century German youth groups into one central intoxication. Hundreds of youth groups would join the Hitlerjugend (many begrudgingly), who appropriated their traditional themes, sentiments, and folk music—call it a hostile takeover of the spirit.

Meanwhile, Nazi-sympathizing musicologists reconstructed folksongs by how they thought they *should* have sounded back before they were "perverted" by oral transmission. These songs were then disseminated to further instill pride in the German state. Dutch avant-classical musician, Jozef van Wissem, noted that "the back-to-nature . . . Wandervogel[s] which started out as an innocent parallel to the hippie movement but later was appropriated by the Nazis were really into herders, folklore, nature, and folk and early music as opposed to jazz and modern classical music. Also probably into yodeling. The fact that the Nazis misused this youth movement which later became known as the Hitlerjugend is your Nazi link to yodeling."

Musik und Volk, a 1930s Third Reich Youth Leadership music publication, published a lengthy article by Fritz Metzler (1935) on the racial aspects of yodeling, which concluded: "The *jodler* is without a doubt one of the most authentic musical phenomena in the folk music of the German tribe. . . . We can assume that the habit of German yodeling harks back to times immemorial. That's why it was often thought that the musical expression of the early Germans was similar to it."

Although no yodel emerged as some rousing "Deutschland Über Jodels," yodels were sung, analyzed, and discussed in Nazi journals in terms of how they defined German character. As author Barre Toelken noted, "Several people told me that yodeling was especially encouraged during the Hitler years because it was considered so centrally Germanic." The Nazis just steered Wandervogel sentiments down a dubiously steep slope of ideological perversion.

REBEL MUSIC

Fred Brathwaite aka Fab 5 Freddy

"It seems like money has killed the ideology that once was strong in American rap," says M.V. Bill, one of Brazil's most popular rappers. The M.V. stands for *Mensageiro Verdade* or Messenger of Truth. We're in Bill's tiny apartment in *Cedade de Deus* (City of God), one of Rio's harshest *favelas,* talking about how materialistic hip hop has become in America. "Hip hop in Brazil," he says, "is like it used to be in the late eighties."

Suddenly there's a blast of automatic gunfire that sounds like it's right outside the window. Everyone in the room freezes like a video on PAUSE. My ghetto survival instincts hit code red, and I look at M.V. Bill. Sipping a glass of ice water, he barely seems fazed.

Raising his diesel, six-foot-six-inch frame, M.V. Bill heads over to the open window and motions for us to follow. With my heart pounding, I look out and see three teens dash into a nearby building carrying what appear to be AK-47 assault rifles. "The police killed two young children here a week ago in a shootout with the dealers," our host explains, rubbing his bald head. He hands me a newspaper clipping with a front-page story about the incident. "We demonstrated in protest and they came in firing rubber bullets and occupied the favela for five days." It seems I picked a good time to visit—the cops just left this morning. "I plan to have a graffiti artist paint the children's pictures on a wall in tribute," he continues. "We will light many candles and have a concert. That's why it's important for me to stay in the favela."

Think of Brazil, and for most people the first images that come to mind are the massive freak-fest of *carnaval*, soccer, samba, and exotic women cavorting on booty-full beaches. But as I saw for myself when I visited in January for two weeks, Brazil is more like a ticking time bomb, especially in its two largest cities: São Paulo, which actually has a section called Brooklyn, and Rio, a glamorous vacation spot where one person dies from homicide every half-hour.

I had heard that the hip hop scene in these areas was exploding, especially in the notorious favelas, the shanty towns on the hilltops where Brazil's predominantly black poor live. I wanted to check it out. Like a growing number of you out there, I've become increasingly frustrated with the direction the so-called rap game has taken. I was there when hip hop was a baby. Better yet, I helped smack it on the ass at birth. But in the past few years, there's been a little too much emphasis on the gleam and glitter—the Bling Blang Boom of it all. Some rappers are so happy to have gotten theirs that they're happy to flash their diamonds and do that shuffling, fake-gangster hustle one more time for the TV cameras. *Represent, y'all, represent! Whatever they'll buy, we'll sell.*

But in Brazil, and especially in the favelas, rap is still about survival, about life and death. Brace yourself for the realest and most important battle hip hop has ever been involved in.

I learn this firsthand when I visit M.V. Bill, one of Brazil's most famous rappers, days into my trip. He is so infamous that Brazilian government officials tried unsuccessfully to censor his hit song and video "Soldado De Morro" ("Soldier of the Hill"), which, they believed, incited young people to participate in gang violence. But in this kill-or-be-killed environment, many have no choice.

Back in M.V. Bill's favela, the action seems to have calmed down, so we step outside in the blazing afternoon sun to look around. "I could have chosen a life of crime," says M.V. Bill, "but I chose rap. And still they treat me like a criminal, because I'm black, and I tell the truth through my music." "Sometimes rap feels like a prayer, calling out to me and no one else. It's like my religion."

Little boys scamper about, flying homemade paper kites. They smile at M.V. Bill, who nods knowingly at each. A small nutmeg-colored girl, no more than six years old, quietly walks over and hands him a note, then turns and runs back to a woman sitting on the curb. M.V. Bill reads the note, then reaches in his pocket while gesturing for the little girl. I ask Paulo Brown to translate the note. Was it some sort of fan mail? "I would like to borrow five reals (about two U.S. dollars) to buy some rice and beans," it says. "I haven't been able to feed my kids in two days."

For years, Brazil's white ruling class has acted as if favelas—and the problems of racism and poverty that created them—don't exist (there are no favelas on any map of Rio). But you can see these clusters of dilapidated dwellings all over the city. They began to spring up about thirty years after, in 1888, when slavery was abolished. While the wealthy chose to live by the beaches, black migrant workers built mud and stone houses at the base of the hills around the city. For many years these squatter settlements were bull-dozed away, but waves of poor people kept coming back to rebuild until the densely packed ghettos expanded to cover the hillsides.

Almost a third of the city's 6 million residents live in these sky-high slums. The minimum wage for a *favelado* (a favela resident) lucky enough to find work is around a paltry $60 a month. No wonder kidnapping, carjacking, and the cocaine trade are out of control—and it's no surprise that the awesome power of hip hop is in full effect, speaking to people's hunger for peace, justice, and self-esteem.

In the 1990s, hip hop caught on with many groups, including homeless street kids who lived in constant fear of being killed by police death squads. Now rap artists openly protest the country's inhuman treatment of its more than 70 million Afro-Brazilians. This is a country where blacks out-number whites, yet the word *preto* (black) is considered an insult. With over three hundred different terms used to describe the different skin complexions and blends of African, Portuguese, and native Brazilian, racial confusion reigns. The country that imported the most slaves in the new world and the last to free them, abolished the race category on its census and encouraged race-mixing in a strategy known as "whitening." The result has been to strengthen the color-caste system since very few people of color choose to identify them-selves as black.

There is no question who the sufferers are—the darker-skinned favelados. A United Nations fact-finding mission recently equated Brazil's widespread malnutrition and brutal crackdowns on the poor with "genocide."

But just like hip hop in its early days, no obstacles—not poverty, police crackdowns, or government censorship—can stop the music in Brazil. One rap group called 509-E formed while they were in a São Paulo prison. They signed to a major label, released hit records, and shot videos during their incarceration. The founding fathers of Brazilian hip hop are the Racionais MCs, a four-man crew formed in a São Paolo train station in the early nineties that went on to sell a half-million copies of their its record, *Urban Holocaust*.

But for most of these rappers, it's not just about the hits and the money. When I visited the Racionais MCs' lead rapper, Mano "Mad Dog" Brown, in his favela, he described himself not as a musician but as a warrior. "For me rap is not a game," he said. "It's war. And in this war, rap speaks directly to those who are suffering." When I ask him what's the most important thing rap has brought to Brazil, Brown pauses to gaze out over the vast sea of slums, then he looks back at me, his ice grill thawing for a second, "To confirm the existence of racial problems and instill a sense of pride in being black," he says. For him the American rap scene, with its diamonds, guns, and Bentleys, is pitiful. "People in the United States are all spoiled," he says. "They cry because their stomachs are too full."

As a lifelong hip hop emissary, I traveled to Brazil under a diplomatic banner that is recognized and respected in ghettos around the world. A few months after my safe return, I learned that not all writers have been so fortunate. Tim Lopes, a well-known investigative journalist for Globo TV in Brazil was working on an exposé about supposed sexual abuse at *Bailes do Funk* (Funk Balls), the local dances controlled by Rio's favela gangs. According to a *New York Times* article, "the captured journalist was first shot in the feet so he couldn't run and then tortured and cut to pieces with a samurai sword." At this writing only the charred remains of his camera have been found. The police cracked down, conducting daytime raids in response to Lopes's murder. On the morning of June 24, 2002, two cars and a van full of gangsters sprayed 132 bullets into Rio's city hall and left several unexploded hand grenades as a demonstration of their strength and resolve.

Days before my visit with M.V. Bill, I visited a favela for the first time. My translator, the longtime São Paulo radio personality Paulo and I hopped into a van driven by Primo—the host of Brazil's version of *Yo! MTV Raps*—and took off into the hot, sticky Rio night. Our first stop was to pick up Catara, one of the biggest rappers on the Funky scene. A dark-skinned brother of average height, Catara is ruggedly handsome but no pretty boy. He strikes me as the kind of cat who's at home and in control on any corner, in any 'hood.

Rumor has it that he was once an active player in the CV, also known as *Comando Vermhelo* or Red Command. Begun in the 1970s, CV is not only a thriving drug syndicate; it is Brazil's largest gang and the government's biggest internal threat—an organized-crime network with revolutionary aspirations. CV's mantra is Peace, Justice, and Liberty, but it could just as easily be "tons of guns"—assault rifles, grenade and missile launchers, night-vision goggles—which they use in their ongoing war with police and rival factions. Catara's supposed exploits in the CV are mythic—from bank robberies and shootouts to prison breaks. But he was encouraged to leave all that behind by other members who saw his passion and skill for music.

148

After Catara gets into the van, he motions to driver and we head for the hills. We approach the outskirts of a slum and begin the drive up a steep incline. Catara gets on a cell phone as he instructs the driver to turn on the interior light of our vehicle, as it's imperative to make eye contact with the guards. We continue up the hill toward a favela called *Morro do Borell*. From a military standpoint, it's an almost impenetrable fortress, a labyrinth of narrow paths and interconnected dwellings. The van stops and a young man about nineteen approaches the car. He smiles and gives the thumbs-up sign and gestures for us to keep going. He has a small walkie-talkie in his hand and something big strapped to his shoulder.

We continue up the steep hill about 100 yards and slow as we turn a sharp corner. The van stops again, just past a store where about a dozen young Afro-Brazilian men are scattered about, ranging in skin tone from light to jet-black. As we step out of the van, Primo looks back at me and says, "Remember, shake everybody's hand." Baseball caps, Bermuda shorts, jeans, flip-flop sandals, and sneakers are the dress code— pretty much typical urban tropical attire, but one accessory is startling. These young men are packing more heat than a blast furnace, in full frontal fashion no less. Most are laden with AK-47s and other high-caliber assault riffles. Pistols, cell phones and clips full of extra bullets are tucked neatly in their waistbands. One cat has two 9mm Glock pistols in holsters that crisscross his bare back and drape under his arms. A grenade is clipped to his waist. My senses are sizzling as everyone, including the driver, shakes everybody's hand. Catara and Primo are speaking to them in Portuguese and gesturing towards me. I can make out that my resumé is being run down as I recognize words like, *Yo! MTV Raps, Wild Style,* and *New Jack City*. Judging from the reaction, the latter must be their favorite. I continue shaking hands like I'm running for office and notice that not one of these Brazilian B-boy commandos seems much older than twenty-five.

A couple of them pull out marijuana and roll several jumbo joints using what appears to be writing paper. The weed is low-grade "stress" compared to the hydro we're accustomed to in the States, but I smoke it heartily in the peace pipe tradition. They seem honored that Catara has brought a well-known black American to their domain. As for me, I'm still getting used to this open display of weaponry, some of which is plastered with the sort of stickers you'd expect to see on a skateboard. "What happens if the police come?" I ask them through Paulo. Several of the CV laugh, and one replies bluntly, "They die."

The joints finish burning and Catara indicates it's time to leave as we shake everyone's hands again and our entourage hops in the van. I remark to Catara about the profusion of arms among the CV. "That's the reality of life in the ghettos here," he says. "It's a real war, and there are so many more, ready to take their place."

I recall a conversation with Grande, the boss of a favela in Rio called *Morro Do Minera*. "The previous boss here was abusing his power and was expelled by the leaders in prison" he explained. I asked him whether he considers himself a gangster or a sort of revolutionary warlord. "Those terms are all relative," he replied. "Our battle here is titanic. The only real money that flows here is our money. We sell drugs. With the money we buy food, medicine, and stock it in the community center that we built. We bring entertainment, rap and samba shows, free for the people. This is how we take the initiative. We need money from the government so the people can live better. We need schools and cultural centers for the children so they can have other possibilities instead of drug dealing."

We spend the rest of the night with Catara visiting other favelas, checking out the Bailes do Funk, or Funk Balls, and the ritual is the same at each. We first meet and greet the heavily armed CV boss and his soldiers that control these ghetto parties. After explaining who I am, Catara then gets on the mike and does a sizzling fifteen-minute set on the giant outdoor sound system as the crowd goes wild, singing along in call-and-response unison, knowing every word. Groups of young girls do intricately choreographed booty-type dance routines. The sound is similar to Miami bass, mixed with a little Midwestern ghetto tech. Simple catchy rhymes, mostly about sex, are scattered over tracks that thump rapidly at upwards of 120 beats per minute. Catara calls his style "conscious funky," incorporating some "reality and upliftment" in his lyrics. His voice—a big, soulful baritone that can be heard at a dozen Funk Balls each week—reminds me of Jamaican dance hall dons like Buju Banton or Bounty Killer. I'm told that some of these are known as Fight Balls, where promoters actually encourage organized gang fighting. Brazil is, after all, the home of *capoeira,* an artistic mixture of dance, gymnastics, and martial arts, but these human cockfights are more like a scene out of *Fight Club.* Partygoers line up on either side of a dance floor, and when the DJ gives a signal, the fierce and the fearless cross a line to try to beat the shit out of each other—sometimes battling to the death.

Next, it's on to *Vigario Geral,* one of the most deadly favelas in all of Rio. Some 20,000 are expected for a concert here tonight. It was here, in 1993, that a battalion of masked police slaughtered twenty-one people in retaliation for the death of four of their own who died in a shootout while allegedly collecting a drug payoff. The cops had fired indiscriminately into a family's home and lobbed a grenade into a local bar.

As our vehicle approaches the concert, we encounter a dozen uniformed police with large automatic weapons, fingers at the trigger. Tension is thick as a hundred or so young favelados stand around outside the venue. As the sun sets, Rapping Hood's hip hop/samba fusion *"Sao Negrao"* ("I'm Black") pumps from the speakers.

Two young Afro-Brazilians—Jose Junior of the group Afro Reggae, and Celso Atayde—organized tonight's free show. Very much an anomaly in his native land, Celso is a young black man making power moves. Born, raised, and self-educated on the streets of São Paulo, Celso has managed and advised some of Brazil's top artists, including Catara, the Racionais MCs, 509-E, and M.V. Bill. Two years ago Celso started the Hutus, the name for Brazil's first rap awards, which keep going on a shoestring budget and a lot of passion. He has even secured limited sponsorship from Globo, the Latin American media giant, for tonight's show.

While rap has developed a considerable audience in Brazil, it has done so with very little marketing support. Celso has closely studied the progress of hip hop in America, and he understands its potential in Brazil. He's also getting involved in politics, organizing favela residents and starting a black political party with M.V. Bill.

Celso leads me around the concert grounds and explains why the crowd barely numbers 5,000 tonight, less than half the expected turnout. "The mayor of Rio is supportive of this concert and helped pay for it," he says. "But the governor is extremely conservative and does not get along with the mayor. He ordered the heavy police presence to stink up the vibe and antagonize the people."

Celso introduces me to Jose Junior, known to most simply as Junior. Junior is from Rio, where he was exposed to gang life from an early age. "The worst of it was going on all around me. Murder, torture, theft, kidnapping," he says. "I remember the night the police came in and killed those twenty-one innocent people," he tells me. "At that point, I decided to turn my suicidal tendencies of street violence around."

With the help of grass-roots organizations and inspiration from the legendary Bahian Afro-samba group, Oladum, Junior formed Banda Afro Reggae with some other favelados who also had no musical experience. Within a few years' time they had signed a major recording deal and were traveling the globe to rave reviews. Theirs is a dynamic combination of rap, reggae, samba and acrobatic capoiera moves, all woven into a dramatic theatrical performance that is riveting and explosive.

Many rap acts that perform at the Vigario Geral concert are very much like their American counterparts. Stalking the stage with swagger and bravura, accompanied by the proverbial hype man, DJs, and some occasional live musical accompaniment, the artists on the bill include some of Brazilian hip hop's best. But Afro Reggae steals the show with a reenactment of the police raid. In one song they wear ski masks and hold their microphones like guns.

The audiences at Brazilian rap shows are similar to crowds in America, but there's something extra. Periodic pools of mosh-pit mayhem erupt during favorite songs, but the overall feel is more like what a political rally or demonstration must have been like during the days of Marcus Garvey or Malcolm X. Long deprived of any strong role models who are black and proud of it, these people pay rapt attention, hungrily absorbing the flows, flavor, and message in the performances.

The American rap business sometimes seems like a maze of carnival mirrors that reflect and distort perceptions, bouncing and flipping reality around so much that it's easy to get lost. I'm convinced that many American rappers truly believe the comic-book personas they've concocted for themselves: the diamond-encrusted gun-toting Bentley-driving super-thug pimp.

According to *Noticias de uma Guerra Particular* (*Notes from a Private War*), a blazing documentary directed by Kátia Lund, (also the codirector of the feature film, *City of God*) and João Salles that aired on Brazilian television in 1999, hundreds of thousands are employed in the drug trade, and the people of the favelas back the dealers all the way. "The youth are in a suicidal spirit," says one favelado with a mask over his face. "They have no fear. All we want to do is protect our community from violent police invasion."

In another gripping interview, Hector Luz, Rio's chief of police, admitted that his force is violent and corrupt. "This is an unjust society," he said with brutal frankness. "Cops are here to protect the unjust society. Does society really want a clean police force? There would be search warrants and doors getting kicked down at the beachfront condos. That's how an honest police force operates, with no restrictions. The middle class supplies the money. With that money the dealers buy more guns. Then they complain about the violence.

"The poor are to be kept under control, so they better watch their step," he continued, staring into the camera with a tired look on his face. "In South Africa they put up barbed wire. Here the poor have TV sets and they watch the *telenovelas*. They're so stupid they just stay inside. The drug dealers have modern weapons that even Libya and the I.R.A. do not have. The day the people in the favelas decide to come down into the streets organized, they will take over." A few months after the documentary aired, the police chief resigned.

After I returned home to Harlem, a friend in Brazil forwarded a translation of a letter from Marcio VP, an imprisoned kingpin of the CV. Though I didn't get to meet with this incarcerated don, he had heard about my visit and wanted to address his "American Brothers in Hip Hop." His letter—which I think is worth sharing in full—begins with a question for "Big Rap Artists":

> Are you not aware that when you sing, you are leaders telling your people how they should behave? You have responsibilities with the listeners you captivate. Today in Brazil, probably 60 percent of us sing and dance pornography trying to imitate you. It's tragic. Where are the Malcolm Xs, the Martin Luther Kings, the Black Panthers? American hip hop cannot ruin itself this way. It doesn't have this right. It is the only channel and compass of the 'marginalized,' 'excluded,' 'underprivileged' people in the world village, Earth.
>
> We are lost, we are disfigured, manipulated puppets of the powerful Citizen Kane. For this reason we do not have time to lose. Sing about the danger of AIDS, drugs, and the Citizen Kane. Sing about unity and strength that hip hop has and creates. We need to

regenerate ourselves, rise from the ashes. The system does not want this to happen, so we need to fight. I wish you brothers in hip hop Peace Justice and Liberty. This is our true weapon: consciousness."

And while the rest of the world may not be conscious of their plight, the battle for Brazil's future rages on.

WILLEM DE KOONING
1904–1997

Peter Schjeldahl

In the mid 1960s I was a kid poet in overlapping literary and art circles, and it made sense that I found myself at a party after midnight in The Springs when Willem de Kooning's mistress (at that time one said "mistress") knocked at the kitchen door. I saw her when the door was opened. She looked horrible: beaten up. "Oh my God," someone near me said to someone else, "Bill's been at her again!" I was sickened and excited. Would police be called? I envisioned a posse of men from the party going to confront the great, evidently mad artist, whom I considered a god and had not yet laid eyes on. I would tag along. From body language accompanying an inaudible conversation at the door, whose threshold the battered woman vigorously refused to cross, the character of the emergency became clear: she and Bill were out of booze. She secured a bottle of scotch and went back into the night. I concluded that I would never understand anything.

Years later, having come to know de Kooning as a brilliant, funny, intensely gracious man when sober, I got a load of him drunk. I dropped in at his studio one snowy morning with Enrique Castro-Cid, a fun-loving and sentimental Chilean artist now deceased. De Kooning was on a round-the-clock bender, attended by a strapping young studio assistant who took the chance of our arrival to drive into town for supplies and probably a breather. Enrique accepted de Kooning's offer of Johnnie Walker Red and was immediately plastered. I declined.

In the vast studio that de Kooning had designed with high windows on either side, unsuspecting birds periodically rammed the glass with fatal plunks, a baleful percussion in the winter hush. He showed us work in progress. "Why do I do all this crap? I don't need the money!" he cried, gesturing at dozens of leaning canvases. "My women will get all the money. They have too much money already. What are they going to do, go shopping forever?" A beat. "I'm a great painter, don't you think? Look at that." We murmured rapturously. "What do you know? It's shit. You don't know anything."

Later de Kooning appeared to take his first notice of Enrique, who was gazing at him worshipfully. "Enrique! My friend!" exclaimed the master, embracing him. With one arm around the handsome, slightly chubby Latin, he addressed me as if I were the world. "This man is my friend. Enrique here is so important to me. I love this man!" Enrique wept with happiness. "But Enrique," de Kooning cooed in a stage whisper tremulous with hurt feelings, "I want you to tell me one thing. Tell me, why are you so goddamned second-rate?"

As I write this, I am looking at my de Kooning: an accidental monoprint. When he used oil paint that he mixed with water in a blender, he would prevent overnight buildups of surface film by keeping wet canvases covered with sheets of the *Times*. Heaps of peeled-off newsprint littered the floor on a day when I visited. De Kooning said, "You shouldn't leave here with nothing." Kneeling, he tossed sheets left and right, "That's no good. That's no good. Hey, this one's not bad. You like it?" "Very much." "Me, too. Which end do you want up?" "I'm supposed to tell you that?" "O.K., this way." He scrawled "to Peter/Bill de Kooning" in charcoal and handed it over.

Framed behind glass on my wall, the pleasantly smudged sheet, its chance composition oddly stately, might be any-body's lucky debris except for a de Kooningesque palette, fea-turing pink and yellow, and the ghost of one blue brushstroke. I fancy that no one else ever born could have left that specific mark, which I have perused for two decades without using up. Vertical, the stroke is about eighteen inches long and two inches wide. It is sinuous, with two slight bends and an abrupt veer. Though liquid and speedy, it is tensile, as if mus-culature and nerves ran within its length. The veer makes space, nipping back into pictorial depth. I don't know how it does this. I must come to a nose's length from the surface, observing the paint's lateral course, to make the illusion stop. That's the spirit, I think as I look at the guided smear. That's how it's done. "It" could be anything. The stroke tells me to be, in all things, deft and economical and at the same time generous, holding nothing back. It doesn't care if I'm up to its program or not, as I fancy it didn't care if de Kooning was. Nothing about him did anybody including himself a lot of good except when he worked. Then everything went into the art as into a bonfire.

He was the last Renaissance painter. Renaissance painting came into its own with Giotto. Now it's over.

We are taught to be embarrassed by nationalist appeals in art, but let's not forget that de Kooning helped wipe out a chronic American inferiority complex regarding Europe. Can we not feel a little lingering gratitude at the European-type mastery that he put in service of "our" yearnings? He described for me his first vivid take on the United States. Jumping ship from Holland in 1926, he ventured into the Hoboken train and ferry terminal. "It was early in the morning and a thousand guys in hats ran in. You know, commuters. A guy at the diner counter had all these coffee cups lined up. He had a big coffeepot, like a barrel, and he poured without lifting it, one end of the counter to the other in the cups. Like this: one pour!" De Kooning balletically mimed a mighty gesture that seemed to express centuries of Netherlandish punctiliousness dissolving, at a stroke, into a more exuberant, soul-satisfying principle.

"I thought, 'What a great country!' I remembered that guy when my Communist friends in Greenwich Village used to say this is a lousy country. I told them they were nuts."

From WILL YOU MISS ME WHEN I'M GONE?

Mark Zwonitzer

The original Carter Family (A.P., his wife Sara, and her cousin Maybelle) began recording music in 1927 and continued until 1941. Throughout those years, they were the most popular group performing what was then called "hillbilly music." Even sixty years after the group's sudden break-up, Carter Family songs such as "Wildwood Flower," "Hello, Stranger," and "Will the Circle Be Unbroken" remain the gold standards of country music. The Carters' high-water mark was the late 1930s. In those shut-in Depression years, the trio was the main draw on the "Good Neighbor Get Together" show broadcast by station XERA, a 500,000-watt shouter on the Texas-Mexico border that could be heard from the top of Canada to the bottom of Mexico, from coast to coast, and just about everywhere in between. From 1938 to 1941 the Carters were in the warp-and-weave of rural life across the country, in people's homes twice a day (morning and evening, live or via acetate transcription disk). This extraordinary reach was owed to one of the oddest characters this odd nation has produced: Dr. John R. Brinkley. Here's how "Doctor" found his way to the dusty town of Del Rio, Texas, where he invented "Border Radio."

D octor John Romulus Brinkley was an American success story suited to his times. When the Carters met him, Brinkley was not only fabulously rich, but as famous as a movie star. He had overcome humble beginnings—a lack of breeding, of inheritance, of formal medical education—to become one of the nation's most successful businessmen and best-known surgeons. "For a poor boy, up from bare feet in Jackson County, North Carolina," Brinkley liked to say, "this, dog me, is something." Even at the pinnacle of his career, while insisting on being called "Doctor," Brinkley never forgot where he came from. And he didn't want anybody else to forget, either. Brinkley was a champion of the common people, he said, and it was only in *their* service that he flourished, a Man of the People in the same generously accommodating mold of that other Great Commoner of the day, Louisiana's Governor Huey Long. Long was once taken to task by the Louisiana legislature over his extravagant spending at New York City's finest restaurants, nightclubs, and brothels. At a hearing, he calmly explained to Louisiana legislators that he wasn't spending the taxpayers money for *himself*. He'd visited New York once before, he told them, as a poor country hick, and was happy enough staying at the YMCA and eating in cheap diners. But on this trip, said the governor, he had been representing the people of the great state of Louisiana. "And the people of Louisiana," he said, "deserved the finest."

Now, Doctor could get right in behind that line of reasoning. Here was a man who, like Brinkley, had to overcome great obstacles, and face down countless small-minded persecutors. And when Long was shot dead in 1936 in the marbled lobby of the grand Louisiana statehouse he built, Doctor must have been ever more confirmed in the wisdom of having commissioned a bulletproof vest, and in his decision to keep Pinkerton guards on the payroll at upwards of $2,000 a month—for protection and for other, more creative services. No, men whose rise engendered so much jealous rage among the ruling class—a class of people Brinkley likened to the Philistines of Jesus's day—could not be too careful.

The rise of John Romulus Brinkley from dirt-poor farm boy to the lofty heights of professional attainment was almost too fantastic to be believed and would likely have been impossible, were it not that Doctor's path to fame and fortune was mercifully free from the bothersome snags of human conscience. In 1918, Brinkley was a country doctor living in Milford, Kansas, and it was beginning to look like the investment of $150 and putting in six weeks of grueling study under the watchful but untrained eyes of the faculty of Kansas City's Eclectic School of Medicine had not been such a great investment after all. Even with the medical degree from that storied institution, a passable understanding of human anatomy, and an impressive facility for tossing Latin terms into casual conversation, the thirty-two-year-old Dr. Brinkley was foundering. *Until,* as he always told the story, a local farmer came to see him about having lost "the pep" in his marriage. Together, the two men cooked up the idea of grafting goat glands onto the farmer's own testicles. A year later, the farmer's wife delivered a healthy baby boy, whom the couple christened "Billy."

At first the medical success was a local phenomenon, with nearby farmers quietly looking for the "kick" the Brinkley operation promised. But Doctor had big eyes, even then. He trotted out young "Billy" in a publicity campaign, and caught the eye of *Los Angeles Times* publisher Harry Chandler, himself in need of a little tune-up. In 1923, Chandler invited Brinkley to California and was so thrilled with his post-op revitalization that he began suggesting the surgery to his prominent friends. When Doctor left California (with the state's medical board fast on his heels) he took with him $40,000 in fees and an idea that would prove even more profitable. While Brinkley was in California, Chandler had showed him around his new radio station, and the Kansan decided that this radio business was another ripe idea.

Doctor erected a sturdy brick studio on the grounds of his hospital, and next to that studio a 100-foot-high steel antenna. In September 1923, after receiving a broadcast license from the Federal Radio Commission, Dr. Brinkley's KFKB (Kansas First, Kansas Best) went on the air. With a ready mike just a few short steps from his office, Doctor could tout his newly christened Kansas General Research Hospital, with its splendid operating theater, its $7,000, electrically-operated, high-pressure steam sterilizing machine, and its highly advanced Victor X-ray equipment, whose cleverly designed "Bucky Diaphragm" eliminated shadows from the photographs. But much of the programming consisted of Doctor's frank talks about the ravaging physical and psychological consequences of male impotence: "Observe the rooster and the capon. The rooster will fight and work for his flock. He stands guard over them, protects them, but the capon eats the food the hens scratch up. He will even sit on their eggs."

The radio-doctor business was a cinch, and Brinkley was soon fetching patients from all over Kansas—Lenexa, Cherryvale, Wakeeny, Parsons. Grant Eden, of Osawatamie, took a week off from his caretaker duties at the John Brown State Park to get fixed up. Pretty soon it wasn't just Kansans. Men were coming from as far away as Cherokee, Oklahoma; Columbus, Nebraska; Corsicana, Texas; Denver, Colorado.

They'd arrive on the Union Pacific spur line from Junction City, met by the Brinkley hospital bus—"the machine"—which sped them to the front door of the hospital. There they were met by the reassuring voice of Doctor's wife, Minnie: "Here come my men." Besides acting as official greeter, Minnie was also a handy assistant in the operating room, where she worked as anaesthetist, side by side with recent Eclectic graduates Brinkley had hired to help him keep up with the stream of patients radio produced.

Behind the hospital was a pen full of four-to-six-week-old goats; Doctor received a weekly shipment of Toggenburgs from a goat and bee man down in Gilbert, Arkansas. Doctor preferred Toggenburg glands because his early experiments with those of the Angora had left a couple of men with an odor that gave pause to even the most ardent and intrepid lady friends. If a Brinkley patient so desired, he could go out back and pick his match from the herd. Occasionally a patient alighted from the train in Junction City cradling his own goat in his arms. No matter, the cost was the same: $750 per operation. Payable in advance. Doctor did not suffer deadbeats. He was a Man of the People, after all, and he wasn't going to let his other patients incur the costs of those who skipped out on a bill.

As performed by Brinkley and his staff, the operation was breathtakingly simple. It could be done under local anaesthesia, in just fifteen minutes. "I took and cut a hole in the man's testicle," Doctor once explained, "and took a chunk out and filled the hole up in the testicle with the goat gland." Despite specific promises in the hospital's literature, Doctor and his doctors didn't waste time connecting arteries and nerves. But how hearts must have leapt when patients were wheeled into the operating forum and saw the agents of their rejuvenation, the tiny dried pellets resting on beds of soft cotton on a gleaming stainless-steel tray. For seventy-seven-year-old Nebraskan A. B. Pierce, the surgery was something of a mystery, but he claimed results nonetheless. "I suppose a goat gland is a good deal like a potato," Pierce once said. "You can cut a potato all in pieces and plant it and every eye will grow. I suppose it's the same with goat glands. Just so you get a little piece in you, it will give you a kick all right."

Doctor was constantly wowed by the results; he was sure he was making real scientific breakthroughs in that knotty thicket of medicine, urology, and most especially in the treatment of the male prostate, that "troublesome *cuckle*-burr . . . that robber gland," he called it. "I began to take out half to an inch of the vas deferens," he wrote. "It seems to me the more of the vas I removed, the better results I obtained so later I resected the vas to the globus minor to the epididymis and ligated there with linen. Also injected the vas with 5 to 10 cc of a 2-percent mercurochrome solution, lavaging the vesicle." After the "compound operation" proper hormone balance was restored, Brinkley said, and the patient was the immediate recipient of any number of unexpected side benefits. Reports of unforeseen benefits always increased at prize time, as when Doctor offered a free Oldsmobile for the post-op patient who wrote the most stirring essay that completed this thought: "I consider Dr. Brinkley the world's foremost prostate specialist because . . ." Brinkley patients claimed the fifteen-minute surgery had cured them of back pain, chest pain, hydrocele, diabetes, Bright's disease and varicose veins. Doctor also claimed he had successfully treated dementia praecox. "My second case of insanity was a young bank clerk brought to me from a State Institution," he wrote in one paper. "Following gland transplantation, his mind cleared completely and he is now head of a large banking institution."

With KFKB (the "Sunshine Station in the Heart of the Nation") running full steam fifteen and a half hours a day, news of these myriad successes didn't have to be hidden away from the people, limited to the stuffy journals of medicine. With a microphone right at the hospital, Doctor could sandwich his talks in between Bob Larkan and His Music Makers, agricultural commodities price reports, French language instruction, "Shut In Program for Invalids," and Roy Faulkner, "the Lonesome Cowboy." He'd spend an entire half-hour reading letters from his reinvigorated patients. Not only could Brinkley trumpet the great—and always greater—benefits of his gland operation, he could also give fair warning to the consequences of delaying treatment: "Many untimely graves have been filled with people who put off until tomorrow what they should have done today."

Doctor plied the airwaves with the honey-voiced concern of a healer, and the canny nerve of an entrepreneur. In 1928, he instituted the fabulously popular half-hour segment, "Medical Question Box." Listeners would write Doctor, detailing their various and vague ailments, and Doctor would answer with stunningly specific instructions, to wit: "Here's one from Tillie . . . My advice to you is to use Women's Tonic Number 50, 67, and 61. This combination will do for you what you desire if any combination will, after three month's persistent use." And it wasn't only Tillie, but other women listening in who, by gosh, were suffering the same symptoms. They'd need the same tonics, which could be purchased at the nearest druggist carrying Brinkley medicine, shipped directly from Milford. For pharmacy owners within reach of the Sunshine Station, a quandary ensued: Doctor's pricey medicines were little more than castor oil or diluted syrup of pepsin, bottled, corked, colored, and numbered. But Brinkley traffic meant as much as a hundred dollars a day in new drug business, and few businessmen were willing to forego the markup on that much product.

So by 1930, Brinkley was more successful than ever, his hospital bigger, his Milford Goats baseball team more stylishly uniformed, his bank accounts bulging. He'd bought his first airplane, his first limousine, his first yacht. He'd even managed to trump his Eclectic degree with a writ of diploma from Italy's Royal University of Pavia, which sheepskin he received after a lavish banquet in honor of the faculty. Doctor paid for the entire affair—the Consommé Frappé àl'Impératrice, the Vol-au-Vent à la Toulousaine, Fléan de Légumes à la Financière, the Glace à la Napolitaine, the bottles of silky Italian Bardolinos and Barolos, the Piper-Heidsieck champagne. He also paid a handsome fee to a local chamber orchestra, which augmented these gustatory delights with the soft strains of Mendelssohn, Puccini, and Irving Berlin. And all this was as pennies compared to the generous donation Doctor visited upon Royal University's College of Medicine.

But 1930 is also when Brinkley started to draw real fire, on multiple fronts. The Federal Radio Commission began an investigation into just exactly how KFKB served the "public interest," angling hard to rescind the station's broadcast privileges. The *Kansas City Star* ran an investigative series on Doctor Brinkley's background, education, moral fitness, and surgical methods. The *Star* reporter found him wanting on all counts. The American Medical Association's *Journal of American*

Medicine began a campaign against Doctor's "blatant quackery" and in April 1930, the Kansas Medical Society made an impassioned plea to the State Board of Medical Registration and Examination to revoke Brinkley's license to practice.

At the board's hearing that July, Dr. Brinkley produced a parade of satisfied customers so long that the presiding judge called a halt to oral testimony, finally agreeing to receive into the record written statements from five hundred other healthy affiants. Unfortunately, by then, Brinkley's character and reputation had been badly wounded. Leading urologists in the field testified that the operation Brinkley performed was, at best, worthless. "Where Brinkley said he borrowed a nerve and hitched into the new gland to give it kick, [Kansas University School of Medicine professor] Dr. [T. G.] Orr said that was absolutely impossible because the nerve he described was not there at all," reported the *Star* "and even if it was it could not be diverted to that use." Brinkley's defense was not much helped by his own expert witness, a former Eclectic instructor who had no formal medical training, signed his own diploma, and touted a cancer remedy that turned out to be a concoction of alcohol, sugar, glycerine, licorice, burdock root, senna, and water. A slew of anti-Brinkley witnesses told grisly tales of being sent home with nasty, open scrotal or abdominal incisions, which led to painful, oozing local infections, and sometimes to blood poisoning. One decidedly unsatisfied customer testified that a Brinkley doctor instructed him to affix a rubber bootheel to the festering incision to act as a drain. This was all damaging enough, but the evidentiary capper was a stack of death certificates numbering forty-two. Each of the departed men had expired as a direct result of their short stay at the Brinkley Hospital, though Doctor pointed out in his own defense that it wasn't the surgery that killed these men, but infection. In September of that year, the medical board revoked Brinkley's license to practice in the state of Kansas, finding Doctor guilty of "gross immorality and unprofessional conduct."

A man of less sturdy constitution might have folded up his tents and left the state altogether. Brinkley decided to run for governor. Just seven weeks before the 1930 election, he threw his hat in the ring. Candidate J. R. Brinkley took to the air-waves daily, promising free textbooks, free medical clinics, a lake in every county, a tax cut, and, for the poor Kansas dirt farmers, increased rainfall. Flying his private airplane from campaign stop to campaign stop, Doctor offered political succor to the forgotten rural masses. Through the beginning of October, political pros in both major parties ignored Brinkley's "sideshow." As the political neophyte had entered after the ballots were already printed, he'd be a write-in can-didate, they pointed out. Maybe he'd poll 30,000, not bad for a man without an organization.

But Brinkley didn't need organization; he had radio. He was on it six or seven hours a day, playing to the sympathy of all those forgotten people who didn't think much of big-city newspapers like the *Kansas City Star* and "that Topeka crowd." Among them, Brinkley's best-loved campaign slogan was, "Let's pasture the goats on the statehouse lawn." As November neared, party pros began to take notice of the pro-fusion of Brinkley bumper stickers, of the thousands of pen-cils inscribed "J.R. Brinkley," of the question most heard on Main Street: "Votin' for Brinkley?" The election pros revised up their predictions for the Brinkley vote to 75,000, but said it was still no threat.

Just days before the election, Brinkley's plane appeared in

the sky over a Wichita wheat field, circling the biggest crowd ever assembled for a Kansas political rally. Once on the ground, Brinkley informed the gathering he wasn't there for politicking at all. It was Sunday, and he told the Easter story instead, reminding them of this: "The men in power wanted to do away with Jesus before the common people woke up," Brinkley said. "Are you awake?" On Election Day, Democratic candidate Harry Woodring polled 217,171 votes to squeak by Republican Frank Haucke by 257 votes. Best estimates are that Brinkley got about 230,000 votes, but with so many write-ins disqualified for improper spellings, his officially recorded total was 183,278. Brinkley had also carried three counties in Oklahoma, proving what Doctor knew better than anybody: radio knows no borders.

Just three months later, KFKB signed off the air for good, stripped of its license by the Federal Radio Commission, citing the station's lack of "public interest." But that's where the radio commissioners had it all wrong, Brinkley knew. The public was nothing if not interested. *Radio Digest's* audience poll of 1930 overwhelmingly voted KFKB the most popular station in the country. Brinkley's station out-polled the *Kansas City Star's* own WDAF 357,000 to 10,000. Alas, popularity could not save Brinkley's license. And when he shut down KFKB, Doctor climbed immediately onto the cross. "Persecution!" he liked to say. "Even as Jesus of Nazareth."

Doctor never wanted for zeal of mission, and he wasn't about to quit his service to the common man. Playing on the Mexican government's anger at the United States government's refusal to share any of its 550–1500 kilocycle radio broadcast band, Brinkley won the right to set up a new station in Mexico. As folklorist Ed Kahn succinctly put it in *American Music*:

"Here was someone who would invest in the necessary broadcasting equipment and at the same time really irritate the U.S. government." Basically, Mexican officials gave Brinkley license to do anything he wanted, and there was Del Rio, a moribund little Texas border town of wool and mohair producers, then lamenting the Depression-era price drops in the greasy shorn domestic wools on the Boston market, and in dire need of a little bump in the local economy. "My dear Doctor Brinkley," wrote Del Rio chamber of commerce secretary, A. B. Easterling, "We certainly hope that you will at least pay us a visit . . . The mayor of Villa Acuna [across the Rio Grande from Del Rio] has already assured the Mexican consul that their city will furnish, free, adequate land for the purpose of erecting your station thereon. However, they will welcome a visit from you and will be pleased to go over any proposition you might have to offer. Del Rio has a splendid flying field, located about one mile northwest of the city. The six-story Roswell Hotel has the name Del Rio painted on its roof and an arrow pointing to the field."

When Doctor arrived in town to stay, the *Del Rio Evening News* gushed: "When a man comes along who can hold his dream of helping mankind in front of him consistently and constantly until he makes it come true, he is a man who stands out and dominates his generation. Such a man is John R. Brinkley, M.D."

ATLANTIC RECORDS: THE INTRODUCTION

Darius James
(dedicated to the memory of Terry Southern)

"What *did* I say?"

With the exception of a few children's sing-a-longs pressed on candy-colored vinyl, the first musical recording I ever owned was a single released on Atlantic's Atco label in the summer of 1959. It was "Poison Ivy" by The Coasters. I'd just turned five years old.

I came by this particular recording thanks to the enthusiasm of my babysitter, Dorthea. Dorthea was an attractive brown-skinned teen with a helmet of stylish, hot-combed hair, whose standard dress consisted of pastel-colored sneakers, sleeveless blouses, and bright shorts emphasizing her shapely and protuberant behind. Not only did she introduce me to the then-current sounds of doo-wop and r&b, via her portable turntable and ever-present stack of forty-fives, Dorthea also hooked me on the no-Negroes dance show *American Bandstand,* hosted by that Dorian Gray of teen pop, Dick Clark.

Skipping in graceful crisscrossed patterns on the balls of her sneakered feet, and jerking her bosomy upper torso while snapping a fat wad of gum, Dorthea made a daily routine of teaching me the latest steps to the day's televised hits. Though her own steps combined the precision of a drill-team majorette with the playfulness of a game of sidewalk hop-scotch, Dorthea's instructions proved fruitless.

Early on, contrary to the rampant mythology concerning my kind, I demonstrated a pronounced inability to coordinate my feet with my other bodily limbs in the rhythmic and orchestrated fashion one might consider 'dance'. Bill Robinson I was not.

This went on day after day until, one afternoon, in the midst of spinning in lead-footed circles around and around on the living room floor, my imagination was seized by a sound that was outright avant-garde to my five-year-old ears. Over-come by the song's lyrics, vocal arrangements, and insistent beat, I instantly dropped to the floor, and flailed about as if I were a monkey infested with fleas—adding to Dorothea's con-siderable irritation by screeching like a chimpanzee.

On that particular afternoon, I displayed a marked genius for acting the fool. And therein lay the song's appeal to my nascent comic sensibility. As if I'd been duped into a false sense of need by the quick-cut edits of a television toy com-mercial, from that moment on, I begged and whined in that incessant way children have until my parents broke down in aggravation and forked over their hard-earned cash to some record-store cashier.

Once in my possession, much to my parents' constant annoy-ance, I played my prized forty-five over and over and over again, repeating my simian antics while warbling in a cracked, atonal voice—"Poison ivaa-eeey! Poison ivaaa-eeeey . . ."

Little did I know I was singing about the *clap*.

My parents' love for jazz was so complete that, by the time I was six years old, I had seen every major jazz musician of the bebop era in live concert. (I've always suspected that my father secretly wished I'd become a jazz musician. It's evident in how I was named: Darius [Milhaud] Hayden [Haydn] James. Why he wished that pauper's tragedy on me I have no idea.) At eight years old, I could boast I once hung out with jazz pianist Romano Mussolini, son of the Italian dictator, after a jazz festival in Genoa, Italy. I'd even met, that same summer, the legendary cigar-puffing Bricktop, formerly a chanteuse with Noble Sisle's band, at her bistro in Rome. And, lastly, sadly, my mother's final deathbed wish, was that a recording of the Modern Jazz Quartet's "No Sun in Venice" be played at her funeral.

Though I didn't choose the musical road (Dwight once tried to teach me piano and quickly discerned I had no talent), my upbringing predetermined my fondness for jazz. And jazz meant Atlantic Records. Jazz meant Blue Note, Verve, and Impulse, too; but mainly it meant Atlantic.

Atlantic Records had insinuated itself into my life (and certainly the lives of many others) in ways I was completely unaware of. For example, by breaking the Stax sound (and therefore, soul music) to a national and world audience, and providing a music that defined the times—its "soundtrack" if you will—Atlantic is as responsible for stoking the fires of black enpowerment in the sixties as were Malcolm, Martin, Stokely, and H. Rap Brown. It was Booker T & the M.G.s, Stax session players who pioneered the transition from r&b to soul music, that provided the soundtrack to Jules Dassin's *Uptight,* the first Hollywood-produced black nationalist feature. This, I think, is a extraordinary testament to Atlantic's power and influence.

Crucial rites of passage in my life were often marked by an

Atlantic recording. With the onset of puberty came the discovery of the hypnotic, trance-like wonders of smoking pot, and I quickly developed an affection for the proto-metal band Iron Butterfly. The first time I dropped acid (four-way brown-dot blotter), Led Zeppelin was my copilot. To this day, I can't listen to "Dazed and Confused" without experiencing a cottony, metallic taste in my mouth. Even my first taste of true sexual pleasure was accompanied by wine, pot, and Coltrane.

My two most memorable Atlantic moments, though, happened while I was still a student in high school. The first was in the men's room of a college outside Boston. I was standing at a urinal, draining a cheap California jug wine from my bladder, when I looked over. And, standing beside me, all done up in feathers and face paint, was the great New Orleans music man and hoodoo hougan, Dr. John.

Needless to say, I was startled by his befeathered presence (though not quite as startled as I would be, two years later, when I shared the men's room in Ben Frank's with L.A.'s glam-queens, The Cycle Sluts). Zipping the fly of my ragged jeans, mustering all the cool I knew, I told Dr. John I had bought his album *Gris-Gris* because I thought I was buying an album by Archie Shepp.

"*Archie Shepp?!!*" he exclaimed, grinning, his eyes lit brighter than a Chrismas tree. "I'm gonna tell Archie that when I see 'im next."

Still grinning, Dr. John reached into the side pocket of his pants, and withdrew a small bottle filled with a thick red liquid. Stamped on the label in fading blue ink was the image of a praying madonna. I eyed it with suspicion.

"Jus' a little oil," he said. He pronounced it 'awl'.

"What kind of 'awl'?"

"You rub it on. It makes you smell good."

I accepted the bottle, not realizing it was my entry into America's invisible but omnipresent culture of voodoo. The details of that story are not appropriate for these pages.

My second great Atlantic-related moment occurred during New Haven's first Duke Ellington Jazz Festival in 1974. The three-day festival, presented on the stage of Yale University's Woolsey Hall, featured the great names in jazz: Duke Ellington and his Orchestra; Slam Stewart; Philly Jo Jones; Max Roach; Tony Williams, and many more than my drug-addled memory can recall. Each evening, resplendent in his signature white tux, Duke Elllington stood before the audience and, with studied elegance, opened with a brief intro-duction detailing the musical legacy of the performers on that night's bill. Upon his introduction's conclusion, he would immediately lead his orchestra through a rendition of "Take the "A" Train." Same thing. Every night. "Take the "A" Train." I take 7th Avenue line.

After each night's set of concerts, the dean of one of the numerous colleges on the Yale campus would throw a party for the musicians to unwind. I attended one such party. And found Charles Mingus lying on the floor in a drunken heap.

It's Charlie Mingus!! I thought. *He wrote the theme song with that cool DUM-DUM-DUM bassline for Spiderman's cartoon show on TV!!!*

Surrounding Mingus was a crowd of stuffy white academics and pretentious Negroes, all of whom ignored his sprawling, whale-like presence. I didn't realize the man was drunk. I thought he was *dead,* having made that kind of discovery once before. So I leaned down, crouching low to the floor and checked his breathing. Mingus opened his eyes and said: "Where c'n I git me a chopped barbeque *po'k* sam'ich?".

Those were the only intelligible words he said to me that night.

After guiding Mingus and his son, Charles III (a painter, playwright and all-round amazing mind), to a joint I knew far and away from Yale's ivy fortress, Mingus spent the remainder of the evening eating grease-soaked sandwiches and mumbling to himself in the backseat of a compact car, no doubt complaining about stuffy white academics and pretentious Negroes.

Now that I've exposed myself for the gushing fanboy I really am, I won't waste anymore time with my music-world misadventures, and get on with the real reason I'm here. And that's to introduce you, gentle reader, to the immortal groove that is Atlantic Records: *Home of the Shit!*

"I don't know why they called it race music. What could they say? Colored music? I didn't come to America until 1935. And the appellation for people of color has changed during my life in America. What was acceptable one year was not acceptable three years later. People were called colored or people were called Negro. Then there was whether you spelled Negro with a capital N or a small n. At the time, people didn't like being called black. There were different appellations: sepia, tan, brown. Nowadays, people call it 'black music'. You're the head of the 'Black Music' Department, right?"—Ahmet Ertegun

There is much more to the story of "race music" in America, and Atlantic Records' role in that story, than I can fit into this introduction. There's the nightclub scene in thirties Harlem, as described in "Repeal of the Blues," when "black or tan or 'yella'" patrons were not allowed entrance into "elegant"

mob-controlled establishments known for their black and tan and 'yella' performers. Then, "race mixing" occurred in "low down joints where dancers . . . wore no panties under their skirts . . . because at curtain time, instead of a bow, they had to snatch money from the ringsiders by first exposing themselves with a wide stance, and then, as a crisp bill was held against their crotch, clapping their thighs together and slowly slinking off with the money held between their lips." (This practice explains why a woman's vagina is sometimes referred to as a "snatch".) This story suggests the history of race music in America is as much about sex as it is about race relations. After all, black music evolved freely in Old New Orleans, flourishing most in the Crescent City's brothels. Jazz derives its name from the "jasper" women who worked there. Remember, too, that New Orleans-style jazz spread throughout the rest of the country as a result of closing down that city's redlight district, Storyville, at the beginning of WWI. There is also the story of how WWII influenced the end of the big-band era, which led to the formation of small, 'Jump Blues' dance combos, producing music Jerry Wexler would name "rhythm & blues."

Nor is there room in my alotted space to examine the role of the shellac shortage during WWII in the formation of independent record labels, the major labels neglect of the "race market" as a result of this shortage, and a related question posed by bewildered filmmaker Arthur Jafar at the 1997 Vibe Music Seminar:

Who decided records should be *black?* Records could've been any color—red, blue, yellow—but someone decided the industry standard was going to be *black!* It was as if they decided to steal the souls of black folks and enjoy the genius of black creativity without the actual physical presence of black people!

I am going to steal space, however, to contradict a cheese-brained film producer for Cleveland's Rock 'n' Roll Hall of Fame I once met with to discuss scripting a series of short films for the museum: rock 'n' roll's evolution does not leap frog from blues man Robert Johnson and his crossroads deal with the sulphorous stinky one to Bill Haley and his silly ass "Rock Around The Clock." If the reverse were true, it would imply that *a black man damned his soul so the white man could invent rock 'n' roll!!*

I ain't goin' for the "lone gunman theory." And I ain't goin' for *that!*

On the other hand, this same producer didn't buy my theory that the roots of rock 'n' roll ran deep in the soil of Southern black gay culture. (What? You thought the queer presence in rock started with Jagger's androgynous pose? Or with London's glitter scene in the seventies? No. There's a tradition of black gay cabaret going back at least to the thirties. In fact, Atlantic has a stake in that history, too. "One Mint Julep" by The Clovers was the song Esquerita taught Little Richard to play on piano.) That, too, is a part of the story.

As I said earlier, the history of race music is as much about the history of sex in America as it is about race. And the discussion always gets confused by questions of proprietorship. Who owns what? And whose story is it?

This brings us to the question, What does a "history" of Atlantic Records mean? The "his" of "his story," in this instance, is Ahmet Ertegun. This implys proprietorship. *What'd I Say?: Atlantic Records Fifty Years On* not only includes stories about the company he founded but the stories of the artists recorded by his company. The artists often tell their own stories here. So whose history is it, really? Whose story?

Furthermore, Atlantic is now owned by Time Warner. The story is now a Time Warner story—a Time Warner history.

In the end, who cares?

Like Dr. John said, "Once you play the music, it's in the air, and belongs to everybody."

Hmmmmm. . . .

According to Jill Jonnes's *Hep-Cats, Narcs, and Pipe Dreams,* Milton Mezzrow, a white man, introduced black people in Harlem to pot smoking. Jones claims that before the Wall Street crash of 1929, pot smoking was "virtually unknown in the north outside jazz musician circles" until Mezzrow showed up in Harlem with his high-grade Mexican pot, dealing and straightening out luminaries like Lionel Hampton and Louie Armstrong. It was "Pops" Armstrong who nick-named great pot "the mezz".

However, this wasn't how *my* Pops remembered it. He grew up in Harlem in the thirties and forties and knew a little something about puffin' som' gauge. He once said the funnel-shaped joint Mezzrow distributed was called a "sidewinder." It was doubtful Mezzrow introduced pot to Harlem. "Too many Jamaicans" my Pops said.

Now, I thought to myself, if this old goateed muthafucka knew "the Mezz," he musta been into som' *shit.* So I asked—

"You *knew* 'Mezz' Mezzrow?!!"

Ahmet looked up from the photograph Perry had laid

before him and stared at me in curiosity. He seemed as surprised by my familiarity with Mezzrow as I was with his.

"Mezzrow was a great friend of ours," he said finally. "He
was a character. They used to call grass the 'mezz' for him,
you know.

"He smoked marijuana, purveyed it for other people, and
gave it to a lot of other musicians. I once asked Lionel
Hampton,'Why did you have him on that date?' And Lionel
said, '*Maan!* He brought the *shit!*".

Ahmet explained that although Mezzrow came from a
family of European Jewish immigrants, he was as "down
home" as a white person could get. "Mezzrow," he said,
"wanted to live a totally hip black life."

His last statement sounded like a reversal of the old joke about
the black man who goes to the rabbi and says he wants to be a Jew.
And the Rabbi says, "Don't you have enough problems?"

So I had to ask *why?* I mean, really, *wha's up wit' dat ?!!*

"To us," he said, "everything black was hip and everything
white was square. That's how most jazz musicians felt. Even
in the South, during the days of segregation.

"Lester Young was the epitome of cool," Ahmet explained.
"We didn't call it that in those days, but that's what he was.
He was natural. He wasn't trying to be hip. It became hip
because he was doing it. All the kids wanted to act, walk, and
talk like the hip musicians they idolized. We all used to do a
thing called Rhyming Harlem Jive. People made up little
rhymes in the way they talked. It was a hidden language.
Louis Jordan did a little bit of that. Harry the Hipster, who was
white, did some. It was like the dozens—those long dirty
poems that were part of Negro culture. You know: '*Your sister
is buzzin' an yo' mama do the lordy lord!*'.

"So when Lester Young toured the East Coast with Count Basie's band, suddenly, all over, in every American city, white saxophone players were holding their saxophones sideways like Prez. Every city had three or four guys who played like Lester Young.

"I used to come from Washington to New York to hear jazz. One night, I ran into Les Paul. In a bar where all the musicians hung out, there was this funny little cat named Herman Rosenberg, who was an agent. Herman Rosenberg was like a walking address book and encyclopedia of musicians. He knew everybody who was playing, like third saxophone in what band. And he knew where everybody was and so on. Les Paul wanted to hear Lester Young. So Herman Rosenberg said 'I'll take you there.'

"We went up to a place in Harlem called the Club Lido. Lester Young was playing with a little quartet. Les Paul sat in. It was one of those moments, just wandering around trying to find the important cats."

Another person Ahmet said "who tried to live the black life" was Diahann Carroll's one-time spouse, Monte Kaye.

"I met Monte Kay on Fifty-second Street in the late thirties or early forties. He was up and down Fifty-second Street, uh, dealing. We'd be standing around on the sidewalk with Billy Eckstein, or with some of the guys in the band between sets. The cops would come by and tell you no loitering. So we'd walk up to this bar on Sixth Avenue called the Three Roses. We'd go there and have a drink for fifteen cents. Beer was a nickel. It cost a dollar in the club.

"Now, Monte Kaye was very hip. Very cool. He would never listen to Mezz Mezzrow and the type of black life he was talking about. It was not the kind of black life Monte was interested in. He was interested in the dincty [yes, you read correctly, Ahmet Ertegun used the word *dincty*], elegant and very sophisticated black life. He liked Charlie Parker, Count Basie, Duke Ellington. You see, there are so many different levels of black music and black life."

The white hipsters' immersion into what Ahmet termed "the black life," and their attempt to replicate the psyche and art of the black musician, could be interpreted, by some readers, as more of the "Samo Samo"—a displacement of American culture's authentic black presence (*"It was as if they decided to steal the souls of black folks and enjoy the genius of black creativity without the actual physical presence of black people in their homes!"*)—the same impulse that led to the public's perception of Tommy Dorsey as the King of Swing, Elvis Presley as the King of Rock 'n' Roll and Tarzan as the King of Jungle. But Ahmet didn't make those claims. He said—*"Everything black was hip and everything white was square."*

That's an extraordinary statement for the head of a huge corporation. What would motivate him to say that? The answer, I believe, lies in two early recollections.

"At the age of two," he said, "I left Turkey when my father had taken up residency in Geneva to become ambassador to Switzerland, and later, to act as a judge at the Court of the Hague. Although my circumstances at school were not comparable to the experiences of black Americans, I did receive a glimmer of what life must be like for them. At that time, the Turks were generally regarded as 'the blacks' of Europe."

The second recollections concerns those first concerts he and his brother Neshui staged in Washington, D.C. "They didn't allow mixed audiences in Washington," Ahmet explained. "Black people were not allowed in the downtown or white movie theaters. The only place blacks were allowed in was the Gaiety Burlesque theater, but they could sit only in the balcony. The whites sat downstairs. The traveling burlesque had one black troop with black burlesque comedians like Pigmeat Markham and Dusty Fletcher. So, we had the first jazz concert, or concert of any kind, which had a mixed band on stage and a mixed black and white audience in Washington.

"We had a lot of trouble in Washington finding a place. The first concert was at the Jewish Community Center. That was the only place that would allow mixed audiences and mixed bands on stage. For that first show, we hired Willie Bryant to be the MC. They used to call Willie Bryant the Mayor of Harlem. He was a tall, light-skinned, very good looking man. He was six foot two, at least. Maybe more, six foot four. He had been on stage as a very young teenager. He was in *Mambo's Daughters,* a play on Broadway. It was one of the first important plays with Ethel Waters. But after that, in the early 1930s, he couldn't get another part. So he became a swing band leader and used to do an imitation of Cab Calloway. That was the only thing a black performer could do then because it was the swing era. He had a really good band with some very famous musicians in it. He himself was not a musician and the band did not become very famous, although they made quite a few records.

"After that, the National Press Club let us use their auditorium. Huey Ledbelly sang at the first concert we gave in the National Press Club. When he saw the crowd, he said: 'Man, you gotta give me double the price otherwise I'm not going on!' "

Though Ahmet would not make the following claim for himself—he would instead say that he and his brother presented these shows "for the love of the music"—it's obvious that by staging these events, and exploiting the " 'extra-territorial situation' offered by the Embassy," he and his family were serving a progressive social agenda.

What these stories imply, rather than the "displacement" of the black body and psyche, is that the early white hipster pose was a counterresponse to white supremacy. It was an antiracist position, an index finger up the rectum of a morally corrupt, white-ruled social order. Similarly, Atlantic's early cultivation of black musical artistry was not simply about marketing and money, it was also about the preservation of a culture and the acceptance of a people.

"They segregated everything" Ahmet said, "but they couldn't segregate the radio dial. The white kid could just turn it on, go a couple of steps to the right and hit the black music station. That's how Elvis Presley was born."

In the end, Ahmet was a pretty cool dude. Turned out he loved him som' collards, too. "I love greens!" he enthused. "I love ribs! I eat *all* that shit!"

Ahmet made one claim, though, that I thought was pretty fuckin' *weird*. He said Glen Campbell sounded like a black man when he played blues guitar. So I slipped a CD into the player behind his desk and asked him to identify the singer. He listened for a few moments and grumbled.

"Sounds like a hillbilly singer. *Who is this?!!*"

"Emmett Miller," I answered.

"Who's that?"

"The last of the old-time minstrel singers."

"I can dig it. The guy's a white man. Horrible playing."

I handed Ahmet the sleeve of the CD. He read the names of the musicians listed inside.

"Can you imagine?" he said, surprised. "That's Tommy Dorsey on trombone and Jimmy Dorsey on clarinet. Eddie Lane, great guitar player. They played corny *on purpose*. These are all good players. These were serious jazz players at that time. Tommy Dorsey was a powerful trombone player. Tommy and Jimmy Dorsey both had big bands. But Eddie Lane and Joe Venuti were the guitar players. They were the stars of the Paul Whiteman band. That's very interesting. It sounded to me like the way they sang the old St. Louis blues songs, like a country singer. They were very corny."

Then Ahmet dropped the *bomb*.

"There's a story about Louis Armstrong," he began. "Milt Gabler was recording him in 1942, '43. They were redoing his theme song 'Dear Old Southland.' And there's a line in it that says 'darkies humming soft and low.' They sang it, Gabler stopped the recording and said, 'You can't say darkies any-more.' And Louis Armstrong says, 'Well, if you're not going to call them darkies, what *are* you going to call them?'

That put my black ass in *check*.

JAZZ AND BOXING

Matthew Shipp

A kinetic chess game—signals being translated at the speed of light—what is the essence of jazz and what is the essence of the killer instinct as defined in boxing? A text of the manipulation of signals in a dance of gestures, can both boxing and jazz be seen as a dance? Is there any connection in the dialogue of two improvisers on, say, sax and piano and the dialogue of two men defining themselves through a repertoire of jabs and uppercuts through each other's flesh—the combination of grace, intelligence, and cunning that both disciplines require if one contends to succeed.

Like free jazz can be, boxing is direct, visceral. There exists both jazz and boxing subcultures—historically sports and arts have been strong alternatives to mainstream economics in the black community.

To an untrained ear jazz can sound crazy, to an untrained eye boxing can seem mad—as the ear and eye become trained one learns the complex patterns that underlie the boxing match or the jazz solo—the theater of Kinetic Gesture—a kaleidoscope of intelligent quicksilver action generates a structure of intense beauty. For the body becomes poetry in motion whether through a keyboard or in the ring—complex patterned action generates a poetic time and space—violent, yet dancelike, uncivilized yet graceful, raw yet sophisticated.

Oldtimers always referred to a great improviser as someone who tells a story—a great boxer tells a story not with words or notes but in a refined language of will and transposed aggression. These acts of self-expression—fighting and playing a musical instrument—a neurological dance—the placement of fluid reflexes that reaches into the rhythmic pattern of a deeper intensity of human motivation—is it a madness? The jazz solo speaks about the beauty of the neurological system for it must mirror what it comes out of.

Thus in both dances (jazz and boxing) we come to the essence (improvisation) which is the unfolding of the space-time of each—a system of symbols that generates the language of each—blue notes and blood—the sensations that dance brings and the rhythmic firing of cells in the brain—a ritual out of time explores the parameters of being in time—the essence of the chromatic scale as it transposes being or the animal lust of the boxing crowd as it senses the knockout of time—being, will, cunning, aggression, the sweet science, placement of tones, hangin' on by some psychic edge.

LETTERS FROM ANNE BOURBON-LEVINSKY TO SOPHIE BOURBON

As channeled by Jon Langford

First published in 1996 in the Mekons art catalog/novel in progress
United these letters were supplied by Sophie Bourbon, guru and
benefactor to the legendary punk rockers since funding the band's
Sin Recordings record label with her divorce settlement in 1985. Jon
Langford has been known to read them aloud at the KGB Bar in
Manhattan to quench a fierce thirst to entertain.

Mom, what's happening? Got your message last night. Call me please, please, please. He never told me you called and now you're not picking up. Are you getting your messages? Dad just won't talk about stuff, you know that, and I'm so mad he didn't tell me you called. I hit FF on the machine and caught half a message, I don't even know when from. A wild, mystical, sympathetic feeling was in me; [your] quenchless feud seemed mine. With greedy ears I learned the history of that murderous monster . . . This will drive. . . . [page missing] . . . shouldn't take sides. I don't know if I'm that big. Anyway the Dead were cool (I took some pictures, I think you'll get a kick out of some of them) and school sucks, so

what. I wish I lived in Chicago with you and Bobbie. Please call!!!!
XOXOX A.

August 12, 1984

Dear Mom,

I'm taking today off and vowing not to have any negative thoughts—wonder how long that's going to last! So the divorce came through, hmmm . . . It's OK but you also forgot my birthday. I know you've got a lot on your mind. Please don't send any more money to that band! You don't know anything about them (really) they could just be a bunch of total losers. Did you talk to them? Whatever makes you happy, I suppose.

Anyway My Birthday: We went to a bar and there was a band playing, we had some pasta, Tony got a bit drunk and then we went and got high out in the woods and found this really old creepy tree and he chased me round it with his trousers round his ankles in the mud. I laughed 'til I cried. He's nice. He likes Jethro Tull. Socially we are fairly big losers, if I had more to do, less time to kill, maybe I'd be less of a loser than I really am.

Anyway I didn't barf like last year. Please call, it was so great to talk to you last week. Did you ever see Hendrix? Give Bobbie a big hug from me.

Love, Annie
XOXOX

August 1, 1986

Dear Mom,

Don't call anymore, I can't deal with you and all your bullshit right now. After all we talked about I can't believe you treated me like that. Where should I start? (Or should I even bother?) Yes, I'm old enough to get the bus from downtown, OK you were busy (drunk) so you couldn't meet me. Yes, I mind sleeping on the floor with a bunch of ugly wasted people I don't even know, shouting all night, crashing into each other, playing stupid hillbilly music, doing drugs or whatever! Yes, I wanted to talk to you, ALONE! It was so disgusting, I was scared to use the towels in case I caught something, I was just using he corner of one to dry myself when some big drunk stumbled in in his underpants, and that guy sleeping in your room, where was he from? I couldn't understand a word he said. Your pillows are ruined, all stained with hair color (!) and the weasily one who was taping everything and the stench and those plastic containers full of green God knows what. What's up with that! Couldn't they just pay for a hotel? They are using you! How do you expect me to feel? Yeah that's my mom's house, the one with the hammer and sickle hanging in the window. I never asked you for anything! And you dare to criticize my life, my politics while you throw your life away on some booze drunk. Can you imagine what it feels like to be called a "little motherfucker" by your own mother? I just don't get it. Mom, what are you doing??? What is it with women of your generation, you come on all pious to your daughters about feminism and then you throw yourselves at these dingy men playing loud ugly music. And don't tell me there are women in the band, that won't wash. You and I know what this is all about!!! Don't call. I can only imagine what Dad would say. Does he know you're like this?

A.

October 27, 1989

Mom, So I finally saw them in this horrible little bar in the University. It was just a horrible noise and shouting and they're on A&M? Sting's label? The support band were cute, the drummer was a cop! Mom if you're gonna get involved in music then get into something that is at least current and real for people today in 1989. This English girl heard one of their records and burst out laughing. She called it "Pub Rock" and said no one under thirty would be seen dead with a record like that—they're all into Acid House. I'm not sure what that is but it's gotta be better than that tired old Mekons shit! Needless to say I didn't introduce myself. They didn't spot me thank God!

I miss you, A
XXX

PS Maybe they can give you your money back now they're POP STARS!!! And in answer to you question; private charities and volunteers would look after the mentally ill. Capitalism is beautiful! OK.

August 23, 1995

Nice joke—bury Garcia—fuck you! Nice to see the joke is always on me, hope you had a good laugh at that one. You were always such a cynic, such an empty ship with your cargo scattered across the ocean floor while you continue to float on uselessly, marinading in your own sad poisonous bile. Sorry, but I mean it. There's a hole in your ship and it is JESUS shaped. PLEASE think about it before it's too late. You can't just go on and on like this. Can you? Where next? Iraq? You're like the Ohio honey hunter, who seeking honey in the crotch of a hollow tree found such exceeding store of it, that leaning too far over, it sucked him in, so that he died embalmed. I will pray for you in your life of pointless excess and loveless perverted coupling.

Yours, Anne

WEIRD SCIENCE

Ada Calhoun

The sign read, "Wanted: Healthy Females 18–35 for UT Psychology Sex Study $200." As a healthy, sexually aware, twenty-four-year-old female, I qualified, felt I had plenty to offer the field of sex research, and was way behind on my bills. So I signed up to test-drive Lilly's IC351, aka the new "Female Viagra." The drug, which, like its male analogue, comes in pill form, is supposed to relax blood vessels in the genital region, thereby increasing sexual arousal and easing the path to orgasm. It was a romantic prospect: bravely contributing to the sum of the world's knowledge, easing the sexual dysfunction of other women in the process. Sixty women were to participate in the study, but each of us went through it alone. In the battle against female sexual dysfunction, I was an army of one.

VISIT #1: THE INTAKE

Do you ever have multiple orgasms?" "How many partners have you had in the last three months?" "Have you ever had a venereal disease?" "Do you orgasm during intercourse?" The interviewer was grim, vampiric. "Uh, is there a more private place to do this?" I asked the tester—a grad student with a mass of dark curly hair she kept carefully pushing back, though it was nowhere near in the way. We were at the nurse's station in the gynecological

197

wing of a women's health center surrounded by bored patients and nurses. Grudgingly, she took me into an empty examination room, then continued her battery.

"Rarely," I replied. "Two." "No." Then, in response to her last question, hoping to add levity: "Not with people who suck in bed." I expected a light-hearted slumber party discussion about men's sexual inadequacies. She looked perturbed.

"Do you mean 'no'?" she asked.

"No, I mean yes . . . yes, usually," I said, flustered. She nodded and made a mark on her clipboard. There would, I realized, be no bonding. I am in the control group, I said to myself, meaning I must be controlled. I was led into a room to wait in a paper gown for a gynecological exam.

About a half an hour later, the gynecologist arrived. An aer-obicized, middle-aged woman, she peered at my vagina over her half-glasses, her sensible gray hair hovering between my thighs. When she found out I was part of the study she became extremely personable and told me all her patients ask her how they can have more and better orgasms. She said it was high time someone came through with a drug that would do for women what Viagra does for men. She told me I was brave and she was proud of me and that I had a perfectly shaped cervix. It was the best gynecological exam ever.

VISIT #2: DRUGS AND PORN, PART I

On the sixth day of my cycle, in the early evening, I got off the elevator on the fourth floor of a university building in which I had once had a class in, of all things, the history of Mor-monism. At the end of a dim corridor I found the curly-haired tester waiting in her white lab coat. She led me into a fairly dingy room with only an easy chair covered with doctor's office paper, a large TV, a scale, tables, and a treadmill. The walls were covered with Monet posters. A Monet book sat by the chair. It was like a freshman dorm room writ large.

"That's your probe," she said, pointing to a plastic tube sitting innocuously on a piece of gauze. It looked innocent enough—very much like a clear tampon, only with wires leading out of the bottom instead of a string. The wires went through a hole in the wall next to the chair, and then into another room, where they were connected to a computer. "Just put that in and have a seat. You can cover yourself with the blanket if you like." A pink faux-felt blanket sat next to the chair. Because I'd planned ahead, I was wearing a skirt and thigh-high tights so I didn't have to take off any clothes. Pretending it was an ordinary applicator-less tampon, I inserted the probe until the rubber guard stopped it from going in any further. The tester had been thoughtful enough to leave the probe on a heating pad so it was warm and felt like nothing so much as an incredibly small dildo. It was so small, in fact, that I could barely feel it inside me. But the wires running out of it and into the wall made me wonder if they weren't going to start pumping alien semen into me.

I sat down, put my feet up on another chair and pushed the intercom button. "Okay, it's in," I said. "Good," said the disembodied voice of the tester. "Now it's just going to register for a few minutes and then I'll show you the first film to get your baseline response."

A few minutes was plenty of time for me to get comfortable and imagine how this would go down. The computer would light up and my vaginal responses would spell out "sex kitten." The pharmaceutical company people would gather around looking at my charts saying "It's not possible! She's off the scale! Let's get her back in for more testing so we can bottle her pheromones." Or at least they would call me to ask for dates and to ply me with the really good sex drugs they'd been saving for just such a femme fatale.

The TV flickered. I put on the headphones, hit the tap-light and watched a five-minute nature film about the maternal instincts of cats. When it ended, the voice came back and instructed me to fill out the questionnaire by my chair.

The questions followed the format "On a scale of one to seven, how do you feel?" I scanned a page of adjectives: sexually aroused, anxious, feminine, loving, guilty, angry. If it weren't for this questionnaire I would never have realized that on any given day I was a solid three or four on pretty much every front. Am I feeling masculine? I asked myself. Well, sure, a little. I've been really bossy lately. Is that what they mean? Maybe like a two or three. Am I feeling depressed? Sure, I had kind of a lousy day. Okay, three. Am I feeling nervous? Fuck, yes. I am in a lab with a probe in my vagina. But still, I am maintaining a detachment befitting a control group member, so four. And so on. I tried very hard to be honest, but how aroused was I? Well, after reading the word "aroused," I started to get a little turned on and went to put down five, but then I noticed I had a run in my stocking and my state of excitement plummeted to three. I averaged it out to four.

When I was done, I intercomed the tester and she came in to give me the study medication. It was a little off-white pill shaped like a piece of candy corn. It arrived in a paper cup along with a paper cup of water. Then she went back to her room to talk on her cell phone while I sat waiting for the drug to kick in. I kept second-guessing my questionnaire answers even though it was too late to do anything about them. Like my sexual arousal in general, my responses had felt completely random. What makes me aroused anyway? Sometimes some guy's eyebrows set me off. I began to wonder how the other women in the study group were faring. Were they all machines of consistency, only feeling one or two emotions at a time and getting turned on as soon as they saw a penis? Is that how things are supposed to work? After ninety minutes of wondering how I stacked up, staring at the Monet posters and reading makeup tips in the *Self* magazines that sat in the magazine rack, I heard the voice on the intercom say the next round (the real round) of films were about to begin. I tapped the light off, saw five more minutes about the nobility of the house cat, and then . . .

Until that moment, I never knew what people meant by the term "Lifetime Porn." In the first of three short films, a boring but "sensual" couple engage in soft-focus foreplay in the sunlight next to a gazebo. I started to think of that crappy seventies song "Afternoon Delight" so by the time the woman had the man's dick in her mouth I was completely turned off. Cut to a slightly overweight businesswoman wearing glasses and her hair in a bun. She and a man in a suit go at it on a desk while phones ring in the background. That was a little more interesting because I could extrapolate a story about their office relationship, which involved lots of power plays and suggestive but mean remarks written on Post-It notes. In the third film, a young couple screws on a rooftop while muttering dirty things to each other in French. I was so proud I understood what they were saying I wanted to intercom the tester and tell her, but I held my tongue.

The porn itself did nothing for me. But the surreal dirtiness of the situation—sitting on campus in the dark under a pink blanket with my vagina hooked up to a computer—did have some effect, although I couldn't figure out exactly what it was, and even if I could figure out what it was I couldn't figure out how much I was feeling it on a scale of one to seven. When it was over, the intercom told me to fill out the same questionnaire again. "Kafkaesque" was unfortunately not on the list.

VISIT #3: DRUGS AND PORN, PART II

On each visit, as soon as I stepped through the door, I was asked to pee in a cup, presumably because pregnancy would have thrown off the results of the experiment. After this third test/third sigh of relief, the tester said she had to have me initial a crossed-out answer on the previous questionnaire. While I had been trying to figure out how much my breasts were throbbing, they stopped, so for "breast sensations" I had crossed out three and circled two. I thought she would commend my attention to detail, but instead she said she could be charged with fraud if any answers were changed without initialing.

Something had been weighing on my mind. "I guess I should have asked you this before," I said, "but am I supposed to think sexy thoughts or anything? Should I try to be aroused?"

The tester looked shocked. "No!" she said. "It's totally passive on your part." I felt dirty for asking, though not as dirty as I guess I would have felt had I started masturbating during the film and been yelled at through the intercom.

Past that, everything was the same as visit two, except that when the drug was supposed to be kicking in, my cheeks flushed and I started feeling more conscious of the probe in me, though I couldn't figure out if it had just moved out of place a little, like when you insert a tampon wrong. I also felt kind of speedy and couldn't stop making weird faces at the TV. The cat films began to take on a sexual significance. I wondered if they had included these particular nature films because of lines like "the soothing sensation of the tongue against fur."

The porn did less for me than the cat film, but it was even more hilarious this time. The first one was of a couple in front of a campfire, with the girl's ass torn out of her jeans, much to her rugged boyfriend's delight. The second was of a couple on the edge of a bed in an L.A. glam apartment with oceans of fog on the floor. In the third, a forlorn-looking sheik and a well-eyelined temptress did it in black-and-white, a ceiling fan above them, a dourly erotic French song playing in the background. They seemed fascinated with each other's toes.

When I opened my bag to schedule the last appointment, I hoped the tester wouldn't notice that I'd swiped the samples of Surgilube she'd left out to help insert the probe. (FYI, it smells too much like a hospital to be useful in a romantic context, unless you're playing doctor and patient.) I asked her why they use porn when it doesn't seem to work so well at getting women aroused. I was told there's no alternative and that even women who register disgust on the subjective questionnaire tend to show a vaginal response on the read-out.

But when I saw my charts I was disappointed by how insignificant all the clusters of lines seemed. There weren't huge peaks, as I was told some of the other women had produced. It seemed like my arousal had in fact dropped when the porn was being shown, and been highest at the beginning, when I was sitting around looking at the Monet picture and the wires and thinking about whether wearing lots of eyeliner on that particular day had bumped my femininity quotient from a four to a six.

"What are those?" I asked, intrigued by the sharp lines that jutted almost to the edge of the page. "That," she said scoldingly, "is where you moved."

VISIT #4: THE OUTTAKE

The nurse checked my vitals, drew some blood, and we bantered about the austerity of the sex study room. "They should at least have a candle in here," she said. After I'd had the blood taken and the nurse and I had discussed design possibilities for the room, the tester came back in to ask me if I'd had any side effects. All I'd really noticed was that I felt a little flushed the second time.

She seemed satisfied, but I wasn't. There are worse ways to spend two evenings of one's life than in a university building being paid to watch lousy porn, one's vagina nestled snugly in the hands of science, but still, I felt a little cheated. Emotionally, it was like a "too much, too soon" romance. After all, who else but an overinquisitive lover would ask so many questions about my sexual history and tendencies? Who else would be so interested in how often my vaginal muscles contracted in a given two-hour period? But one minute I'm being deluged with attention and probes and tests, free to fantasize about being discovered as the most sexual being on earth and recruited into some sexual intelligence agency, or at least being impregnated by aliens; the next I'm standing on the steps with a check in my hand and a stash of smelly Surgilube in my bag.

204

And from a more detached, clinical perspective, what exactly do they think they're measuring, anyway? I can't help but think that if I'd wanted to I could have thought sexy thoughts at any point and started having sexual responses irrelevant to the drug, porn, or situation. Let's face it, female sexual arousal isn't as simple as men's (if it goes up, the drug works, if it doesn't, it doesn't). I wasn't turned on, at least not in the way it appeared I was supposed to be. Being stoically passive in the face of such invasive psychological and physical probing was hard. Being emotionally passive and aroused at the same time proved pretty much impossible. Drug or no drug, it was only when I started eroticizing the clinical setting that I felt anything like arousal. More power to the drug companies for trying to find something that will help sexually dysfunctional women, but what it is they're learning from this process, surreally replete as it is with supple Monet haystacks, informative videos on feline science, and European pornography, doesn't seem like anything that's going to coax the female orgasm out of its scientific hinterland, far from the medicine cabinets of America.

FROM THE DREAM LIFE: MOVIES, MEDIA, AND THE MYTHOLOGY OF THE SIXTIES

J. Hoberman

urther evidence of image war and positive polariza-
tion: On the evening of January 14, 1970, in New
York, Leonard and Felicia Bernstein held a cocktail
party at their Park Avenue home to support the twenty-one
Black Panthers charged with a conspiracy to implement the
Battle of Algiers scenario by bombing five midtown Manhattan department stores. The Bernstein bash, whose guests
included wealthy socialites and show business personalities—
Otto Preminger, Sidney Lumet, and Mrs. Arthur Penn
among them—inspired Tom Wolfe's essay on "radical chic"
and was cited as symptomatic of liberal lunacy in a secret
memo Daniel Moynihan was then writing the President on
race relations. Had not the year's first issue of *Time* designated the Panthers the "most authentic villains" in white
America?

"American self-hatred has reached such a point that the
movies are selling it, and projecting it onto the American
past," Pauline Kael complained in her review of Abraham
Polonsky's *Tell Them Willie Boy Is Here*. Whereas the critic
had praised *Bonnie and Clyde* for popularizing contempo-
rary attitudes toward violence and authority, she attacked
Willie Boy as if frightened of the revolution *Bonnie and*

207

Clyde wrought. The audience believed that America was collapsing:

> They're on the side of apocalypse: since they feel it's all going down anyway, it seems to make them feel better to see these movies saying that it should go down, that that's right. And now here's a movie that goes all the way—turning white Americans into a race carrying blood guilt, a race whose civilization must be destroyed.

Willie Boy was only the first. The most overtly ideological of revisionist Westerns addressed the subject of the Indian wars. In their open identification with Native Americans, such movies were the equivalent of marching for peace beneath a Vietcong flag. Hollywood contra Hollywood: Cavalry Westerns *Little Big Man* and *Soldier Blue* were in production when My Lai was exposed and the revelation of American atrocities only reinforced their argument that the slaughter of Native Americans was the essence of the white man's war.

Kael had called *Willie Boy* an incitement to "genosuicide" made for "black kamikazes and masochistic white Americans." What then was *Soldier Blue,* a conflation of the Sand Creek Massacre and Battle of Wounded Knee, which Ralph Nelson was then filming in the Mexican high sierras? Sole survivors of a Cheyenne ambush, a released captive (Candice Bergen) and cavalry private (Peter Strauss) make their way through Indian country to the fort only to arrive as the cavalry ignores a white flag to slaughter a Cheyenne village. Paraplegics and amputees were bused in from Mexico City for this climax. In her memoirs, Bergen recalled the "prosthetics truck" stocked with wooden legs, severed heads, and blood bags. She herself was required to wear "lifelike plastic breasts."

Predicting the "most gut-clutching film in history," *Time's* February 2 production story described one of *Soldier Blue's* more sensational bits in which a cavalryman rapes and mutilates an Indian maiden, noting that "even the Sharon Tate murderers might have blanched at such a scene."

Could *Soldier Blue* be Hollywood's future? Were the old entertainment verities gone? Hollywood seemed fixated on the events of "1968": "Gutter language, nudity, casual permissiveness point up the fatal mugging of puritanism on stage, on screen, and in rock music," *Variety* complained in their January 7, 1970, front-page story, "B.O. Dictatorship by Youth": "There are no subtleties in today's young. Theirs is the vocabulary of anger, violence, destructiveness."

The counterculture mega-hits *Easy Rider, Midnight Cowboy,* and *Butch Cassidy* were still in release and straggler *Zabriskie Point* had just unfurled its colors to a fusillade of derision. As the horrifying Manson was promoted for the role of America's number one hippie, so My Lai commanding officer Lieutenant William Calley came to personify the Vietnam War. America needed a military hero and, like a miracle, one suddenly materialized. Now there was *Patton*—the last 20th Century-Fox road show but the first true Nixon movie—which premiered at New York's Criterion Theater, two days after the opening of the Panther 21 trial, on February 4, 1970.

His celluloid portrait subtitled *Portrait of a Rebel,* the colorful and controversial four-star general George Patton was positioned not only as an authority figure but even a Righteous

From THE DREAM LIFE

Outlaw. Although *New York Times* critic Vincent Canby called *Patton* "the story of a man about whom only the Establishment would become genuinely sentimental," reviews were mainly favorable. Unlike *The Green Berets, Patton* created a consensus: *Variety* marveled that the movie appealed to hawks and doves, "ultra-liberals" as well as the American Legion. Director Franklin Schaffner, writer Edmund North, and even producer Frank McCarthy thought *Patton* was antiwar—at least, considering its hero's dubious behavior, by implication. But that questionable subtlety was soon lost.

Time's January 5 issue had named the Middle Americans as their Man and Woman of the Year—choosing, over the Silent Majority, a term coined by pundit Joseph Kraft in late 1967:

> Everywhere they flew the colors of assertive patriotism. Their car windows were plastered with American-flag decals, their ideological totems. In the bumper-sticker dialogue of the freeways, they answered MAKE LOVE NOT WAR with HONOR AMERICA or SPIRO IS MY HERO. They sent Richard Nixon to the White House and two teams of astronauts to the moon.

> While the rest of the nation's youth has been watching Dustin Hoffman in *Midnight Cowboy,* Middle America's teenagers have been taking in John Wayne for the second or third time in *The Green Berets.*

By mid-March—when *Patton* went wide and General Lon Nol deposed Prince Sihanouk in Cambodia—Schaffner's movie was widely understood to articulate Silent Majority yearnings. Observers were struck by the long lines of middle-aged or elderly whites queued to see the movie, zombie ghouls tottering back to the box office.

Why? *Patton* began on the grisly battlefield of national defeat—a massacre in the Sahara with Bedouins and buzzards stripping American corpses. But, *Patton* ended three hours later in total American victory. How did the general prevail? First, he had to create a fighting force. "They don't look like soldiers, they don't act like soldiers" was Patton's initial response to the lackadaisical American troops. *Patton's* key scene, played just before intermission, has the general browbeat, slap, and nearly pull his gun on a sniveling "yellow-belly" private hospitalized for battle fatigue. (Patton actually struck two such soldiers, one suffering from malaria.) The scandal becomes a national issue. The U.S. Senate delays Patton's promotion and he is further humiliated by the Allied Supreme Commander, General Dwight D. Eisenhower—compelled to make a public apology to the private, the medical staff, and the entire unit. His career seems over but, in the movie's second half, the irascible general bounces back to win the Battle of the Bulge. In the end, Patton's former adjunct promoted to his superior officer, General Omar Bradley (Karl Malden), tells him that the slapped soldier "did more to win the war than any other private in the army."

As impressive as *Patton's* triumphant narrative was the movie's pop art prologue. The first image is the screen-filling red, white, and blue of a monstrous American flag—greeted, Stanley Kauffmann noted in *The New Republic*, by a smattering of "defiant applause." Presently, to the cry of "ten-SHUN!," the tiny figure of Patton emerges. Close-ups feast on the fetishistic details of his outfit—the shiny helmet embossed with four stars and the letter A, the blue sash, the riding crop, the jodhpurs and boots, the pinky rings, the ascot, the pearl-handled revolvers, the chest layered with medals. Canby joked that this bizarre presence might be mistaken for "a member of the chorus of *The Student Prince*." Yet the critic "felt the audience lunge toward [Patton] with relief. Everything was all right again, the old values were safe."

By now the so-called old values had come to encompass telling-it-like-it-is. Framed by the flag, the general bids his audience be seated, then launches into an outrageously tough-talking speech. Although wearing the orders and decorations given to him after the war, Patton speaks as if the war were just getting under way. "Men, all this stuff you've heard about America not wanting to fight—wanting to stay out of the war— is a lot of horse dung," he rasps. The recruits to whom Patton speaks are never shown; it is the viewer who is addressed:

> Americans traditionally love to fight. All real Americans love the sting of battle. When you were kids, you all admired the champion marble-shooter, the fastest runner, the big-league ballplayer, the toughest boxer. Americans love a winner and will not tolerate a loser. Americans play to win all the time. I wouldn't give a hoot in hell for a man who lost and laughed.

At this point, Canby noted the audience giggle in embarrassment. But titters stopped as Patton continued: "That's why Americans have never lost and will never lose a war—because the very thought of losing is hateful to Americans." How long had the nation been waiting to hear that?

When the Oscar-bedecked picture was rereleased fourteen months later on a double-bill with Fox's other military success *M*A*S*H,* a significant portion of the audience was reported remaining in their seats to savor Patton's opening exhortation a second time.

Movies continued to offer imaginary solutions to real problems. *Variety* suggested that audiences were flocking to *Patton* to see "a hero who is egocentric and personally unpleasant, but has the know-how in achieving military victory." In England, the *Times* of London stated the obvious: "I daresay the Americans now fighting in Asia could do with him if he could manage another of his reincarnations."

Patton's most public fan was, however, the president of the United States. Richard Nixon would repeatedly screen the three-hour movie throughout the spring of 1970. The most conservative estimate has Nixon watching *Patton* twice—on April 1 and, then again, on April 25. Other commentators, noting that the president obtained a personal print, believe he projected *Patton* at least a half-dozen times both at the White House and at his San Clemente, California, retreat.

Nixon's biographer Stephen Ambrose tactfully writes that the president "started watching" the film in late March. Months later, Secretary of State William Rogers told Darryl Zanuck that the president found a way to bring almost every conversation around to *Patton,* he was a "walking ad for that movie." Soon, syndicated columnists Evans and Novak revealed that presidential assistant H. R. Haldeman advised young White House staffers to see *Patton* if they wanted a handle to grasp the Commander in Chief's mindset; the movie persuaded the president that "the true American spirit was Patton, not the New Left."

The same day the Evans and Novak column ran, a jury convicted five of the Chicago Seven of crossing state lines with intent to foment a riot. Patton, too, had also had to contend with undisciplined, cowardly young people—and when he lost his temper and attacked the hospitalized "yellow belly" it was for the bastard's own good, as well as the country's. After the "slap heard round the world," liberal journalists had called for Patton's court-martial but, as the movie points out, Patton was supported by a great Silent Majority; the mail that followed the slap was 89 percent in his favor! Nixon likewise endured an acrimonious adversarial relationship with the treacherous press—like Patton he was forever drawing unwelcome, unsympathetic media attention. Only two days after the president ordered B-52s to secretly bomb the Plain of Jars in mid-February, *The New York Times* blew his cover.

Patton survived an image crisis, endured disappointment, withstood personal attack and came back to win World War II. He was absolved by History as well as by Hollywood. Patton had even designed a uniform, just as Nixon proposed one for the White House guards. More: Patton's eccentric belief in reincarnation, his mystical connections to ancient battlefields were part of a larger pattern. "The men can't tell you're acting, sir," an aide-de-camp informs him after one cursing, screaming display. "It's not important for them to know," is Patton's reply. "It's only important for me to know." Thus, Patton anticipated what Nixon privately called his Madman Theory. "I want the North Vietnamese to believe I've reached the point where I might do anything to stop the war," he explained to Haldeman in 1969.

As spring arrived, power barometers registered mounting pressure. The same day that Majority Leader Hale Boggs denounced FBI surveillance of Congress, and rock star Grace

Slick attempted to sneak Abbie Hoffman into the White House tea to which, as Tricia Nixon's former classmate at Finch College, she'd been invited, Nixon was spooked by his own vice-president. Spiro Agnew was asserting that anything less than total invasion of Cambodia was mere "pussyfooting." With stocks falling on Wall Street, the April 25 screening proved crucial. JFK had *Dr. No*, LBJ had *The Alamo*, SDS had *Bonnie and Clyde,* the Panthers had *The Battle of Algiers*, Abbie Hoffman and Tom Hayden had *Wild in the Streets*, Norman Mailer had *Maidstone* and the president had . . . *Patton*.

The movie, so Evans and Novak later revealed, served to reinforce Nixon's "resolve to risk the Cambodian intervention." National Security Advisor Henry Kissinger understood that he had gained admittance to the president's inner sanctum when he was asked to join Nixon, Attorney General John Mitchell, and Florida businessman Bebe Rebozo on the presidential yacht for an official wargasm—a martini-fueled, pre-invasion Potomac River cruise of which Kissinger wrote that "the tensions of grim military planning were transformed into exaltation by the liquid refreshments."

The outing was capped by a White House presentation of *Patton* which Kissinger's memoirs hint may actually have been Nixon's second screening of the day. Haldeman's notes reinforce Kissinger's account of the president's overwrought state. Nixon was on a manic jag—drinking heavily and going without sleep, throwing tantrums, worrying where to put his new pool table, cursing his aides, and invoking Patton whom he told Haldeman was, for him, an inspiration.

Thursday evening April 30, five years and twenty-three days after LBJ offered his Indochina rationale; the president went on television to announce he had ordered Americans ground troops into Cambodia. *The New York Times* reported Nixon seemed as "grim" as Johnson in using the "toughest" rhetoric of his presidency. Other viewers were less restrained. Nixon appeared at once drunk and hung over, perhaps even suffering the DTs. The president was "strident." He slurred his words. His upper lip was beaded with sweat and "his vision" was apocalyptic:

> We live in an age of anarchy. We see mindless attacks on all the great institutions which have been created by free civilization in the last five hundred years. Even here in the United States, great universities are being systematically destroyed. Small nations all over the world find themselves under attack from within and from without. . . .

So do larger ones:

> We will not be humiliated. We will not be defeated. It is not our power but our will and character that is [sic] being tested tonight.

> If, when the chips are down, the world's most powerful nation, the United States of America, acts like a pitiful, helpless giant, the forces of totalitarianism and anarchy will threaten free nations and free institutions throughout the world.

Rather than speak from his Oval Office desk, Nixon chose the White House war room, standing with a pointer before a map, as though it were a military briefing. The president cast himself as Patton: Total victory or political death!

> I would rather be a one-term president and do what I believe was right than to be a two-term president at the cost of seeing America become a second-rate power and to see this nation accept the first defeat in its proud hundred-and-ninety-year history.

The White House switchboard reported that incoming phone calls supported the president six to one; antiwar demonstrations began on many college campuses within the hour.

May Day: The following morning, the president met at the Pentagon with the Joint Chiefs of Staff, Secretary of Defense Melvin Laird, and Kissinger. The assembled officials were disquieted by their commander's behavior. Nixon didn't appear to pay much attention to their briefing. Distracted, he broke into the discussion with a disjointed, impassioned, profane monologue worthy of you-know-who. Nixon reiterated his determination to "clean up those sanctuaries" and shouted at his mortified advisors that "you have to electrify people with bold decisions . . . Let's go blow the hell out of them!" Was he still acting? As the president left the Pentagon he suddenly turned to reporters, shifting his focus from the Vietcong to their student supporters: "You see these bums, you know, blowing up the campuses . . ." he mumbled. Had the president recalled General Bradley's last line about the slapped soldier winning the war?

EAST SIDE,
WEST SIDE,
WEIRD SIDE:
UNRESTRAINED
URBANITY

BRAVING THE HEAT

Chris Smith

He is running. He is running up West Street in clunky knee-high rubber boots that cut into the backs of his knees, in a bulky black-and-yellow firefighter's coat, with a thirty-pound air cylinder strapped to his back, and Howie Scott is running faster than he ever has before in his thirty-nine years on this earth. Ten seconds ago, he was about to step into 2 World Trade Center. For no reason, he glanced up. The tower exploded. The whole freakin' thing exploded! Now Scott is running from a black cloud of—what? Ash? Soot?

A shrapnel storm of steel and glass and stone is smashing all around him. A concrete boulder the size of a garbage truck thuds into the ground. "John! John! John!" he is yelling as he runs. John Ceriello, also from Squad 18, was standing right next to him outside the building. Where is John?

Scott is diving. He sees a walkway and leaps for cover. He is flying through the air as if something is pushing him, something more than his adrenaline—the force of the explosion? The hand of God? He travels at least fifty feet in the air. As he hits the asphalt, the oxygen tank delivers an iron punch to his lower back. Scott lands under the walkway as 110 stories of pulverized office tower smack like an industrial hailstorm, shredding and demolishing every car and storefront and abandoned doughnut cart in sight. The walkway shields him from the debris. The walkway saves his life.

After thirty seconds on the ground, Scott starts to save other people's lives. He pulls his air mask back into place. He crawls, bumping into—what is this shit? It's too dark, just black, black, black everywhere, to distinguish animal from mineral. It is weirdly quiet. No sirens. No screams. There are people streaming out of an undamaged building, dazed and staring. "Just go!" Scott yells. "Don't even look! Just get out of here! Go! Go! Go!" Men in expensive business suits coated in thick dust, women with bloody bare feet, everyone is sprinting.

Scott runs, too. North again, he thinks. His back aches. His lungs are heaving. He is picking up speed. He runs straight into a plate-glass window.

He fights not to lose consciousness. Must be the only damn unbroken window, and it's nearly knocked him out! He gets up again. There's some daylight. At least it appears to be daylight. This time Scott walks. Up West Street, toward the daylight. He stops when he arrives instead at the edge of the Hudson River. Holy shit, he thinks. Where the hell am I?

Scott slowly picks his way back toward the improvised command center at the corner of West and Vesey. There's supposed to be a main gas line over there, underneath Battery Park City; everyone is being herded clear. The chiefs are getting a little control over the situation now. They're formulating a plan . . . then BOOM! The second tower comes down. It sounds like when a pilot lowers the hammer for takeoff, Scott thinks. The first one, we had time to react, we had a moment to make a move. This one? Anyone there got crushed. Holy Christ.

Now all the radios are out. Bosses are talking about sending firefighters back in, but among the men there's a lot of skepticism: "Is there more?"

"Is anything else coming down?"

"Did they wire this building?"

Figures are emerging like apparitions, stumbling. Firefighters are hugging as they recognize fellow survivors. Scott doesn't see anyone from Squad 18. Where's John? Where is Timmy Haskell, who wouldn't wait for Scott to finish getting dressed and roared off from their Lafayette Street firehouse in the Hazmat truck? Where is Eric Allen, the guy everyone ragged about collecting old junk? Where is Manny Mojica, the Harley-riding Puerto Rican from Astoria with biceps like an NFL lineman's?

Scott's eyes are burning. He knows rubbing them is the worst thing to do, that more of the black gunk will get in his eyes, but he can't help it. Suddenly, thankfully, a familiar face materializes, alive, out of the gloom. It's Larry Cohen. He was scheduled to be working this shift, but Scott had asked to trade. Larry was at home upstate when he got the call. He raced across the Tappan Zee, stopped off at special-operations command on Roosevelt Island, then continued downtown.

On his way into the city, Cohen picked up Joe Downey, a Squad 18 captain and son of Ray Downey, chief of special operations. In 1995, Ray Downey had been dispatched to Oklahoma City to help direct rescue efforts after the bombing; in 1998, he'd pushed the FDNY to create units with extra training in terrorism response, particularly in anticipation of the millennium. One of those units was Squad 18.

Ray Downey's uncanny ability to find order in the worst chaos earned him the nickname "God." Teasing colleagues

223

nicknamed his son "Jesus." Now the World Trade Center has fallen on God, and Jesus is searching for him.

On West Street, Scott tells Cohen about the other members of Squad 18 who are unaccounted for. "Let's go," Cohen urges. "We gotta get them out."

"GOD BLESS PADDY BROWN," WE CRIED AS WE TOSSED HIS ASHES INTO THE AIR

Michael Daly

SEPTEMBER 8, 2002

In keeping with the humble spirit that Fire Capt. Patrick (Paddy) Brown shared with all great men, most of us took only a modest handful of his cremated remains.

"Anybody need some more?" asked his brother, Mike Brown.

Mike went back down the line of thirty mourners and we each scooped a little more from the cardboard container. The gray ash was gritty to the touch. It rested in the palm as if disbelief had taken substance, as unreal as the thought we would never again see our gallant friend.

"Oh, Patrick," Vina Drennan said. We had arrayed ourselves along the top of the Great Lawn in Central Park, the place Paddy had marked on the map he had enclosed in a letter should anything ever happen to him. Paddy had often passed this way on the long jogs that kept him fit enough to have lived another half-century. You had only to gaze downtown to know why he had chosen this spot. On this sharply cold January night four months after the attack on the World Trade Center, the remaining spires of Manhattan stood beyond the dark trees with incandescent majesty. These surviving towers seemed to have been constructed to be admired from exactly here at precisely this hour. The sky above was so clear we could see the stars not often glimpsed over this city Paddy had served so valiantly.

"This is kinda beautiful, you know," Mike said.

Mike was echoing words Paddy had uttered seven years ago, after Fire Capt. John Drennan lost a forty-day struggle to survive terrible burns he suffered in a fire on Watts Street.

"We cried over his body and stuff," Paddy said. "It was kinda beautiful, you know."

Vina and the rest of us now followed Mike's instructions to turn toward the moon that shone big and bright behind us. We cast our handfuls into the icy air and called out in one voice.

"God bless Paddy Brown!"

The breeze caught the ash and it stayed aloft, swirling and sparkling in the moonlight. The one and only Paddy Brown, the firefighter who was always first in and last out, seemed to have become a kind of magic, heavenly dust.

We all still had gritty ash on our palms and fingers. The one who knew what to do was the pregnant widow of a firefighter who perished with Paddy in the north tower. Her husband and Paddy had been as close as brothers, and she now rubbed her hands on her face in a gesture of pure and perfect love.

In a hush, we walked over to a silver maple that had been planted in Paddy's memory. Nobody had wanted to take the last of the ashes from the cardboard container, and Mike gently poured what was left around the base of the tree. Somebody set down a holy card that had a smiling Paddy on the front and a photo of a rope rescue on the back. Somebody else added a small, flickering candle.

With the unadorned, genuine voice of a former grammar

school teacher, Vina broke into the Marine Corps Hymn. We sang along and she led us straight into "God Bless America." We placed our gritted hands over our sorrowing hearts.

Just as we ended with ". . . my home sweet home," an airliner like the planes that struck the twin towers flew overhead as if in a variation of the traditional military tribute.

"The hardest thing was to get that plane to fly over," Mike joked.

We proved we could still laugh. We did not seem to leave behind even the smallest fleck of what was important about Paddy as we went down the winding, sloping path leading from the park.

On the way out, we passed the uptown end of the Metropolitan Museum of Art, and through the glass we could see the Egyptian Temple of Dendur. No ancient ritual could have held more power than had Mike Brown with his cardboard container.

The whole city seemed to be Paddy's temple as we headed downtown, but then again that was how the city had seemed when he was alive. We crowded into a long table in one of his favorite restaurants, a pizza parlor as unassuming as Paddy himself.

A waitress whose eyes were welling at the memory of Paddy set down our orders. Fingers that had just scattered his remains into the moonlight now moved sustenance to mouth.

"Nobody washed their hands," Mike would later note.

At night's end, we shook those hands and embraced, each carrying our love of Paddy with us when we parted. Some of us could still feel the faintest traces of the grit between our fingertips the next morning.

The pregnant widow who had shown such magnificence of

heart when she rubbed the ash on her face went on to have her baby, a girl. Vina returned to her life of writing and doting on her grandkids. Mike went back to his life as a Las Vegas emergency room doctor, his hands doing the daily work of a true Brown.

Up at that perfect spot at the top of the Great Lawn early Friday afternoon, the breeze carried the scent of newly mown grass. A boy about 5 years old, in an FDNY T-shirt, pedaled by on a bike with training wheels, the spires of Manhattan standing off in the distance against a porcelain blue sky liable to remind anyone older of another September day.

Five other youngsters, four girls and a boy, ran barefoot on the cushiony lawn, laughing as if the air still held some kind of magic dust. You rubbed your fingertips together and a year later you missed Capt. Patrick (Paddy) Brown even more than on that sunny morning we lost him.

KARAOKE NATION—OR HOW I SPENT A YEAR IN SEARCH OF GLAMOUR, FULFILLMENT, AND A MILLION DOLLARS

Steve Fishman

I have a pretty good idea where the business started for me. The why is fuzzier. I was at a Tribeca loft, attending a quiet midweek cocktail party, an after-work fundraiser for a worthy politician who had no chance. There were perhaps thirty people there, broken into small groups. I stood near a long, gray counter. Really, the entire apartment seemed as gray as a factory floor. "It needs updating," I could imagine my wife Cristina saying. The gray counter was chest-high which is too high for a counter. I'd set down a beer and almost missed it. Recovering, I poked the blue wire-frame glasses up the bridge of my nose, a not entirely attractive gesture, smiled, paused, considered a story I'd just heard, and then, as if the outcome of the miscue and the slight embarrassment, the story, and who knows, but my recent past as well, found myself thinking, "Today I set out to make a million dollars."

I didn't immediately know why I had this thought. After all, it wasn't like I suddenly knew how to make a million dollars. I hadn't gone fumbling for a pad in the middle of the night, struck by a "vision" of a new way to do things, which people would later impress upon me as important. Nor did I have a unique "skill set," "a core competency," a dynamic new "business model," all things that, eventually, I'd hear were

229

helpful in business. Frankly, I didn't know what a business model was. Soon enough, I'd meet a shaggy-headed fellow who'd shut himself in a closet—he insisted it really was a closet—and emerged six months later with a brainy software package. ("I was so excited," he told me, "many nights I couldn't sleep.") That wasn't something I was likely to pull off; I spent too much time on the phone with tech support. I could go on. The list of business-y things I didn't have or didn't know was stunning.

Plus, it's probably worth mentioning, I didn't really think of myself as someone motivated to earn a million dollars. Growing up, I'd worked my share of part-time jobs, the kind that someone would later tell me indicated an entrepreneurial disposition. I'd delivered newspapers and cut lawns. I'd sold flannel shirts at college, seconds at bargain rates, and worked in a neighbor's basement assembling gaudy costume jewelry. My family had always gone in for a fair amount of vocational experimentation. At a time when my father held an executive position in New York City, he nonetheless stacked jewelry catalogues in the small entryway of our suburban house. He'd sold inexpensive necklaces and bracelets through the mail, the type, coincidentally, I'd been putting together in that neighbor's basement. Later, my parents would look into a laundromat business, then a tutoring center. Briefly, they'd spend time in pay phones, collecting bagfuls of quarters in their Ford Escort.

Moneymaking, though, hadn't gotten its hooks in me. (I'm not sure it had really latched onto my parents either. My father literally whistled while he worked.) As a primary focus, money seemed pushy, limited, obvious; the stakes, measly. I was after bigger fish, I assured myself.

And, anyway, journalism, which I'd done for twenty years, was a fine, useful profession; the work was varied, interesting, worthwhile. A person could do it forever. I had prospects and didn't have to get up too early. I wrote long feature stories about colorful characters. Oddball extremes was how I sometimes thought of them. Johnny, a favorite, had tried to blow up his hometown. "You had to really like Johnny to like Johnny," his best friend told me. I liked Johnny. He never really fit in, but I thought I understood him, and through him, appreciated something about those who did fit into a safe, settled environment. I suppose my preference was for outsiders, people like Johnny, or the hoboes I rode trains with, the scared volcanologist, the Harlem kid with a genius for chess, the hustlers on the outskirts of Hollywood—people with unusual, even uncontrollable urges. I even—and I can't account for this—took to a serial killer I'd first met when he picked me up hitchhiking.

And yet, lately, I had to admit, journalism wasn't exactly riveting. In fact, I'd recently found myself perseverating on a disturbing encounter from my first newspaper job. Two decades ago I'd worked for the *Miami Herald*. One day a fellow reporter told me of meeting a farmer near Lake Okeechobee. The farmer asked my friend what he did for a living. Actually, his formulation was more pointed.

"You go around and ask people things and then put them in the paper?" the farmer asked.

"Yes," my friend told him, a little surprised himself.

"And they pay you for that?" he pursued.

Lately, when I thought of what I did for a living—the patient notetaking, the patient listening—it all seemed absorbing of course, fascinating; still, these days my job seemed to lack intensity, an essential drama, a connection to a larger story. What was it I was doing? Accomplishing? Back in Florida I'd brushed off that farmer's pointed questions with a laugh. Recently, they seemed troubling. Let's face it, I was pretty much indifferent to work in the categories that made sense these days. I was a feature writer, and wrote the human-interest stories that used to get printed in a newspaper's Women's Page—before it became the Style or Living section. I often felt, like my colorful characters, a bit peripheral. I'd started to wonder what I'd do if I left journalism.

Then one evening I'd attended that cocktail party for a movement Democrat, a liberal from New York's Upper West Side who sometimes championed the kinds of people I wrote about. He was a short man. Perhaps that encouraged me; a physical squaring-off seemed possible. I told him to wise up. The world had changed. It was leaving his good-natured outlook behind. I rattled on. He grew a smile that I thought might never leave his face, the kind you give someone else's misbehaving kid.

"You're husband's something else," he told Cristina when I finally let him go.

I turned to listen to a handful of nearby people, some of whom I didn't know, not entirely concentrating, the way one does at New York parties. I was distracted by some laughter from across the room, a few isolated words, and then a guy next to me began telling a story. He was tall, mid-thirties, with a full head of dark hair, black rectangular glasses, and an inviting style of speech. He called people he'd just met "brother" in a half-familiar, half-ironic way. I thought someone said he was a novelist; apparently, he'd recently been an entrepreneur. He was describing how you'd go about meeting with venture capitalists in order to raise money.

"You want one of the people on your team to be button-down, your banker, your grownup," he said. He may have rapped his knuckles on a chair.

"Grownup?" I asked. In context, the term was intriguing.

"He's got to instill confidence," he said and adjusted his head to an ever more precise angle.

"Oh," I said. "And who else?"

"A flashy guy. In an Armani suit maybe. This guy has to promote the vision," he said. "Then you want someone, maybe a celebrity, somebody who could casually say, 'I was just playing golf with Quincy and he loves this idea.' "

My eyes lit up. It was as if this guy had let slip that he was a Navy SEAL. The drama of a meeting like that! Anything could happen! I knew magazines were writing about lone entrepreneurs upending entire industries. Perhaps this fellow had been one of those. My imagination raced. I pictured stare-downs with investors. Shouting matches. Had he, I found myself wondering, ever been double-crossed? I'd lately thumbed through the business pages. Who hadn't? They read like sports pages. You could almost hear the cheering. People in business seemed to be having the time of their lives.

"Which guy were you?" I asked him.

"Brother," he said to me, "I used to own a black Armani suit."

It was just about then that I'd placed my beer on the counter, the one I'd almost missed, and experienced, jumbled with self-consciousness, a vague . . . what was it? What I seemed to experience was an urge, though now that I say the word aloud—urge—that sounds wrong. It wasn't all that forceful.

It was probably just a mood. As close as I could tell, this one had to do with wanting something—something other than what I had. Everybody wanted something else, I assured myself reasonably. You can't get away from it. I want, I want. It was a roar. I thought, "I want more than anything . . ."

But there I hesitated. My aptitude for wanting hadn't ever been all that high, not for focused wanting, the kind you heard so much about these days. With me, desire headed into the cosmos, disappearing like radio waves in search of distant life.

It was a little embarrassing. After all, my family boasted serious goals. In past generations there'd been choppy crossings in the dead of night. I had a great uncle who swam a river (I forget which) to escape. (Talk about focused wanting!) My energetic father had eventually walked away from an established career. Together he and my mother had started a small school.

Then, at that party in the gray room, I suddenly knew what I wanted, wanted with an intensity I am tempted to describe as ancestral. I wanted my fill. I wanted to give as good as I got. To get into arguments. Some tussling. A showdown or two would be fine. Maybe I could be double-crossed. I wouldn't mind having a hand in the future. Not at all. I wanted something that landed me. Landed me. I wanted to be in the thick of things. And I wanted stories to tell.

And that was the precise moment when I reached for the chest-high counter, almost missed it, smiled, paused, pushed those blue wire-frames up along my nose, and thought triumphantly: "Today I set out to make a million dollars." Though, on reflection, I may have uttered these words aloud, seeing as how nearby partygoers tightened the grip on their drinks. Two women, I noticed, shared a wide-eyed look.

I hardly cared. Look what I'd been missing, I thought suddenly.

I gazed at my brown bottle of beer, which made a sweaty *O* on the gray counter. The million-dollar project suddenly struck me as a whole lot more invigorating than the doughy work currently at the center of my life. The roughhouse of commerce. That's where it's at these days. Business, I'd recently read, "wakes up [a man's] inventive genius, puts his wits to work. . . ." That's what I wanted. What I'd always wanted. I thought about the manly adventure of business, and the entrepreneurs I'd tangle with, and imagined that I'd soon go on about the real engine of the economy, and the shape of things to come. Before long, I just knew, I'd cut people off with a look. "What's the bottom line?" I'd say. I'd start sentences with 'I believe' and float a finger in the air to let people know I meant it. They wouldn't walk away, a grin fixed in place.

I took up my drink, wiped the ring of condensation from the counter with my sleeve. Perhaps, on reflection, I wanted to impress the guy next to me, the one in a brown suede jacket, who I now thought of as the Armani guy. I made a motion with my elbows like a washing machine. "I want to throw some elbows," I said sincerely. I did this with beer in hand—spilling a drop—as I tried to explain to this person I barely knew, how things would go if—where did this inspiration come from?—he were willing to pitch in. I believed, I think, it would be more fun. Yes fun was the word that came to mind.

So business wasn't traditionally kind to the naive. "Come on," I said to this guy, the one I now seemed to be addressing. I may have been shouting. Who could blame me? I was suddenly intent, a fine development in and of itself. I saw my future. A bunch of them. "Let's make a million dollars! Why not?" I snapped. "Let's give it a year," I said. "If it takes ten months, then we'll take two off."

I liked the precision of the million-dollar goal. It seemed robust, vital, martial, the way I used to feel playing touch football, breathing quick, steamy bursts into fall air. And it seemed full of possibilities as if—looking back, I can still hardly believe I thought this—it was something original. I felt springy, full of purpose. Taken together, it was one sharp feeling. I took a sip of beer and grabbed for a chair, at which point the knot of partygoers dispersed, perhaps a bit relieved.

Simply declaring my million-dollar intention—however mismatched it and I appeared to be—put me in a group which seemed for a time just about everywhere. It was, for instance, at about that period I met a fidgety Ivy League graduate, a good-looking, slightly reedy woman with intense red hair and a sharp, insistent manner. Mary was one of those people, I soon understood, who always seemed to have a hand in the air indicating something smart and entertaining to say. "I'm an insecure overachiever," she explained. Apparently she knew lots of them.

We were at a café drinking lemonade as Mary explained she had a future to plan. She seemed optimistic more or less. (Optimism, I sensed, wasn't Mary's strong suit.) Until recently, she'd been involved in an entrepreneurial venture with two other employees, both friends, both unpaid, and all working out of her apartment. I gathered that the business had something to do with bonds and the Internet. Mary didn't feel I'd get it and so spared me a detailed explanation. In any case, the venture collapsed when the investment house of Goldman Sachs decided to go into bonds in just the way Mary had contemplated.

Suddenly Mary's narrow shoulders pulled taut as a birdcage. I sensed some discontent, though I wasn't sure why. She said she hadn't gotten the pop she wanted, a term which apparently meant money. Still, Mary was entertaining job offers. She was the kind of applicant people sought. And tomorrow she was off for vacation.

She signed. Did she have to spell it out?

Perhaps that would be best.

So she did. "Why aren't I a millionaire?" she asked forlornly. Then she straightened, her vertebrae clicking into place, and added, "I'm thirty—well, almost."

You didn't have to be approaching thirty to experience the special tug, or accompanying ache, in that question. You didn't even have to be a businessperson, not one of longstanding in any case.

To set out to make a million dollars connected a person to what seemed for, for a time, the country's most popular ambition. It was almost run-of-the-mill. For a while, it hardly seemed much of an ambition at all. According to what I read, most people expected to make a million dollars. In 1997, a survey of American college students found that a stunning 77 percent believed they would someday earn a million dollars.

Were they wrong?

At one point, *The New York Times* reported this perversely precise statistic: On any given day, said the paper of record, sixty-four new millionaires were minted in California's Silicon Valley alone, which is a rate of 23,360 a year—about the population of the town in New Jersey where I grew up. By about 1999, someone had counted 84,000 millionaires in the Silicon Valley region. (Another 134,000 were half-millionaires, at least on paper.) These new wealthy weren't just computer programmers, those who suddenly seemed to know everything worth knowing. They were managers and manual writers; they were in PR, in sales. They were people in your circle, or just outside it. In 1998 a reporter at *Fortune* magazine would write, "Everyone I know knows somebody, or knows somebody who knows somebody, who's made $10 million. . . ." Wealth suddenly seemed a routine chore and—reversing a decades-long trend—was being achieved at a young age.

In New York, too, people I kind of knew appeared to be doing very well. I heard about the person whose son was on a friend's son's soccer team and whose company was going public. (And, still, worried about his son's playing time.) It was always a regular guy, someone you might have a beer with, a person who seemed to have no particular aptitude. As one friend with an unusually compromised attention span exclaimed, "This guy answered an ad in a free newspaper"—I think the free part got to him in particular—"and now he's worth $35 million," he added, his attention riveted. The process might be baffling—free newspaper? $35 million?—but the import was clear. Riches were as available as air, if you just knew where to look.

In a few minutes, the Armani guy wandered over.

"You're tic-y," I said from my seat. It was mainly in his foot and occasionally in his head which could shift with camera shutter speed.

"I'm a ticker," he concurred.

"Do you ever feel . . ." I pursued, looking for the right word, "pent-up?" Lately, I did. I had it in my legs, shot through like a drug.

"All the time," he said quickly. Then, without a segue, he offered to help. "I have some experience with business plans," he mentioned casually, "I could look at one for you."

I thought that was terrific, though I didn't have a firm idea what a business plan was. I'd never seen one. No matter. I told myself things were falling into place. I had a team forming. (Team. I already liked saying the word.) From the start I thought of the Armani guy as my business *consigliere*. His name was Steve Reynolds. Consigliere was what I liked to call him. Later, when I got to know him better, I'd sometimes call him Consig.

In time, I'd learn a few salient details about him—not that it was ever easy. (It was like pulling teeth, as my mother would say.) Consigliere, it would turn out, had ample business credentials. Before becoming an entrepreneur, he'd been a leading Internet consultant, often quoted in *Fortune* and *Business Week*. He occasionally referred to this as "my business act," which led me to think there were others. And indeed he'd enrolled in an MFA program and written an inventively titled novel, *The Impact of the Energy Crisis on Haircuts and Other Matters of Inner Peace*. Consigliere, I sensed, had a dose of ambivalence. He was a business guy who longed for a three-book deal. No wonder he seemed to keep a lot of energy under wraps.

At the party, Consigliere abruptly put his elbows at his sides. He twisted his arms in his suede jacket, a gesture that at first confused me. Then I got it. My first company would be called Throwing Elbows, a Limited Liability Corporation. All I needed now was an idea, a business idea.

"Ideas come from everywhere," Consigliere reassured me. He would always be reassuring.

KARMANDU

Mark Jacobson

T hings happen when you have a car in the city. Back in the early eighties, when I was crazy enough to be living on St. Mark's Place, I had the battery stolen from my '68 164 dual-carb Volvo. Some wretched skell reached up through the broken grille and opened the hood latch. My sister-in-law told me I better get the grille fixed immediately because once I moved the car the thief would know I had a new battery and take that one, too. Since I never listen to anything my sister-in-law says, I did not get the grille fixed. My new battery was immediately stolen. Pissed, I locked the third battery in the trunk and taped a note on the car saying "Fuck you." The next morning I returned to find "Sorry, man" scrawled at the bottom of the note.

Alas, all that remains of that beloved Volvo is the driver's-side-window hand crank, which I keep as a souvenir. The rest was donated to the Westport, Connecticut, volunteer fire department, which ripped open the car's roof like a can of creamed corn with its Jaws of Life as an "extrication" exercise. In this way, the Volvo joined so many of my other autos: my '65 Sunbeam Minx (totaled on the West Side Highway), my Ford Econoline van (sold for $200 to a guy named Malcolm, to haul fish from South Carolina), my Dodge Dart (scavenged for parts, crushed to a three-foot-by-three-foot steel box), my Buick Special (also crushed), and my Ford Galaxie (bought because Lemmy Caution in *Alphaville* drove one, then stolen, never found). I mourn all these departed conveyances, to various degrees.

I was thinking of all these ruined vehicles while riding out to Willets Point Boulevard, site of the vast automobile graveyard and open-air parts bazaar just east of Shea Stadium. It was a mission, a quest. Looking for a bench seat for a twenty-two-year-old Chevy can be called nothing else.

The car in question was my buddy Terry Bisson's 1979 maroon-and-silver Chevrolet Caprice Classic. When it comes to the automotive, Terry is my man. Firmly ensconced in Brooklyn for the past couple of decades, T. B. grew up in Owensboro, Kentucky. This was where, like dem Southern boys like to do, he learned how to double-clutch and speed-shift at about the age of twelve, screaming along in his uncle's '53 Ford with a beer between his legs. It was hell-raising, and if you're going to raise hell sans seat belts you might as well do it dodging the planes on the runways of the town airport, which had just been built by a company run by the grandfather of Johnny Depp, Owensboro's most famous son (if you don't count Bill Monroe, and NASCAR champ Darrell Waltrip). Having rebuilt a '48 Willys Jeepster before he was seventeen, T. B.—an erstwhile grease monkey turned famous sci-fi author and official biographer of Mumia Abu-Jamal—has a healthy respect for the potential life span of a good car, which in his case is as long as he can possibly make the fucker run.

It was a bench-seat-in-the-haystack sort of deal, we understood, approaching the banks of the fuming Flushing River, the great junkyard looming beyond like a deeply oxidized Oz.

Still, T. B. was hopeful. After all, Cairo has its City of the Dead, but Willets Point, the forty-acre former site of Gatsby's ashpits, is the City of Dead Cars. If there was a Chevy bench seat to be found, it would be here.

Karmandu, I call it, owing to Willets's frontierlike, unpaved, and sewerless streets, which, depending on the weather, are either dust-choked or flooded. Also reminiscent of the Third World is the way dozens of hitherto unseen hawkers fly from their corrugated tin offices to bang on the hood of your vehicle, demanding you purchase a used fender, a used transmission, a used windshield, a used CV joint. With John Rocker's number 7 train rumbling through the monoxide-saturated air, Willets Point is a post-*Mad Max* caravansary, catering to all nationalities. Homesick cabbies from Quito seeking replacement glass can find solace at the Ecuador Body Shop. For refugees from the Taliban in need of a radiator, there is Kabul Auto Repair, Inc. (for Spanish-speaking Afghanis, the shop sign adds *reparación de autos*). It is impressive to be here on evenings when the Mets play. You squint into the vapor lamps to see 40,000 rise to do the wave or boo John Franco, the bum, one more time. But nothing beats Willets seen during a winter's sunset, when silhouettes of ice-gleamed steering columns stacked on rooftops point upward like shrunken spaceships straining to the stars. It is enough to make any gearhead weak.

We stopped first at Sambucci Bros., Inc., Auto Salvage. Mario Cuomo, who used to be the governor, said he knew a guy there. When he was a young lawyer he represented the Sambuccis and several other Willets Point automotive pioneers against Robert Moses, who was looking for Lebensraum for his 1964 World's Fair. "Moses wanted to build a ball field, he thought it would be easy to get rid of a few little oil-covered guys with a baling press machine. . . . We took Moses on and beat him," remembered Cuomo when I called him, clearly still relishing this vanquishing of the power broker. "Strange you bring up Willets Point," the former governor remarked. "It was a big case for me, it led to several others. Willets Point was really the beginning of my public life . . . a career begun in the junkyard."

Forty-one years later, hearing that Cuomo was still "miserable" over not receiving his full fee in the case, Dan Sambucci, Sr., now seventy and leather-faced from a life of hard work, said, "Well, he got my part of the money. The governor was educated, way up there, but we got along. He always got a kick out of how I talked, you know, from the street." Sambucci, who was born in Corona and bought his first wreck in 1949 with $20 borrowed from his mother, recalled when "this was country, green fields, and we'd burn those punk things to keep away the mosquitoes.

"Everything is different these days," said Sambucci, whose office sports a six-foot-tall statue of Jesus. "We got a League of Nations here now." Plus, he continued, with leasing and 100,000-mile warranties, people don't look for parts the way they did. "Mostly it's dealers who come in. You don't get the individual like before." Then again, the old wrecker reflected, with the city making intermittent noises about condemning the junk-yards to build a new park for the Mets to lose in, life at Willets Point has taken on the ephemeral, doomed aspect of the cars that end up here. "You know: Here today, gone tomorrow," he said.

After that, Sambucci told us what we already suspected: he didn't have a bench seat for a '79 Caprice Classic. "That's pretty old," he said.

Over the next couple of hours, as we stepped gingerly over glass pellets strewn on the streets, the story was the same. There was no bench seat at Panjoti Body, no bench seat at Malek Motors, no bench seat at El Salvador Glass, no bench seat at F&F Auto Salvage near the La Guadalupana Restaurant's lunch wagon, and no bench seat at Agnello's, where the large letters on the to-do blackboard spelled MAKE MONEY. Over at Budget Wrecking they had a couple of black leather buckets, hidden away in a spider-filled trailer, that the Rastaman attendant said he might "bend to fit," but this seemed chancy at best. Over at Sunrise Auto Body Shop, a massive yard out by the old stone coal silos left over from the ashpit days, paydirt appeared palpable. There, beyond twin handwritten, bilingual remonstrations—no pissing and *no orinar*—magically revved up and running just for our benefit, was a 1985 Caprice, which, when it comes to bench seats, is close enough. The condition was good, too. Nice gray velveteen with no rips.

"How much?," T. B. inquired.

Natan, the doleful Semite in charge, scratched his head. "I give you for $60, no installation."

Unfortunately, the deal was soon dashed. Whoever purchased that old '85 Caprice, however many owners ago, must have been relatively flush. He'd ordered the power seats, an option the buyer of T. B.'s '79 model had eschewed. The '85 seats would not fit.

It was about then that T. B., veteran of such situations, became apprehensive. By now it was clear: Even amid the immense disassemblage of Willets Point, there was likely only one bench seat to fit a 1979 Caprice. That seat was inside T.B.'s maroon-and-silver rocket, or at least it was when we parked in the mud puddle at the far end of the lot. Now, with word of our search no doubt buzzing around the yard, the next scene was easy to imagine. Some local chop-shopper would tap us on the shoulder and lead us down a grease-stained pathway to show us the object in question. He'd want $50.

To which T. B. would reply, "Fifty?! Why, that seat's no better than what I've got now."

This would cause the price to drop to $40. When it got to $25, we'd buy the thing, install it back into the Caprice, and drive off feeling, well, at least we'd gotten the guy down on the price.

Hearts sinking, we drove back to Brooklyn, to the automotive neighborhood on the southern end of Utica Avenue. Past the Bluebird Diner and Paco's Tacos, we came to the blocks containing John's Auto, Bim's Auto, and Mr. Auto Trim. But none of these establishments could help us. Last stop was nearby on Foster Avenue, at Hammer's, a cheery wrecking yard with joyous folk art of dead and dying vehicles painted on the yellow exterior.

By now, however, T. B. had changed his focus. The bench seat quest forsaken for the moment, he now sought to replace the long-busted cover of his left front turn signal. Hammer's seemed the place for that. Thousands of taillight and signal covers hanging on hooks festooned the three-story wall inside the wrecker's iron fence like red and yellow plastic ivy. Suspense filled the summer South Brooklyn air as the Hammer attendant picked through the seemingly endless array.

"I have '80," the Hammer guy, a Russian gentleman in a Banlon shirt and gold chains, said with an accent fresh from the steppes. "Best I can do. Can you use '80?" T. B. could not. For reasons known only to the Detroit brain trust, GM had seen fit to change the front-turning-light setup between the '79 and '80 model years.

"Guess not," T. B. said, slowly sinking back onto the bumpy springs of his unreplaced bench seat.

Then, as if we didn't already know, the Russian leaned in the window and said, "Take it from me. What you look for is not a part. It is an antique. Try a museum."

FUN, FUN, FUN

Daniel Jeffrey Ricciato

G ood evening, my name is Daniel Jeffrey Ricciato and I am addicted to fun. If you see me on the street there are two options: I'm either going to, or coming from having fun. There is a third option, though: I could be having fun right then. I have driven across four states sleeping only three hours in two days for one magnificent hour of fun. When I order Chinese food, I always get Shrimp Mei Fun.

The first time I had fun was probably around age two. We took a little trip to my grandmother's house in Connecticut. She gave me a ball to play with and it was the best thing that ever happened to me. Just a ball, that's all, no robotic-spark-flying-attention-derailing-mr.-pickle-make-you-cry-on-the-floor-of-the-toy-store-and-kick-out-your-pouting-leg-if-you-don't-get-it thing. Like the earth and quite possibly the shape of the universe itself, that ball was perfect and encapsulating. I rolled on the ball, the ball rolled over me, and at that moment I knew there was some sort of higher power in this world that consumed me, some glowing cosmic radiance I had become connected with. It was like being born again, only better.

The thing is, once you have fun like that there's really no

going back. Fun becomes everything in your life and you will do anything, go anywhere, or try anything to attain it. Sometimes I will be walking down the street and just out of the corner of my eye I will see that bouncy blue-and-red ball and I will leap away from my friends or push the woman I am trying to make swoon out of the way in an attempt to capture that ball, hold on to it, and embrace the plastic softness of it, inhale the memories and days of innocence when fun was as simple as a ball. I still occasionally wake up from a sound sleep because I think I hear the ball bouncing outside, or pushing ever so softly against my bedroom door in the middle of the night; the experience when I was two was so profound, it created what can be comparable only to a compass and magnetic north.

Eventually though, we fall from grace and fun becomes more technically precarious. No longer did the radiant ball instill the same relentless mirth it once had. In a moment of myopia I remember intentionally roofing that blue ball. It was both sad and eloquent and ultimately I cried a little, on the inside of course, and then moved on. At the age of ten my family was vacationing in Vermont. There had been torrential rain and it had come streaming down from the hills with the force of a renegade herd of buffalo for four days straight, washing out the dirt road. This magnificent act of God created a temporary, but wide, stream. The next morning, the rain stopped and I meandered out to see what kind of fun could be had by the washed-out road. Like a Buddhist receiving enlightenment I was struck by a force so strong I can still feel it resonating in me today, right now, right here. In the middle of where the road had been flooded was an island of fun waiting for me to occupy. It was the sovereign state of fun that I had been looking my whole life to claim as my own for so long and now it was my chance to live the dream. My heart beat like a voodoo drum at the mere thought of what kind of glorious action would take place. I pictured my running start down the road, and the fluid, panther-like pounce I would erupt with, soaring over the water and landing like Mary Lou Retton in the 80s, a perfect score of ten for fun. However, it was not to be. What I thought was an island of bliss turned out to be a mirage of sorts: just a pile of dirt that was floating on the surface that had dried in the cursed summer sun. There is a silver lining to this fun cloud of fun and that is instead of landing on the island of bliss I ended up neck deep in filthy, sediment-ridden road water. After the initial shock of not landing on solid land and scurrying up and out I examined what had happened and became quite enamored with myself. I wore my mud-soaked clothes back into the house as a king who returns triumphantly from battle. That, my friends, is some serious unexpected fun that I have still not had the pleasure or even opportunity to recreate, nor do I care to.

As I've gotten older the fun has changed. Instead of tug of war, cupcakes with extra frosting, and beating frogs to death with sticks, I find I have fun in other ways. It might be walking around Soho on a Saturday night with a large piece of lumber slung over my shoulder, or trying to convince the person next to me on the subway that I smell like a pork roast. My ultimate philosophy is that I don't choose to have fun, the fun chooses me, but I will always, without fail, bring the fun to the fun cause nothing is more fun than having fun. Call it a metaphor, call it a matzoh ball, I could care less. I've modeled my life around having fun, I cannot avoid it. It has cost me money, a few scrapes, a few scars, and most of my humility, but I know that even if scientists were to prove that there is indeed an afterlife, it couldn't be as much fun as the one I'm living now.

THE UNKNOWN SOLDIER

Luc Sante

The last thing I saw was a hallway ceiling, four feet wide, finished along its edges with a plaster molding that looked like a long row of small fish each trying to swallow the one ahead of it. The last thing I saw was a crack of yellow sky between buildings, partly obscured by a line of washing. The last thing I saw was the parapet, and beyond it the trees. The last thing I saw was his badge, but I couldn't tell you the number. The last thing I saw was a full shot glass, slid along by somebody who clapped me on the back. The last thing I saw was the sedan that came barreling straight at me while I thought, it's okay, I'm safely behind the window of the doughnut shop. The last thing I saw was a boot, right foot, with nails protruding from the instep. The last thing I saw was a turd. The last thing I saw was a cobble. The last thing I saw was night.

I lost my balance crossing Broadway and was trampled by a team of brewery horses. I was winching myself up the side of a six-story corner house on a board platform with a load of nails for the cornice when the weak part of the rope hit the pulley sideways and got sheared. I lost my way in snowdrifts half a block from my flat. I drank a bottle of carbolic acid not really knowing whether I meant to or not. I got very cold, and coughed, and forgot things. I went out to a yard to try and give birth in secret, but something happened. I met a policeman who mistook me for somebody else. I was drunk on my birthday and I fell off the dock trying to grab a gold piece that looked like it was floating. I was hanged in the courtyard of the Tombs before a cheering crowd and people clogging the rooftops of the buildings all around, but I still say that rascal had it coming to him. I stole a loaf of bread and started eating it as I ran down the street, but there was a wad of raw dough in the middle that got caught in my throat. I was supposed to get up early that morning but I couldn't move. I heard a sort of whistling noise above my head as I was passing by the post office and that's all I know. I was hustling a customer who looked like a real swell but when we got upstairs he pulled out a razor. I owed a lot of rent and got put out and that night curled up in somebody else's doorway and he came home in a bad mood. I was bitten by that black dog that used to hang around and I forgot all about it for six months or so. I ate some oysters I dug up myself. I took a shot at the big guy but the hammer got stuck. I felt very hot and shaky and strange and everybody in the shop was looking at me and I kept trying to tell them that I'd be all right in a minute but I just couldn't get it out.

I never woke up as the fumes snaked into my room. I stood yelling as he stabbed me again and again. I picked up a passenger who braced me in the middle of Broadway and made me turn off. I shot up the bag as soon as I got home but I think it smelled funny when I cooked it. I was asleep in the park when these kids came by. I crawled out the window and felt sick looking down, so I just threw myself out and looked up as I fell. I thought I could get warm by burning some newspaper in a soup pot. I went to pieces very slowly, and was happy when it finally stopped. I thought the train was going way too fast but I kept on reading. I let this guy pick me up at the party and sometime later we went off in his car. I felt real sick but the nurse thought I was kidding. I jumped over to the other fire escape but my foot slipped. I thought I had time to cross the street. I thought the floor would support my weight. I thought nobody could touch me. I never knew what hit me.

They put me in a bag. They nailed me up in a box. They walked me down Mulberry Street followed by altar boys and four priests under a canopy and everybody in the neighborhood singing the *Libera Me, Domine*. They collected me in pieces all through the park. They laid me in state under the rotunda for three days. They engraved my name on the pediment. They drew my collar up to my chin to hide the hole in my neck. They laughed about me over the baked meats and rye whiskey. They didn't know who I was when they fished me out, and still didn't know six months later. They held my body for ransom and collected, but by that time they had burned it. They never found me. They threw me in the cement mixer. They heaped all of us into a trench and stuck a monument on top. They cut me up at the medical school. They weighed down my ankles and tossed me in the drink. They gave speeches claiming I was some kind of tin saint. They hauled me away in the ashman's cart. They put me on a boat and took me to an island. They tried to keep my mother from throwing herself in after me. They bought me my first suit and dressed me up in it. They marched to City Hall holding candles and shouting my name. They forgot all about me and took down my picture.

So give my eyes to the eye bank, give my blood to the blood bank. Make my hair into switches, put my teeth into rattles, sell my heart to the junkman. Give my spleen to the mayor. Hook my lungs to an engine. Stretch my guts down the avenue. Stick my head on a pike, plug my spine to the third rail, throw my liver and lights to the winner. Grind my nails up with sage and camphor and sell it under the counter. Set my hands in the window as a reminder. Take my name from me and make it a verb. Think of me when you run out of money. Remember me when you fall on the sidewalk. Mention me when they ask you what happened. I am everywhere under your feet.

TALKING DOT.COM INFERNO BLUES

Bruce Stutz

On my journalistic journeys I'd traveled near and far
even walked barefoot through the jungles of Madagascar,
tracking the rare and precious ring-tailed lemur
as they flung themselves from dangling lianas.
I had paddled a native dugout on the Amazon,
fished for pirahna, kayaked among the Alaskan
glaciers, trekked miles with reckless abandon
through Jordan's Dead Sea desert canyons.

From my first job on a suburban Jersey weekly
I had worked my way up to editor in chief
of a magazine with a half-million readers monthly
and a 3-million-dollar budget sheef.
But with prideful vision, boundless vanity
a little insanity, a hungering urgency
I left behind my job security
Placed my family in financial jeopardy
So I might write my way through the world of the literary
And here, I point you to Dante,
at least the first two verses which I had read
each night before falling asleep in bed:

TALKING DOT.COM INFERNO BLUES

"Midway on our life's journey, I found myself in dark woods, the right road lost. I found myself at Petplace.com. I'll tell what I saw though how I came to enter I cannot well say, being so full of sleep whatever moment it was I began to blunder off the true path."

Now, passing through an unmarked door,
I found myself in a dusty, moldy, eighth-floor
office in a crumbling building on Beekman
in lower Manhattan where the balky elevator
enveloped in murky vapors ascended, I'm certain,
on the fumes of french fries percolating
in cauldrons of hot golden fat fermenting
in Virgil's Stygian sandwich shop below.
Here, at Petplace, is what we want to know:
How do you get a ferret
to piss where you want it?
How do you bathe your chinchilla?
Housebreak your squirrel monkey?
When do you know your ailing iguana
Has begun to get a little too funky?
What do you feed your tree frog?
What if your cat drinks the eggnog?
How do you post-mortem your angelfish?
And keep your bird's shit out of its dish?
This, we were told, was what people want to know.
Not your elegant harangues on endangered species in
Borneo
Or craven political animals in their sinking archipelago.
Face it, you wouldn't be here if you were Italo Calvino.
There were few things worse for the ailing ego.

258

They were:
First, I agreed to do it.
Second, I needed to do it.
Third, there were others there doing it, too.
Lost souls who'd fallen into this first circle
Of dot.com hell and awaiting some acquittal,
Or some mercy now that fate had put
The shoe on the other foot.

My guide was Arthur, a man my own age,
who himself had been cast out of the page
and ink world. Once the much feared
editor of a New York daily tabloid
and now on a ghostlike trail of tears
Through the darkening dot.com void.

And there were others glum
who sat at their desks mum
As if the gates of hell
Were not far beyond
The french-fry smell.

Yet another New York daily editor
And a veteran staff reporter
A woman who'd run a team of journalists
And one who's career I'd match yours against.
All stared at computer monitors
Minds focused by some hypnotic spell
On dogs and cats and pets that dwell
In yards, cages, or glass enclosures.
I saw the best journalistic minds

Of my generation
In icy veneration
Of useless information
That any student
Who had thumb and forefinger intact
Could find in a library bookstack.

Then there were the real dot.com heads.
Here was Scott, bald and pie-eyed
With power, cache rich, RAM tough,
the systems hipster growing bolder
by the gigabyte, bold as his bowtie
Palmtop in his beltclip
Just chomping at the databit,
Ready to upload our downloads,
Transmography our content
Boot us when we crashed ignobly
Innoculate us against the virus
That once loosed will inevitably
Infect the ignorant and Web-weary.
While we mourned our losses,
Scott talked us through the process
Of getting our words to show up
On the screen without screw up.
Oh, Scott, for you, Dante's special grace:
May the Gods split you open
From your chin to the farting place.
And that, Arthur whispered, is Eisen.
Lost in a hell of which he's ignorant.
He's the third vice-president.
And that he must truly have been,
For in his seat was barely a dent,

But the man dressed well,
and strode with significant aplomb
to his desk where at times I glombed
A bit of his hard sell for his new CD-rom.
"Where in hell are *they* getting *their* money?"
And planning his son's bar mitzvah,
And downloading music from Napster,
And shouting to Scott, "I'm down
again, Scott, I guess it's time for lunch."
Or, "I'm going to the West Coast, big guy,
I'll be back next week on the red-eye."

And this, Arthur said, pointing
To a desk with no chair,
Is where you sit.

Our log on is petplace
Our provider is petplace
Our domain is petplace
Our password is petplace.

My job was to be a content provider
Which is not, I found, the same as a content provider.
The provisions with which we were to stock
The infinite miles of virtual shelves without surcease
were how-to's for the owners of all manner of beast:
fish, snakes, ferrets, frogs, birds, rabbits,
describing their habits, their cages and tidbits
of advice for their care.
Cats and dogs
Spiny hedgehogs

261

Rumpled chinchillas
Passing scintillas
Of knowledge
Or what passes
For knowledge
In five-hundred-word
Database-worthy,
Down-to-earth friendly
Nothing too meager
No first person singular
Installments.
I read you some of my best stuff:

You will find that each rat
Has his own personality
Some will eat and get fat
Others will be bullies.
Parents, I'm told out flat
Will devour their own babies.

Know that your hedgehog can really be fun
Although at first it seems
like you brought home a dead one.
But beware, be very aware
Of the dreaded Wobbly Hedgehog Syndrome
At present there is no cure
For this slow paralysis of the hedgehog hind limbs.
Dr. Grasser, however, is sure
That, quote, "You should try massage and homeopathic care."
And Laura Roberts of Pullyap

Swears she kept her Tommy alive on crystals, herbs, and
prayer.

Even blind ferrets
can do the litter-box bit
Just spread vanilla extract
Where you want them to shit.

If you prefer pre-killed mice
To live ones that squirm
Try the frozen food section
Right next to the worms.
Get the size that your snake can eat whole
For skin, bones, and internal organs all
Are vital for the nutrition of your animal.

Mosquito larvae make great food for your fish
But if the fish don't eat them you'll wish
They had.

Sir M, the Bunny of suburban Denver,
received the Human/Animal Bond Award
with its owner Vinita this last September.
This rabbit, says Vinita, saved my life
When medication failed
to cure my depression
And I was this close to suicide
I bought this rabbit, a glum little guy,
who looked about as depressed as I.
Now whenever I feel a bout
Of melancholy coming

I call Sir M and he comes running
and pet him and I even out.
He understands me, I tell you, like no other
For I'm sure he was taken too soon from his mother.

Koto the ferret got stepped on one day
His hindquarters crushed in a horrible way.
But Gloria Horton, a vet with a heart
Strapped a roller skate to his hind part
And now Koto can pull himself around
The office and someday, he's bound,
Hopes Horton, to run and play
Like other ferrets. Some days
He tries to make his legs go.
And some day, well, you never know.

Have fun with your chinchilla.
Give him a carpet remnant to sit on
and watch him move it around.
Never pick a gerbil up by his tail
it may break off.
Call the vet if you
Hear your hamster cough.

Oh, not in Dante's wildest imagination!
Not by the Furies most fevered imprecation!

"Here we encountered no laments that we could hear—except
for sighs that trembled the timeless air: they emanated from
the shadowy sadnesses, not agonies of multitudes of children
and women and men. He said, "And don't you ask, what

spirits are these? Before you go on, I tell you: they did not sin. Some lived before the dot.com faith, so that they did not worship aright—and I am one of these many worthy souls enduring suspension in this Limbo. "Did ever anyone go forth from here—by his own good or perhaps another's to join the blessed, after?"

My friends you see me here unstrung
And whether I deserve to be among
your blessed fellowship, judge what you see,
For I was too weak to escape my own misery.
Rather, the vicissitudes of the virtual universe
Brought an end to my wandering and my curse.
The word came from the main office
From the unseen masters of cyberspace
From God knows where
And God knows why
But this Petplace we were told
was corpus delecti.

I stopped back to the office the other day;
No trace was left of the computers or desks
A few cables lay on the floor; and the dust
from which we came had settled.
My virtual world had vanished
And the only reality that remained
Was the sickening smell of french fries.
I turned and left without remorse or goodbyes.

THE BATTLE FOR NEW YORK

Mike Wallace

I n mid 1863, with the city rancorously divided, Confederates invaded the North. On June 27, Lee's Army of Northern Virginia moved up the Shenandoah Valley, crushed the Union garrison at Winchester, crossed over the Potomac, and by June 29 was within ten miles of Harrisburg, the capital of Pennsylvania. Thousands of troops poured out of New York City to join General George Meade's army which, on July 1, engaged Lee at the town of Gettysburg.

The emergency left the city virtually stripped of defenses and wide open to invasion by southern ironclads. If Lee eluded Meade he could be in Jersey City, and at New York's throat, in a matter of days.

To make matters worse—far worse—it was at just this moment that the Federal Government's new Draft Law was to go into effect. Back in March, reacting to heavy losses, dwindling recruitment, and soaring desertion rates, Congress had passed the National Conscription Act. The legislation authorized government agents to go house-to-house, enrolling all 20-35 year old men (and all unmarried men 35-45), and then hold a lottery to choose draftees from this pool. The law also created federal Provost Marshals in each congressional district and gave them unprecedented power to summarily arrest

267

draft evaders, draft resisters and deserters. Finally, in a crude assertion of class privilege, the law provided that draftees could provide a substitute to fight in their place, or pay $300—a prohibitive sum for working people—for the government to use as a recruiting bounty.

This was not a popular law in New York. It represented, together with emancipation and the new tariff and banking laws, yet another massive increase in the intrusion of the Federal government into the city's communities, workplaces, even households. As the *Daily News* put it: "Conscription, that does not dare to invade a cottager's dwelling in monarchial Great Britain, steps arrogantly upon our Republican soil and draws lots for its victims from among the sons of industry, leaving the rich man to his luxurious repose."

The enrollment process proceeded peaceably enough in May and June, in part because leading Democrats like Governor Seymour vowed to initiate legal challenges to the act's constitutionality. Seymour also argued, correctly as it turned out, that Republicans had set unfairly high quotas for the heavily Democratic metropolis. Other voices counseled harsher tactics. Seymour, at a mass protest meeting on July 4th at the Academy of Music, used words he would later regret, telling the crowd: "Remember this—that the bloody and treasonable and revolutionary doctrine of public necessity can be proclaimed by a mob as well as by a government."

On July 4, news of the Union victory at Gettysburg began to trickle in over the telegraph wire, but the general jubilation was tempered by reports of the heavy casualties local soldiers had taken.

One week later, on Saturday, July 11, the lottery commenced. Seymour had failed even to get it postponed. Anticipating trouble, and still without military resources to back up the police, the authorities chose to begin the process on the city's periphery, at the Ninth District Headquarters on Third Avenue and 47th Street, an area of vacant lots and isolated buildings. It went reasonably well. While a large but good-tempered crowd watched, the Provost Marshal read off names drawn from a large barrel. By late afternoon, 1,236 draftees had been selected, at which point the office closed, leaving the remainder of the 2,000 man quota to be filled two days later.

The next morning, working class families pored over the names published in the Sunday papers. In bars and taverns around the city, men discussed their response over glasses of whisky, and large numbers of working class wives and mothers (the *Herald* reported) "mingled their wildest denunciations against the conscription law." A variety of protest activities were decided upon for the next day, Monday, July 13.

DAY ONE

Between six and seven in the morning, four hours before the lottery was scheduled to begin again, hundreds of workers from the city's railroads, machine shops, shipyards, and iron foundries, together with building and street laborers working for uptown contractors, began to stream up the west side along Eighth and Ninth Avenues. Beating copper pans as if they were gongs—a tactic familiar from labor protests— they closed shops, factories, and construction sites, moved on to a brief meeting in Central Park, and then marched, with "No Draft" placards aloft, toward the Provost Marshal's Office on Third Avenue. At 10:30, with a huge crowd gathered outside, the selection process started up, guarded by sixty hurriedly gathered police.

At this point another group arrived—the Black Joke Engine Company No. 33, in full regalia. The volunteer firemen, enraged at having lost their traditional exemption from military service, had decided to destroy all evidence that members of their unit had been drafted. They stoned the building, drove off the police, smashed the draft wheel, poured turpentine everywhere, fired the structure, and then drove away the arriving fire companies.

Word of all this reached the Provost Marshal's General Bureau headquarters. A thirty-two man squad of the Invalid Corps (composed of wounded or disabled veterans reassigned to light guard duties) was dispatched uptown on a Third Avenue horse-car through jeering and ever thicker crowds. When they reached 43rd Street they were met with a fusillade of hurled paving stones. They broke and ran. A similar experience awaited Police Superintendent John Kennedy. On hearing of the attack he hurried most of the way uptown by buggy, then tried to walk the remainder of the way up Lexington through the now huge throngs around the Ninth District Office. Recognized and identified by a former policeman, the crowd beat Kennedy about the head until he was unrecognizable.

By now the day had grown hot and humid; it made one feel "as if you had washed yourself in molasses and water," one participant recalled. The streets fumed with the usual rotting debris and excrement, the stench worsened by the stifling heat and humidity. Tremendous numbers of people poured out of the tenements. Crowd members began to isolate the area, cutting down telegraph poles that connected local police precincts to the Central Office. They stopped Second and Third Avenue Railroad cars. New Haven commuter trains were stoned, then Irish women crowbarred up the tracks of the Fourth Avenue line above 42nd Street. Rioters pulled down fences surrounding vacant lots to make clubs. The skirmishes spread into the East 40s around Third and Lexington. As small isolated detachments of police reserves were sent into the area they were routed, stomped, their bodies stripped, their faces smashed. Homes suspected of giving refuge to fleeing policemen were burned. Fury at the Metropolitans, banked for years, blazed up viciously.

Targets identifiable as Republican came under attack. On Fifth Avenue, a crowd menaced Republican Mayor Opdyke's house until dissuaded by Democrats. Sumptuous Fifth Avenue mansions were sacked, looted, burned. George Templeton Strong, watching the stoning of a house on Lexington off 45th rumored (wrongly) to be Horace Greeley's, concluded that "the beastly ruffians were masters of the situation and of the city." Some of the crowd now hived off downtown toward an armory at 21st Street and Second Avenue, really a rifle factory operated by a son-in-law of Mayor Opdyke, which contained a thousand weapons. The rioters so far had had few guns. The Broadway Squad arrived to defend the armory, but soon found themselves surrounded and stoned by thousands of men and women. Strong, who had followed along, depicted a crowd of Irish day laborers, including "low Irish women, stalwart young vixens and withered old hags" "all cursing the 'bloody draft' and egging on their men to mischief." Finally they stormed and occupied it around 4:00 PM and began carrying off carbines. When police reinforcements arrived, the crowd torched the building, trapping some rioters inside on the upper floors; of the thirteen who died at the Armory, ten perished in the fire.

At about the same time, a ugly second front opened up across town, as crowds hitherto focused on rich whites turned their fury on poor blacks. Patrick Merry, an Irish cellar-digger, led 200-300 men and boys down Broadway to West 29th Street where, at 5:00, they burned the deserted Eight District Provost Marshal's Office. Then they began attacking homes of African-Americans in the West 30s. The race riot had gotten underway.

Bands of Irish longshoremen, with quarrymen, street pavers, teamsters and cartmen following along, began chasing blacks, screaming "Kill all niggers!". Blacks were dragged off streetcars and stages around City Hall. The owner of a colored sailor's boardinghouse on Roosevelt Street in the Fourth Ward was robbed and stripped, his building fired. A crowd tried to attack black waiters at Crook's Restaurant in Chatham Street but was repulsed. Uptown, at Fifth Avenue and 43rd, rioters attacked the Colored Orphan Asylum, screaming "Burn the niggers nest". The 237 children (most under twelve years old) escaped—young Paddy McCafferty heroically shepherding them to the 20th Precinct house—while the crowd smashed pianos, carried off carpets and iron bedsteads, uprooted the trees, shrubs and fences, then set the building ablaze. Crowds would attack other moral reform projects, even those not associated with blacks. They stoned the Magdalene Asylum on Fifth at 88th Street and burned down the Five Points Mission.

When night fell, the racial assaults worsened. Some blacks were attacked on the corner of Varick and Charlton Streets by a crowd led by an Irish bricklayer. One of the pursued turned, shot the bricklayer with a pistol, and escaped; the maddened crowd grabbed one of the others, lynched him and then burned the corpse. Gangs attacked and torched waterfront tenements, dance houses, brothels, bars and boarding houses that catered to black workingmen. Bands of small boys would mark the victims' houses by stoning windows, then return with older men to finish the job. Racially mixed couples, white women who consorted with blacks, anyone who defied taboos on "amalgamation" were specially targeted. By mid-week rioters had virtually emptied the downtown waterfront of blacks.

The same evening a debate broke out amongst the authorities about how to respond to the upheaval. During the day, Mayor Opdyke's approach of dispatching small bands of police to the uptown working class wards had proven drastically counterproductive; it had enraged the crowds and provoked massive and murderous retaliation. Now Strong and some Union League Club colleagues proposed another strategy. They hurried over to the St. Nicholas Hotel, where General Wool had established his headquarters, and begged him to declare martial law and summon federal troops to enforce it. Wool refused, though he did order troops moved in from Fort Hamilton to assist the police. Disgusted, Strong and the others telegraphed Lincoln directly, asking for troops, and then went to the home of David Dudley Field in Gramercy Park where friends gathered with muskets.

At 11:00 P.M., drenching cooling rain brought the day to a close.

THE BATTLE FOR NEW YORK CITY

As Tuesday dawned hot and dry, crowds crystallized all over the city, broke into gun shops to arm themselves, and launched firefights against a variety of targets. Far from being random anarchic outbursts, the attacks focused on those in command of the new industrial and political order.

Rioters swept the streets clear of wealthy individuals— readily identifiable by their clothes and bearing ("There goes a $300 man!" "Down with the rich men!"). They attacked genteel homes and trashed (more often than stole) the fancy furniture.

They lit into Republican enterprises. Crowds attacked and sacked Brooks Brothers, hated for being hard employers and shoddy contractors; went after German clothing stores along Grand Street; and would have marched on Wall Street had it not been the best defended area in the entire city. Customs House workers prepared bombs with 40 second fuses. Employees of the Bank Note Company readied tanks of sulfuric acid to spill on attackers. At the Subtreasury Building on the corner of Nassau Street, guns and bottles of vitriol were passed out to employees stationed at windows, troops with howitzers were stationed nearby, and a gunboat anchored at the foot of Wall Street.

The crowds, particularly the women, beat policemen and soldiers, the agents of upper class and Federal power. When Colonel Henry O'Brien of the Eleventh New York Volunteers used a howitzer to clear Second Avenue and killed a woman bystander and a child, the crowds (when they found him the next day) beat his face to a pulp, then stripped, tortured, and shot him in the head, and hung his broken body from a lamppost.

Rioters began erecting barricades, cordoning off their waterfront neighborhoods from center-island bourgeois districts. On the east side, industrial metal trades workers used cut-down telegraph poles, carts, wagons, lumber, boxes, bricks, and rubbish to run a line along First Avenue (particularly solid from 11th to 14th Streets) and along Third Avenue on up to 26th Street—areas with high concentrations of large metal-working establishments. On the west side, waterfront laborers drew their lines along Ninth Avenue, most solidly from 36th to 42nd Streets, from where they could dominate most of the upper west side. To hinder the summoning of outside reinforcements, they cut telegraph lines—as Indians did out West—and assaulted ferry slips and railroads.

Rioters also pursued the race war. Brandishing poles and clubs, they hunted blacks on the streets, mauled them along the docks, went after black workers in restaurants and hotels. They attacked black homes and stores around Bleecker and Carmine Streets, except where blacks tore down chimneys for bricks to hurl at attackers, or, as in Minetta Lane, guarded their homes with guns.

Divisions now appeared in the rioters' ranks. Many original protestors had envisioned at most a one day anti-draft demonstration, and certainly not a general onslaught on private property. Large numbers of them—particularly the Germans, though many Irish Catholics and native Protestants as well—abandoned violence and even joined with the authorities. Squads of Turnverein and Schutzenverien patrolled the streets of Kleindeutschland. Volunteer fire companies (including the Black Joke men who had started the riot) turned out to defend their neighborhoods against riot and arson. Crowds, at times led by Irish priests like Father Treanor of Transfiguration, intervened to halt lynch mobs.

While the battle raged on the streets, two sharply opposed factions within the city's upper classes argued over how to respond to the uprising. On one side were those businessmen and Democratic officials who, in effect, treated the riots as an appeals to elites to respect and protect customary working class rights and privileges. Governor Seymour dispatched gentlemen and clergymen to negotiate face-to-face with the crowds, displaying the confidant paternalism of the old upper class. On Tuesday morning, he himself, flanked by Tammany leaders A. Oakley Hall and William Tweed, pledged a large crowd at City Hall (whom he addressed as "My Friends") that he would work for postponement of or relief from the draft, while repudiating violence.

At noon, Mayor Opdyke asked Secretary of War Stanton for troops. Stanton complied that evening but had the request come even a day earlier it would have put him in a difficult spot. After Gettysburg, Lee's army, wounded and dangerous, had remained in the area, and Union forces had been tied down in blocking a possible move northward. As it happened, Lee escaped south across the Potomac the night of Monday the 13th, leaving Stanton free to divert five regiments.

Troops began arriving Wednesday evening, a day of atrocities during which crowds had hung, drowned, and mutilated black men, looted and burned black homes up and down Sixth Avenue, attacked Republican mansions and Protestant missions. In Brooklyn hundreds of men, including some disgruntled ex-employees, invaded the Atlantic Docks and burned two of the hated grain elevators, and along the East River north and east of Fulton Street, blacks were beaten and killed, their houses ransacked and destroyed.

Promptly on arrival, the soldiers from Pennsylvania took up arms against the rioters, aided by volunteer companies set up by merchants and bankers who mobilized their employees. Fighting continued all Wednesday night and throughout the next day. Troops assaulted "infected" districts, using how-itzers loaded with grapeshot and canister (primitive fragmen-tation bombs) to mow down rioters, and engaged in fierce building-by-building firefights. Rioters defended their barri-caded domains with mad desperation. Faced with tenement snipers and brick hurlers, soldiers broke down doors, bayo-neted all who interfered, and drove occupants to the roofs, where many jumped to certain death below.

By Thursday evening it was all over. The city filled with 6000 troops. Seventh Regiment pickets manned Third Avenue. The Eight Regiment Artillery Troop trained mountain howitzers on streets around Gramercy Park. The 152nd New York Volunteers set up camp in Stuyvesant Square. By Friday, telegraph lines were being repaired, west side rails relaid. Omnibuses and horsecars ran. Laborers returned to work. It was over.

ON THE WATERFRONT

Budd Schulberg

How *On the Waterfront* managed to reach the screen is a story with more ups and downs than the plot of the movie itself. Oddly enough, it has never been told. And yet it deserves its place in Hollywood film history as one of those rare moments when the writer succeeded—with massive help from his director/collaborator Elia Kazan—in getting his work to the screen despite the resistance of all the major studios, the Hollywood Establishment at its most stubbornly reactionary—or to put it more gently, blindly conservative—back in the 50s when studios could still be called "major."

Once upon a time—so our fairy tale fades in—this writer was living on his farm in Pennsylvania doing novels, and thinking he would devote the rest of his life to that nice, quiet work, when he received a visit from the famous director of *Gentleman's Agreement, Viva Zapata,* and *A Streetcar Named Desire*: Elia Kazan. Kazan wanted to know if the writer would like to do a picture with him—not a Hollywood movie, but a film to be conceived, written, and shot in the East. Since I had just finished a novel and didn't feel ready to start another, the idea appealed to me. I felt I had left Hollywood as a place to live and work because the screenwriter was low man on the

279

totem. Producers and directors used a writer's work but never seemed to respect him as the true source of the production. Even famous writers, be they Dorothy Parker, Scott Fitzgerald, Aldous Huxley, or John Van Druten, were treated as dispensable and expendable hired hands. Screenwriting, it seemed to me, was simply not a self-respecting line of work. Once in a while a Dudley Nichols enjoyed his work with John Ford, a Bob Riskin with Frank Capra, or a Ben Hecht would light up the screen for a month, make his twenty-five thousand, and get the hell back to "21." But until I got talking to Kazan about the possibilities of an "Eastern," I was quite prepared never to write another script for the rest of my life.

But if I worked with him, Kazan promised, instead of the Hollywood imbalance, he would respect the writer and his script as he had respected Arthur Miller, Tennessee Williams, and other playwrights with whom he had worked closely in the theater.

At first we discussed a film on "The Trenton Six," a northern version of the racist persecution of "The Scottsboro Boys." For a few weeks I researched the case in and around the grubby Trenton area. As Gadg (the familiar nickname for Kazan) and I sifted the complication of the Trenton case we came back to a subject we had touched on at our first meeting: the waterfront. The great harbor of New York—from the luxury line piers on the Hudson to the hoary docks of Brooklyn. Coincidentally, both of us had been bitten by the waterfront bug. A project Kazan had begun with Arthur Miller had aborted. I had been approached by a nephew of Harry Cohn to dramatize Malcolm Johnson's Pulitzer Prize–winning *Crime On the Waterfront,* but, ironically, the hard-mouthed Cohn would have none of it.

Now Kazan and I decided to plunge in again. The first step was research, not merely to read the soundly documented Johnson material but to go down to the docks and get the feel of it for myself. "To go down to the docks" is an oversimplification. What I actually had to do was work my way into what I soon discovered was a self-contained city-state: 750 miles of shoreline, with 1800 piers, handling ten thousand oceangoing ships a year, carrying over a million passengers a year and over thirty-five million tons of foreign cargo with a value of around eight billion dollars.

What I was soon to discover, following leads from Mike Johnson, was this seagoing treasury was in the pocket of the mob—the Bowers mob on Manhattan's west side, the Anastasia family in Brooklyn (including "Albert A," chief executioner of Murder, Inc.), the Italian and Irish Mafias murdering each other for control of the Jersey waterfront. "Cockeye" Dun (who later went to the chair) and his partner "Freddie McGurn" (who later retired in style to Miami) ran the Chelsea section on Manhattan's lower west side as if it were their private hunting and killing preserve.

At least 10 percent of everything that moved in and out of the harbor went into the pockets of these desperados. And if you were one of the 25,000 longshoremen looking for work, either you kicked back to a hiring boss appointed by mob overlords with the connivance of "legitimate" shipping and stevedore officials, or they starved you off the docks.

As inevitably happens under a system of oppression and vicious exploitation, a handful of braves were refusing to take this lying down. Such a group fascinated me when I met them with "the waterfront priest," Father John Corridan, at St. Xavier's in the dangerous Dunn-McGrath neighborhood.

Father John's effect on me was nothing less than to revolu-
tionize my attitude toward the Church. I approached it with
the prejudice of a liberal freethinker. In Father John, a tall,
fast-talking, chain-smoking, hardheaded, sometimes profane,
Kerryman, I found the antidote to the stereotyped Barry
Fitzgerald-Bing Crosby "Fah-ther" so dear to Hollywood
hearts. In the west-side saloons I listened intently to Father
John, whose speech was a unique blend of Hell's Kitchen,
baseball slang, an encyclopaedic grasp of waterfront economics, and an attack on man's inhumanity to man based on
the teachings of Christ as brought up to date in the Papal
Encyclicals on the reconstruction of the social order.

When I told Kazan about my discovery, he had to see this
cassocked phenomenon for himself. Father John was in great
form that day. He was furious at "Spellman," as he called the
cardinal, for recommending Bill McCormack as a recipient of
the highest honor a layman could receive in the Church.
McCormack was the "Mister Big" of the waterfront, into sand
and gravel, trucking, stevedoring, and virtually everything
that moved in and out of New York. The ILA president, Joe
Ryan, was "his office boy". What upset Father John was that
these waterfront powers not only condoned but fronted for
and benefited from organized crime: "Sunday Catholics"
who defied, in the words of Pius XI, "the clear principles of
justice and Christian charity." "The damn Power House could
clean this mess up in five minutes if it really read the riot act
to those SOBs," Father John exploded. "But the whole trouble
is, they see all that cabbage. So we gotta help the boys on the
docks do the job, from the bottom up."

After that session, Kazan and I paused to catch our breath
at a corner saloon. "Well, what do you think?" I said, as proud

of Father John as if I had created him myself. "Are you sure he's a priest?" Gadg asked.

"My God, he's wearing a cassock—and we meet him in St. Xavier's."

"Maybe he's working there for the waterfront rebels in disguise . . ."

"Gadg, you've been seeing too many movies . . . Hollywood movies!" We both laughed, overjoyed, excited. Father John was a priest, a ruddy-faced Irish version of one of those French worker-priests, and we both knew we had to write his character and his morality into our picture.

The research took a dramatic turn. One of Father John's most devoted disciples was little Arthur Browne, proud of the fact that he was one of the stand-up "insoigents" in the Chelsea local run by the fat cats and their "pistoleros." With his flattened nose, his cocky laugh, and his stringpiece vocabulary, Brownie reminded me of those tough little bantamweights who used to delight the New York boxing fans.

Brownie promised to take me in hand and "walk me through the waterfront," but first we had to work up a cover story. Even in the bars friendly to the "insoigents," his pals would wonder what he was doing with this obvious outsider. They would think "reporter" or "cop" and in either case Brownie (and I) would be in jeopardy. Since I knew boxing and co-managed a fighter, and since longshoremen are avid fight fans, Brownie would tell the curious that we had met at Stillman's gym, fallen to conversation about fighters and had simply drifted over to the west side to quench our "thoist." "I'll point out the various characters and shoot the breeze and you listen 'n drink your beer."

It worked fine. We drank boilermakers, Brownie got a

group talking, I listened and made mental notes as to how I could work the dialogue into the script. One night we worked our way from bar to bar until we were opposite Pier 18. A saturnine man in a grey suit was at the bar and somehow, on my fifth boilermaker, I forgot my usual role and asked the stranger what he did. Brownie grabbed me, and the next thing I knew we were running down the street toward our "home block."

"Jesus, Mary, n' Joseph, you wanna get us both killed? Y'know who that guy was? Another Albert A. He's topped more people 'n Cockeye Dunn. I'm gonna tell Father John you're fired! We need a smarter resoicher."

Then he gave that undefeated laugh of his. The cowboys had flattened his nose, thrown him through a skylight, and even into the river unconscious. "Lucky it was winter and the cold water revived me!" I lived with this sawed-off Lazarus and his wife Anne in their coldwater flat. I sat at the kitchen table and wrote down lines I could never make up: "Ya know what we gotta get rid of—the highocracy! Wait'll I see that bum again—I'll top him off lovely." And for revenge: "I'll take it out of their skulls!"

Sometimes it seemed as if everybody I talked to on the waterfront said something usable. I had left Hollywood because there were too many collaborators. Here I was surrounded by them—and welcomed every one of them.

The research became a year-long experience that I shared with Kazan. Out of day-and-night talkfests at my farm and his house on 72nd Street, with his critical-minded wife, Molly, sometimes sitting in as catalyst—"a helpful pain-in-the-ass," one playwright described her—we thrashed out the characters, the story line, the theme. Involved in the rebel longshore movement and writing articles on their behalf in the *New York Times Magazine*, the *Saturday Evening Post*, and *Commonweal*, I finished the screenplay in a high state of excitement. Kazan shared my enthusiasm for it. In fact, he went further, "It's one of the three best I've ever had! And the other two where *Death of a Salesman* and *A Streetcar Named Desire!*"

Owing Zanuck a picture at 20th Century Fox, he had written Darryl a zippy "Here we come!" letter about the zinger of a script we had sent out to him. I was a little worried. We had chosen a tough subject. We had taken real characters and put them through a struggle that was still being waged. Was it too somber, too real for the Hollywood Dream Machine? Gadg tried to allay my fears. Zanuck wasn't your typical big studio rajah. No L.B. Mayer who only wanted to make happy family pictures. Had I forgotten the Zanuck who made *The Grapes of Wrath, How Green Was My Valley,* and the then-controversial *Gentleman's Agreement*? "Darryl will love it," Gadg kept assuring me on the long ride out on The Super Chief. It was a writer's dream trip, long lunches in the dining car, with my director exclaiming, "I don't think you realize how great this is!" and the writer saying with belly and ego stuffed, "No, Gadg, tell me how great it is . . ." whereupon my Greek friend would go into what was becoming almost a religious litany . . . *"Salesman . . . Streetcar . . . Waterfront . . ."*

It was the nicest trip to California I ever had, and I hoped it would never end. When we pulled in to the old Santa Fe station in downtown Los Angeles, there was no studio limousine to meet us. When I remarked on this omission, Kazan, the prosperous proletarian, snorted, "C'mon, Budd, who the hells needs a studio limo?—let's grab a cab."

In our suite at the Beverly Hills Hotel (where my mother

had brought me in 1920 to get away from the sinful Alexandria), I noticed that there were no flowers. "Flowers!" Gadg exploded, "What are you—some kind of fruitcake? Who the hell needs flowers?"

"We're in trouble," I said.

"F'christsake, stop worrying. We've got a gutty script. Darryl has guts. He's got to love it."

"I think he hates it," I said.

"Budd, we just got here. Give the man a break. He's running a big studio. Wait 'til he sees us."

But I had been raised in Hollywood. I knew the unspoken language. No limo and no roses, no loving welcome note, and no invitation to come down to Palm Springs for the big Sunday croquet match spelled big trouble.

After an anxious weekend of intense tennis and Polo Lounging, we called Darryl's office at 20th first thing Monday morning. Apparently Darryl was still on his croquet field. We should "stand by." His secretary would call us as soon as she could set up an appointment. "Darryl hates it," I said, "or he would have called us from Palm Springs to say hello."

"Let's not jump to conclusions," said a now slightly nervous Kazan. We waited through Monday morning and were finally summoned in the early afternoon. In the outer office was Bella Darvi, the latest European import. My Hollywood upbringing warned me which of us would be called in first. We put in perhaps another half hour while Miss Darvi was in conference with Darryl. Finally we were in the Mussolini-sized office of the fearless producer of *The Grapes of Wrath*.

"Know what I love about this business—there's always something new happening!" Zanuck greeted us. "First there weren't enough frames to a foot, so the picture flickered. Then they got smooth natural movement. Then sound. Talkies! And just when the public was getting tired of black and white talkies, in came color, Technicolor—and now Cinerama! Can you imagine *Prince Valiant* in Cinerama? All those beautiful broads in silky gowns practically on top of you! I tell you, this is an exciting business!"

Gadg and I were exchanging looks. Our picture, he had written Darryl, was to be *black-and-white,* just plain flat black-and-white.

"Darryl," Gadg asked, "have you read our script?"

Kazan has a voice developed in the theater, but Darryl did not seem to hear it. As he went on about Prince Valiant and the wonders of Cinerama, Gadg interrupted, louder: "Look Darryl, we didn't come all the way from New York to talk about your effing *Prince Valiant.* What about *Waterfront*? Have you read Budd's script?"

There was a long pause. Darryl took a step backward. We pressed forward. It could have been a scene out of one of the gangster movies Darryl had made at Warners. "Yes, Darryl, what about it?" I echoed Gadg. Darryl kept edging back toward the security of his desk. We kept moving forward.

"Well . . . I read it, and boys, I'm sorry, but I didn't like a single thing about it."

A stricken writer: "Not one thing?"

A furious director: "Not a single thing about it? Darryl, you gotta be kidding!" And Gadg recited his lexicon of the script's virtues: "It's unique—something different—it catches the whole spirit of the harbor—the way you caught the Okies in *Grapes*."

"But the Okies came across like American pioneers." The

mark of a tycoon is to have answers ready for any challenge. "Who's going to care about a lot of sweaty longshoremen?"

Sweaty longshoremen! I thought of Father John's gritty group: unsinkable Brownie, the heroes of Pier 45, Tony Mike in Hoboken . . . were they not waterfront Joads who would endure? But Darryl was rubbing salt in the wound: "I think what you've written is exactly what the American people don't want to see."

There were angry accusations about broken contracts and our "handshake deal" with the porous Spyras Skouras who had made large promises and cooed, "Make it a beautiful love story."

We had been given an office in the directors' building and when we ran out of Darryl's throne room we could think of nothing better to do than to trash that office—turn over the desk, throw the chairs, hurl the telephone . . . When our rage was spent, a little, we decided to confiscate the typewriter, typing paper, and office supplies and retreat to our foxhole in the Beverly Hills Hotel.

"Don't worry, Buddy. Screw Darryl. I'm still very hot in this town. Every studio in town wants me to do a picture for them. Jack Warner—"

"Don't tell *me*, tell *him* . . ."

I was feeling a little sore at Gadg. His Darryl Zanuck and all that brave bullshit about Grapes of Wrath. A few minutes later he had Jack Warner on the phone. "Hello Jack, listen, baby (Gadg can do the Hollywood bit pretty well when he wants to)—I've got a great property for you—a powerful story— *Public Enemy*—*Chain Gang*—the kind you guys do better 'n anybody else in town!" He told our story, crisply, vividly, and then I heard a lot of "Buts . . ." "But it isn't just a labor story. . . . But it isn't downbeat and grim, it's got. . . . But there is a love story tied into the main plot. . . . But. . . ."

When Gadg hung up I already knew we were dead at Warner Brothers. And a day later ditto at Paramount and MGM. A messenger picked it up at dawn to rush it over to Columbia and it seemed we had hardly finished breakfast when the script was back on our laps. Belay that. Make it teeth. We didn't have any laps. We were pacing up and down in our bathrobes, all day, all night. Friends called to ask us out to dinner at Chasen's but we felt too beaten-down to get dressed, or be seen. Anybody who's ever worked in Hollywood knows how tough it is to go out on the town a loser. In my hometown losing and leprosy are interchangeable.

The *Hollywood Reporter* drove the final nail into what seemed to be our coffin with an item in its gossip column explaining that all the studios in town were cold-shouldering our project because it dealt with waterfront radicals and was pretty communistic.

Gadg wondered if we could do it as a play. And to his everlasting credit, after every Hollywood studio had thumbed us down, this director commanding a $250,000 salary—if only he would direct what *they* wanted him to do—swore to me, "Goddamn it, I'm going to stick with this thing if I have to get a 16mm Eyemo and shoot it myself on the docks."

Since 20th Century had shut off our expense account, I decided the better part of valor was to get the hell back to Bucks Country and try it as a novel. Meanwhile, whether it was determination or just nervous energy, we kept banging away at the typewriter we had liberated from 20th. Despite our depression, we kept getting new ideas for scenes, tightening, sharpening, rewriting. We took turns at the typewriter.

The floor was littered with paper balls of discarded pages. Romantics might describe the atmosphere as inspired. Realists would call it manic.

Occasionally our door would open for room service or a friend from Suicides Anonymous, just as the door directly across the corridor opened, offering us a glimpse of the international producer who fancied himself as "S. P. Eagle," whose square handle was Sam Spiegel. Spiegel had been in Berlin when Hitler came to power. He fled Vienna, Paris, London, Mexico, New York, and finally back to Hollywood, where he had been fired by Paul Bern in the late '20s. Spiegel had gone down as often as Primo Carnera. But he had gotten up more often. With his keen mind, courtly manners (to those he courted), and sybaritic tastes, he was a very special kind of Wandering Jew, a throwback to the days when pirates were heroes if they were *your* pirates. When he was up he was very up and when he was down he knew the Hollywood and Middle-European game of behaving even more successfully. He had been up with *The African Queen* but now he was down with *Melba,* a costly mistake no theater even wanted to book. But the way Sam was living it up you would have thought he was celebrating an Oscar winner. We saw beautiful ladies enter his suite and heard Sam's ingratiating "Darling!" Waiters arrived with buckets of champagne. Sharon Douglas. George Stevens. If ever anyone knew how to ride out a loser, it was S. P. Eagle.

Enter Mr. S. In his elegant suit of midnight blue, smelling of expensively crushed French lilacs, he looked around in disdain at our paper-littered floor, our unpressed bathrobes, our unshaven faces, and urged us to clean ourselves up and come across the corridor to his party.

"Thanks Sam, but we're in no mood for parties."

S. P. stared at the crumpled paper. "Are you boys in trouble?"

We each grabbed him by the arm and poured out our Hollywood horror story.

He looked at Kazan and became thoughtful. "Why don't you come by my room tomorrow morning and tell me the story?"

"It's got to be awful early," I said. "I'm flying home in the morning. Leaving the hotel at eight sharp."

"I'll see you at seven," said S. P. Eagle, and then, thinking ahead as always, "I'll leave the door unlocked so I won't have to get up."

Next morning on the dot of seven I walked through the party litter of the living room to the bedroom where S. P. Eagle lay inert in the splendid bed, as if in state.

"Sam?"

"Hmmm. . . ." Snores.

"Sam, it's seven o'clock, I'm here to tell you the story."

"Hmmm."

I didn't have much time before catching my plane so I began . . . haltingly, as it's not easy to talk into a cave of silence. But the muscle of the story began to stir me—damn it, there was a reason why Gadg and I had clung to it so desperately—and I began to pace around the large double bed ignoring its motionless occupant as I followed Terry Malloy through his waterfront ordeal. Occasionally I would pause and say "Sam? . . . Sam?" receive a faintly reassuring "Hmmm" and press on. When I reached the climax, the eyes of the listener—with a sheet and blanket drawn up over his chin—remained shut. There was a long silence, during which I thought about my waiting plane and the retreat to my Bucks Country farm. Then there was a slight stirring under the blanket. The head managed to raise up a few inches. "I'll do it," a murmur rose from the pillow. "We'll make the picture."

Later that same morning I flew East with the Eagle, who proceeded to set up a low-budget deal with United Artists. But there was still to be many a slip between script and production. Gadg sent our brainchild to Marlon Brando and he promptly sent it back. I claimed he hadn't bothered to read it. From my OSS days I had learned a sneaky trick of inserting tiny bits of paper between the pages of a book or manuscript. If they have not moved or fallen out, the work has not been read. The Brando script came back with the paper slips in place. Then a tough little Hoboken kid agreed to play the part: Frank Sinatra. UA wouldn't put up more than $500,000 for Frank. Gadg felt we needed a minimum of eight. Then Spiegel and Kazan went to work on Marlon. Spiegel wined, dined, wooed, and seduced. Gadg reminded him how he had fought to give him the lead in *Streetcar* when producer Irene Selznick preferred a bigger star, also very right for the role, John Garfield. Ironically I had talked to Julie—as we knew him— about possibly playing Terry Malloy when we were first getting into the research. But Julie's career and life were being destroyed by his pathetically "Un-American" activities, and he died of a heart attack before our project was under way. He would have been good, maybe great. But as Gadg rightly insisted about Brando, he brought that extra something, the magic, the mystery, the gift of doing the unexpected that makes for genius.

With Brando on board, the wily S. P. was able to jettison Sinatra and UA and bring our project to Columbia who now accepted what they had twice rejected. We were in business at last. Kazan plunged enthusiastically into the casting, mostly

from the Actor's Studio: Lee Cobb for the dock boss, Karl
Malden for "Father John," Rod Steiger for Marlon's mobby
brother, even the small parts, Marty Balsam as a waterfront
crime investigator. For the innocent Catholic girl we thumbed
through the entire *Players' Guide Directory* and finally came to
Eva Marie Saint for her screen debut.

The screenplay that Gadg had fought for so uncompromis-
ingly still went through a lot of rewrites. Spiegel was a
taskmaster. A bear for structure. He thought it was overlength
and sometimes discursive. Lots of times he was right. I
respected his story mind. Still do. But he could be madden-
ingly manipulative. In his suite at the St. Regis, where our
daily story conferences were held, I used to hate to go to the
bathroom because I would return to the sitting room to find
S. P. whispering to Gadg. I finally exploded. "I've been on this
goddamned project for two years. I've taken practically nothing
up front. I'm gambling like you on a percentage of the profits.
It's beginning to break me. I've actually had to mortgage my
farm. Sam hasn't paid me the lousy five thousand dollars he's
owed me for months. I've written my heart out on this god-
damn thing. So what the hell can you two bastards be whispering about?"

I walked out. Gadg followed. We walked around the block.
He was sympathetic. He didn't blame me for being sore. Sam
did have maddening ways. He was naturally conspiratorial. He
was jealous of the fact that Gadg and I worked so closely as a
team. Just as he tried to separate me from Marlon or Marlon
from Gadg. Divide and rule. He had to feel that he was in control. But, Gadg reminded me, there was one thing I should
remember: with "S. P. Eagle" we were coming to bat with two
outs in the bottom of the ninth. If we couldn't score with him,

Waterfront was dead. "Let's face it, Sam Spiegel has saved our ass." I had to agree. Back to St. Regis. The fight went on.

One tough round I won: the scene in the hold when Brownie—whom I called "Kayo"—is crushed in an "accident" and "Father Pete Barry," climbs down into the hold to deliver the last rites. There he makes a fighting speech about "Christ in the shape-up," comparing the feisty "insoigent's" death to the Crucifixion. His dialogue—taken almost verbatim from Father Corridan's daring Sermon on the Docks—ran over three pages, and Spiegel insisted that while a speech that long might hold in a novel, it had no place in a screenplay for a picture that ought to be taut and spare. Day after day he hammered at this until, each time he asked me for the cuts in the Father Barry scene in the hold, rather than repeat myself, I would simply go to the window, open it, lean my elbows on the sill and stare out in silence.

At last, as he did so often, Gadg came to the rescue. "Sam, why don't we drop this and go on? I know it *reads* long but I know how to shoot it. Against all the tension between Kayo's pals and the mob. And Marlon caught in the middle, torn, feeling the guilt. I'll be cutting to him, and Tami Mauriello and Tony Galento (the fighters I had brought Gadg, along with Abe Simon, Lee Oma, and a lot of other old heavyweights to play the goons). It won't be static or talky, believe me. Let me handle it."

And finally when we got into production, in bitter winter on the Hoboken docks, Gadg handled that scene, and every other one in the script, with a fierce veracity that proved how effectively cinematic theatricality and cinematic verité can be combined in a unified dramatic experience. Often I would sit with Gadg late into the night while he mapped out his next day's shooting. He would point out what dialogue he thought was dispensable because of his visual attack on the scene. There were dawns when I sat with him on a frigid Hoboken rooftop, or in a squalid cold-water flat, or in the riverfront saloons that became "sets" for the picture, rewriting scenes that needed adjustments to fit the actual demands of those rugged locations.

At the outset Gadg had made his promise not to change a line of the script, but I would have to make a counter-promise: either to be on the set with him every day or to be on call to make the changes accommodating the practical and creative exigencies. Even though he had to shoot the picture in hostile territory, with police protection to guard him and the embattled company from an aroused waterfront under-world, Gadg kept his promise. Oh sure, lines overlapped, good, fresh words were thrown in spontaneously, but scene by scene Gadg stuck to the script, inventing and improving with staging that surprised and delighted me.

One day, fighting weather, fighting light, trying to hold together a crew so cold, miserable, and contemptuously treated by S. P. Eagle that it was ready to mutiny, Gadg fell a day behind schedule. Sam came to the "set," a frozen, dingy alleyway, in his slick limousine with his compulsory accessory, a lovely lady. The scent of Chateaubriand from "21" was still on their breath . . . Sam had called Charley Maguire, the heroic assistant director, at four in the morning to ask him, "if he couldn't get Gadg to go faster." Although I had not been talking to Sam on the eve of the first day of shooting—when I said I would not show up unless he promised to stay away—we had made up one more time and he had also called me at some ungodly hour to urge me to urge Gadg to shoot faster.

Gadg walked away from Sam and came to me. "Budd, I've had it. I warned that son of a bitch, if he came on this set once more and broke our concentration, I was gonna quit!"

And now it was my turn to coo, "Gadg, one thing you've got to remember. We were down to our last out. Let's face it, Sam Spiegel saved our ass."

Gadg laughed, somehow finessed Sam and his lovely back into their limo and "21," and to on with the job he shot so brilliantly in thirty-five days.

When our picture went on to win its record number of Oscars, and break box office records, revenge was more bitter than sweet. We kept hearing Darryl's deadly, "What you've written is exactly what the American people don't want to see." But just for once, getting a script to the screen in the spirit in which it had been conceived—thanks to that rare director who refused to make a distinction between playright and screen-playwright—was victory enough. Find me a director who respects the *play*, as Kazan respected not only this one but Bill Inge's, Tennessee Williams's or Paul Osborn's, and the *auteur* theory will float away from the hollow, gaseous thing it is. What will remain will be solid screenplays, and solid directors who will not only embellish but vivify them.

SEX,
POLITICS,
AND THE
INEFFABLE

DARK MATTERS

Neil de Grasse Tyson

There is no way to put it gently. The twentieth century ended without us knowing the composition of 90 percent of the matter in the universe. What we call "dark matter" emits no light in any form and does not interact with ordinary (household) matter by any known means. Its identity remains a mystery, although its gravity is immediately apparent. In an example from our home galaxy, the outer regions of our Milky Way revolve around the galactic center ten times faster than they otherwise would, were it not for the actions of dark matter. Ordinary matter and dark matter coexist, not in parallel universes, but side by side in the same universe. They feel each other's gravity, but otherwise do not respond to each other's presence.

Perhaps astrophysicists are at the dawn of a new era of scientific discovery, just as physicists were in 1900. At the time, various loose threads in prevailing theories began to unravel. They eventually unraveled completely, opening the door to entirely new branches of physics. One of them, called quantum mechanics, accurately accounts for nature's behavior on its smallest scales—those of molecules, atoms, and particles. Nearly a dozen Nobel prizes were awarded to the scientific leaders of that effort. Dark matter may be a rich assortment of exotic subatomic particles, as some theories have proposed. But it may be something yet to be imagined. The dark matter dilemma in astrophysics at the dawn of the twenty-first century may force a revolution in our understanding of gravity and (or) matter that rivals the scientific revolutions of the past.

Occasionally, I cannot help but personalize, even personify, dark matter's place in the universe. Especially the part about matter and dark matter feeling each other's gravity but not otherwise interacting. This schism came home to me during the spring of my sophomore year at Harvard; I was well into the course work of my declared major, taking an (un)healthy dose of physics and math classes as well as the requisite other nonscience courses that a full schedule requires. That year I was also on the University's wrestling team, as second-string to a more talented senior in my 190-pound weight category. One day after practice, we were walking out of the athletic facility when he asked me what I had been up to lately. I replied, "My problem sets are taking nearly all of my time. And I barely have time to sleep or go to the bathroom." Then he asked me what my academic major was. When I told him physics, with a special interest in astrophysics, he paused for a moment, waved his hand in front of my chest, and declared, "Blacks in America do not have the luxury of your intellectual talents being spent on astrophysics."

No wrestling move he had ever put on me was as devastating as those accusatory words. Never before had anyone so casually, yet so succinctly indicted my life's ambitions. My wrestling buddy was an economics major and, a month earlier, had been awarded the Rhodes Scholarship to Oxford where, upon graduation, he planned to study innovative economic solutions to assist impoverished urban communities. I knew in my mind that I was doing the right thing with my life (whatever the "right thing" meant), but I knew in my heart that he was right. And until I could resolve this inner conflict, I would forever carry a level of suppressed guilt for pursuing my esoteric interests in the universe.

During graduation week of my senior year of college, an article appeared in the *New York Times* that broadly profiled the 131 black graduates of my Harvard class of 1,600 people. The *Times* made public, for the first time, that only two of the 131 graduates had plans to continue for advanced academic degrees. I was one of those two. The rest were slated for law school, medical school, business school, or self-employment. (The other "academic" was a friend of mine from the Bronx High School of Science who graduated college in four years with both his bachelor's and master's degrees in history.) Given these data I became further isolated from the brilliant good-deed-doers of my generation. Nine years passed. Having earned my master's degree from the University of Texas at Austin, I spent several more years there before leaving to teach for a year at the University of Maryland and finally transferring my doctoral program to Columbia University. At Columbia, I was well on my way to completing the Ph.D. in astrophysics when I received a phone call at my office from the local affiliate of Fox News. I had already been the Astrophysics Department's unofficially designated contact for public and media inquiries about sky phenomena so this call was not itself unusual—except that it would change my life.

Some explosions on the Sun had been identified by a recently launched solar satellite and the Fox News desk wanted to know if everything would be okay in the solar

system. After I offered my assurances that we would all survive the incident, they invited me to appear in a pre-taped
interview to convey this information for that evening's broadcast. When I agreed, they sent a car to pick me up. Graduate
students are generally not known for fashion or neatness, and
I was no exception. Between the time of the phone call and
when the car arrived I ran home, shaved, and put on a jacket
and tie. At the television station I was interviewed by their
weatherman in a comfortable chair in front of a bookshelf
filled with fake, sawed-off books. The interview lasted two
minutes, within which I said that explosions on the Sun
happen all the time, but especially on eleven-year cycles
during "solar maximum" when the Sun's surface is more turbulent than usual. During these times, high doses of charged
subatomic particles spew forth from the Sun and fly through
interplanetary space. Those particles that head toward Earth
deflect toward the poles by the action of Earth's magnetic
field. Subsequent collisions of these particles with molecules
in Earth's upper atmosphere create a dancing curtain of
colors, visible primarily in the arctic regions. These are the
famous northern (and southern) lights. I assured the viewers
that Earth's atmosphere and magnetic field protects us from
these hazards and that people might as well take the opportunity to travel north in search of these displays.

The interview took place at three p.m. and was scheduled
to air during their six o'clock news. I promptly called everybody I knew and rushed home to watch. That evening, while
eating dinner, the segment aired. In the middle of my mashed

potatoes, I had an intellectual out-of-body experience. At
home I was part of the general public, yet on the screen before
me was a scientific expert on the Sun whose knowledge was

sought by the evening news. The expert on television happened to be black. At that moment, the entire fifty-year history of television programming flew past my view. At no place along that timeline could I recall a black person (who is neither an entertainer nor an athlete) being interviewed as an expert on something that had nothing whatever to do with being black. Of course there had been (and continued to be) black experts on television, but they were politicians seeking support and monies for urban programs to help blacks in the ghetto. They were black preachers and other clergy offering spiritual leadership. They were black sociologists analyzing crime and homelessness in the black community. They were black business executives talking about enterprise zones in the most impoverished regions of town. And they were black journalists, writing about black concerns.

For the first time in nine years I stood without guilt for following my cosmic dreams. I realized, as clear as the crystalline spheres of antiquity, that one of the major barriers to successful relations between blacks and whites is the latent supposition that blacks, as a group, are just not as smart as whites. This notion runs deep—very deep. It's fed in part by differences among IQ scores and demonstrated in other standardized exams such as the SATs, where whites score higher than blacks. Its influence is felt in debates on academic tracking, affirmative action (in schools and the workplace), and the international politics of Africa. The most pervasive expression of the problem is the casually dismissive manner in which many whites treat blacks in society. I have never had an IQ exam, which is possible in this world if you attend only public instead of private schools. I nonetheless know all about them and what they look like from reading extensively on the subject. Among the claims of IQ proponents is the claim that a single number, your intelligence quotient, is largely inbred and is an indicator of your innate intelligence and your like-lihood of succeeding in life. Data show that blacks, on average, score a full standard deviation lower than whites. The prevailing notion is that you cannot substantially increase your IQ at any time, so one might conclude that whites are genetically higher scorers, independent of upbringing, accu-mulated wealth, or birthright opportunities.

Since humans can get better and better in everything else that matters in the world simply by practicing, I have always questioned the relevance of the IQ exam to one's promise and performance in life. If one's ability to succeed were strongly dependent on a heritable IQ, then why do some whites fear integrated schools? Why the high anxiety and the intense com-petition that surrounds school-choice, from pre-kindergarten through college? Why the heavy monetary investment in education among those who can afford it? This collective behavior betrays a deep notion that it is wealth and choice of schools, not IQ, that are the most significant factors to influence one's chances of success in life.

Since the adjectives "smart" and "genius" get applied to scientists far more often than to people in other professions, this most fundamental barrier in "race relations" had yet to be crossed. Indeed, the barrier's true nature had yet to be identified.

The incentive to achieve knows no bounds. My father's high school gym instructor singled him out in class as having a body-type that would not perform well in track events. My father's muscular build did not fit the lean stereotype of a runner that the instructor had formulated. My father had never run before. But almost out of spite, he went on to become a world-class track star in the 1940s and 1950s—at one time capturing the fifth fastest time in the world for the 600-yard run. After college, my father continued to run for the New York Pioneer Club, an amateur track organization whose doors were open to blacks and Jews and anybody else who was denied admission to the WASP-only athletic clubs. One of my father's longtime friends and Pioneer Club buddies once competed in a race where he was barely ahead of the number-two runner as they approached the final straight-away. At that moment, the other runner's coach loudly yelled, "Catch that nigger!" In the world of epithetic utterances, this one ranks among the least intelligent. My father's friend, having overheard the command, declared to himself, "This is one nigger he ain't going to catch" and won the race by an even larger margin.

An academic counterpart to the phrase "Catch that nigger" may be found in my growing collection of scholarly books published over the centuries that assert the inferiority of blacks. One of my favorites comes from the 1870 study *Hereditary Genius: An Inquiry into its Laws and Consequences,* by the English sociobiologist Francis Galton, founder of the eugenics movement. In the chapter titled "The Comparative Worth of Different Races" he notes:

> The number among the Negroes of those whom we should call half-witted men, is very large. Every book alluding to Negro servants in America is full of instances. I was myself much impressed by this fact during my travels in Africa. The mistakes the Negroes made in their own matters, which were so childish,

stupid, and simpleton-like, as frequently to make me ashamed of my own species.

Whenever I need energy to fight the pressures of society, I just reread one of these passages and, like my father's track-buddy, I instantly summon the energy within me to ascend whatever mountain lay before me.

By winning four gold medals and four world records in track and field, Jesse Owens wiped the slate clean of Aryan claims to physical superiority during the 1936 Berlin Olympics. So, too, will a black American Nobel laureate (in a category other than Peace) forever change the dialog on innate intellectual differences. Who knows when that time will come. In the interim, I play my small part in this journey. I've been interviewed on network television fifty times over the past five years for my expertise on all aspects of modern cosmic discovery—from discoveries in the solar system to theories of the early universe. And I have refused all invitations to speak for black history month on the premise that my expertise is neither seasonal nor occasional. I had finally reconciled my decade of inner conflict. It's not that the plight of the black community cannot afford having me study astrophysics. It's that the plight of the black community cannot afford it if I don't.

THE NUDIE CUTIES (1950–1969)

Legs McNeil

John Waters (film director): There was a theater in Baltimore—where I grew up—called the Rex Theater, that showed all the nudist camp movies—which was what we had before porno.

I'd read *Variety* since I was twelve years old, which was the only paper that covered the pornography business at the time. *Variety* reviewed every film—and I saw them all. Not just the exploitation movies, but the nudie movies.

So I saw every nudist camp movie, and they had to be the most ludicrously un-sexual films ever made; like a girl on a pogo stick, or a nude volleyball game. You just saw their backs—asses and tits but never dicks.

Dave Friedman (exploitation film producer): The exploitation business was only an extension of the circus carnival. What's the carnival? Girlie shows, freak shows, gambling games, rides, ballyhoo, hullabaloo—all done at a local level. But think about this: if you're in the carnival business, you can only be in one place at one time. And if you get rained out, you're dead.

But what if, all of a sudden, you can put this stuff inside? And be in more than one place at one time? That's when these guys started figuring out, Hey, we'll put this crap on film!

John Waters: Kroger Bab was one of the first great exploitation filmmakers. He went around to bingo halls and fire houses with his movie *Mom and Dad* that played for ten years all over the whole world. Why? Because *Mom and Dad* showed the birth of a baby. That was the big deal. It was the only way to show parental nudity at the time. So I guess men liked looking at the vaginas—and ignored the baby—which is really scary. Birth as an erotic act. And they would show it in bingo halls and have men see it in the day and women see it at night. They also had fake nurses selling sex education literature.

So Kroger Babs is one of my heroes. I mean, I have the poster for *Mom and Dad* in the hallway of my house.

Dave Friedman: The exploitation filmmakers quickly realized they could make a picture about any controversial subject— as long as it was done in bad taste.

They only had to do one thing: they had to "square it up," like you do in the carny.

For those of you who don't know, the "square-up" is the pitch at the beginning of the picture where they say, "The producers of this picture show you these scenes not in any terrible attempt to exploit this subject, but to make the public aware that these things exist in our beloved land, and that through education it will be brought to the attention of the proper authorities, so that child marriage can be stamped out, so that dope can be stamped out, so that miscegenation can be stamped out, so that juvenile delinquency can be stamped out . . ."

John Waters: The exploitation film business was an industry based on slowly and sneakily showing what the studios wouldn't show—like the nudist camp movies.

Dave Friedman: These nudist camp movies were about as erotic as walking through the cold-storage room of Swift and Company in Chicago. You got these poor, tired old dames with their breasts hanging below their navels, and these old guys walking around . . .

Nudist camps were the salt mines of sex, so to speak.

Roger Ebert (film critic): The nudist camp movies were one of the most pathetic and least significant of the 1950's sub-genres, and were of interest largely because of the actors' difficulties in manipulating bath towels and in standing in shrubbery. Their inevitable strong point was a volleyball game made somewhat awkward by the need for the male actors to keep their backs to the camera.

Dave Friedman: Nudist camp movies couldn't show "pickles and beaver"—which was the trade term for genitalia.

Ann Perry (film maker): Pickle meant that "something" was showing. So if accidentally you got a shot of a man's frontal nudity, the cameraman would yell, "PICKLE!" and they'd have to reshoot the scene.

John Waters: Maybe you'd see a girl with a hairbrush crotch . . . but no, you couldn't even see pubic hair. That took a long, long time—to show pubic hair. So you really had to use your imagination—because naked people hidden by pogo sticks is not exactly erotic.

Bunny Yeager (model/photographer): Doris Wishman made all her nudist camp movies down here in Miami. I did a lot of her movie stills. Doris was a pioneer, of sorts, because nudist camp movies were pretty bold for that time, even though she wasn't making total nudity—everybody's holding a towel or a beach ball over their privates.

I think the first one was called *Nude on the Moon*.

Doris Wishman (film director): I don't care what people say. I just do my very best. I make my films with love and care, and as I always say, "Not Eastman Color, but Wishman Blood."

Bunny Yeager: Another funny thing about Doris's movies was that she couldn't afford to put real sound in them, so when somebody's talking, you only see the person from the back of the head—and the other person's reacting to what they're saying.

Doris Wishman: I think Chesty Morgan was from Poland. So I had to dub all of her lines because you couldn't understand what she was saying. And a lot of the people that I worked with couldn't speak properly, so I had to go back and dub in their lines, which was more costly—but at least it was professional—and you could understand what they were saying.

Dave Friedman: Bunny Yeager was very important in those early days because she had a stable of chicks in Miami that you couldn't believe. You see, Bunny had something going for her as a woman. She would see a beautiful girl walking down the street, and she could walk up to her and ask her to pose.

Bunny Yeager: I was always out looking for girls, because at that time I had a rivalry going with Russ Meyer. We were both selling pin-ups to the same magazines. And Russ always had the big-busted girls—bigger than anybody. And I just thought, "Where does he find them?"

Dave Friedman: Bunny would say, "Excuse me, dear. I'm Bunny Yeager. Have you ever considered modelling?" The girl would say, "No." And Bunny would say, "Well, would you consider it? Maybe with underwear or maybe . . . uh, nude?"

If that would've been me, the girl would've smacked me in the mouth. So Bunny got lots of girls to pose for her, and of course, later on, Bunny shot the famous *Playboy* centerfold of Betty Page.

Bunny Yeager: I was a high-fashion model. I posed in furs and dresses and did runway work. And if you did that, you weren't supposed to do bathing suit modeling. I don't know why you weren't supposed to, but I liked bathing suit modelling—so I went out and got my own work.

I was kind of a maverick at the agency; I did what I wanted to do. They didn't like it, so I said, "As long as you get paid your fee, what do you care?"

FBI Special Agent Bill Kelly: I was in love with Bunny. When she was thirty years old, she was the best-looking thing on two legs you ever saw.

Chuck Traynor (Linda Lovelace's husband and manager): Was Bunny Yeager good-looking? Well, you know, to a sixteen-year-old, anybody with long blond hair and big boobs is good-looking. That was enough for me.

Bunny Yeager: I was called "The Prettiest Photographer in the World" by *American Weekly* magazine—which was a Sunday supplement to newspapers across the country—who did a big spread on me.

You see, Roy Pinney—who was a New York photographer—came down to Miami every year to shoot stock photos. You know, daily living-type photos—a woman pushing a grocery cart, or a woman holding a baby—and he used me as a model for them.

After we finished, Roy said, "Let's go out and shoot some cheesecake—you know, in some bathing suits."

So while he was shooting me, he said, "What are you doing these days? Anything new?"

I said, "Oh, I'm going to photography school."

He said, "That's a good angle. I'd love to do a human-interest story on you."

I said, "Well, you know, that's lying, because I'm not really a photographer, I'm just taking this course for the fun of it."

Dave Friedman: That's another way Bunny used to get all those girls—she used to model with them. Also, back then, there were thousands of young girls and guys that lived up north, and come winter time, they'd do anything in the world to get out of that weather.

So they'd come down and become waiters, waitresses, whatever—anything to make enough money to spend the winter in Miami.

Bunny Yeager: That's how I met some of the girls, because I'd modeled with them. But most of them were too highbrow to pose in bikinis, so I was kind of looked down on, you know?

But that's how I met Maria Stinger—"Miami's Marilyn Monroe"—because she modeled, too.

So one day I said to her, "Would you like to pose with some cheetahs? Some live animals?"

And Maria said, "Oh, I love animals. I'd love to do that. Yes."

So I said, "Let's go up to Africa, U.S.A. in Boca Raton. I'll make you a little leopard bikini and we'll take some pictures with live cheetahs."

It was actually for a school assignment—we had to shoot something in color.

So when the instructor critiqued the photos, he said, "These are pretty good. Maybe you should try to sell them to a magazine or something."

I said, "Are you kidding?"

He said, "No. I'm serious."

So I did, and it sold for a cover right away.

Chuck Traynor: One of the first jobs I got after I married my first wife was driving a dump truck for the Three Bays Improvement Company, who were digging the Kendal Canal.

And while I was working there, I found out that along the Kendal Canal lived Maria Stinger, one of the first nudes who came out in a centerfold the same year that Betty Page did in *Playboy*. Well, for some reason I had this fascination, and thought—like most guys—that if a chick poses nude for a magazine—she must run around her yard nude, too.

So I used to climb this fucking crane to look over the top of the trees to see into Maria's yard. I did that every chance I got—climb this damn crane and look into her yard—but I never saw her.

FBI Special Agent Bill Kelly: Of course Bunny knew I was an FBI agent, but she used to talk to me anyway—half-way. She would never implicate anybody. She was reluctant, and I don't blame her. Bunny wasn't into it very heavily.

But it is true that Bunny Yeager was America's most prominent female nude photographer at that time.

Bunny Yeager: After the *American Weekly* did a big spread on me, *U.S. Camera* picked it up, and they're the ones who put "The World's Prettiest Photographer" on the cover. And that was great, because I started getting phone calls from people all over the place, and one of those people was Betty Page, the famous pin-up model.

I just shot what I felt like; you know, cute little shots. Betty had a couple of bikinis that she had made—which I found very interesting because I had never met anyone who made bathing suits like I did—I designed the leopard suit she wears in the Africa, U.S.A. pictures that are so popular. But Betty said, "Here, give me the material. I'll take it home and sew it."

I thought, "Whoa, I'm off easy here. I don't have to do anything."

Bettie was a lot of fun to work with. I like to shoot outdoors—so we did that—but after a while I thought, "Maybe I should shoot something in a studio—do something for a calendar."

Chuck Traynor: Lo and behold, one day I stopped in front of Maria Stinger's house and there was this woman outside unpacking some stuff, and I said, "I always wanted to meet . . . uh . . . Maria. . . ."

And this lady looks at me and says, "Why?"

I said, "Well, because . . . I . . . you know, I'm a fan, and I always wanted to meet her."

She said, "You ever wanna be in a movie with her?"

I said, "Sure."

She said, "Well, my name's Bunny Yeager and we're gonna be doing a movie here and if you wanna be in it, I sure could use you."

Bunny Yeager: Chuck Traynor said that when he was sixteen he knocked on the door? No, I don't think so. Maybe he would've liked it that way. Maybe he called me up and offered his services—I don't remember that—but I do remember Chuck Traynor.

I always liked Chuck. He was always a good old country boy from Homestead, Florida—very likable, very charismatic, very laid-back type; easy to get along with, quick to laugh. You know, just a nice guy.

Chuck Traynor: I was supposed to screw Maria Stinger in the movie, but at that time, they only did simulated sex. So I played with her tits—but that's when they used those real hard implants in girls' tits—and they felt like plastic.

Bunny Yeager: If Chuck called me and said, "I have a pretty girl for you to shoot," I knew she would be pretty. Not everybody has that taste.

You see, I just think commercially, you know? If I'm going to shoot a girl, all I'm thinking about is, "Can I sell this?"

That's why I took a chance on shooting Betty Page completely nude, because the only place that used nudes back then were nudist magazines and calendars. And the nudist magazines were only paying like five dollars a shot—and I didn't know of any calendar companies—so I was lucky to run across this new magazine, *Playboy*. And when I saw *Playboy*, I thought, "Gee, they run pictures of pretty girls. Maybe they'd like this. I think I'll send it to them. Try them out first."

FBI Special Agent Bill Kelly: Bunny Yeager was a friend of Hugh Hefner's, and supposedly the word "Bunny"—the idea for *Playboy* bunnies—was based on her. Now, whether that's fictitious or not, I don't know.

Bunny Yeager: I get a call from Hugh Hefner—but I have no idea who Hugh Hefner is—because he isn't anybody yet. He was just this kid out of college who'd started this magazine. And he started telling me all his dreams for his magazine and I liked him. I thought he was very charismatic.

Hefner said, "We're looking at these pictures you sent us and we think we'd like to use them." So that's how I got my first *Playboy* centerfold: Betty Page.

Dave Friedman: I first met Bunny Yeager when Herschell Gordon Lewis and I were down in Miami making a nudist camp picture. A friend of mine, Wally, who worked for *Playboy*, gave me Bunny's phone number. So I called her, and she said, "How did you get this number?"

I said, "Wally at *Playboy* gave it to me."

She said, "Oh, you know Wally?"

I said, "Yeah, we're very good friends in Chicago."

So she said, "Oh, yeah? Well, I guess you're okay then. See, I get all these creeps that come down here and say they're gonna make a nudist camp movie just to get girls, and I can't stand them!"

Chuck Traynor: I was sixteen or seventeen years old when I first got in the movies—a nudist camp movie—and that was when they did nude volleyball. A lotta nude volleyball.

But they wasted a whole roll of film—when I squatted down with my back to the camera—because my balls were showing.

Dave Friedman: You had to hire some good-looking models to appear to be nudists at the nudist camps. We learned that the hard way.

See, one time Hershel and I went to make a nudist camp movie at Miss Zelda's Nudist Camp. Well, Miss Zelda was like this Creature from the Black Lagoon, and she said, "You boys will have to take off your clothes if you want to come in here."

Now neither of us are exhibitionists—but we needed a place to shoot this movie—so Herschell and I stripped down. So we go have lunch with all these nudists—and they're eating Franco-American spaghetti—and Miss Zelda's breasts are in the spaghetti.

I said, "Herschell, enough of this."

That's why we called Bunny Yeager. When we met her, she said, "What can I do for you?"

I said, "We need some girls."

She said, "How many?"

So Bunny sends over half a dozen nice-looking girls.

Bunny Yeager: I had worked on a lot of movies, because

people like Doris Wishman would hire me to take stills on the sets. So I learned how to make movies by watching.

Then Russ Meyer came along with *The Immoral Mr. Teas*. As I said, Russ Meyer and I were always competing with each other, so when Russ branched out into movies, my husband and I thought, "Maybe we could do that, too."

Dave Friedman: Even though Russ Meyer and I were both in the signal corps during World War II, I was just an instructor, I never got overseas. But Russ was a real hero—he filmed Patton's march across Europe.

So I didn't meet Russ until Pete DeCenzie—his original partner—introduced us, after the war.

One day I got a letter from Pete that said, "My friend Russ Meyer and I have made a picture and we'd like you to play it in a couple of your houses."

So I went up to San Francisco, and Pete had a little theater down on Church Street and a burlesque house—the El Rey Theater in Oakland. The first thing he and Russ had ever done was a picture with Tempest Storm called *The French Peep Show*.

Roger Ebert: After the war, Russ Meyer, like most service cinematographers, failed to find a job inside the Hollywood union system. So he moved to San Francisco, shot some industrial films, gained a reputation during the 1950s as a leading pinup photographer, did about a half dozen of *Playboy*'s earlier Playmates and shot an obscure mid-1950s burlesque film, which starred Tempest Storm.

Tempest Storm (stripper/burlesque queen): I met Russ Meyer at the El Rey Theater and he did a movie of me.

Dave Friedman: The Tempest Storm film wasn't a short, it was a feature, because you know, with girls like Tempest Storm, they knew how to sell themselves so beautifully.

And some of those burlesque stars weren't the greatest looking women, but they just exuded sex, and they knew how to present it. They could get these guys so excited it wasn't even funny. They had more body movements than a Swiss watch.

Tempest Storm: Yeah, I picked up a few of Elvis's movements. We did talk about dancing and compared notes. He gave me a few pointers, and I gave him some.

I met Elvis Presley in Las Vegas in 1957, when I was working the Dunes, and Elvis was the headliner at the Riviera. Funny how the first time he played Vegas he was a big flop. Anyway, he came over to the Dunes to see my show, and I just thought that he was adorable.

Oh, I fell in love with him, are you kidding? Was Elvis a good lover? Yeah! He was the King. Yes. Definitely. No complaints. It was a wonderful night.

But the next night, when I went into the show, the big boss said, "Did you have a good time last night?"

I said, "Yes. I went to sleep."

He said, "But did you go alone?"

Here I was, trying to be very discreet—be a lady about the situation—and the whole hotel knew about it.

Russ Meyer (film director): When I first met Tempest Storm I was so in awe of her great big cans that thoughts like performing badly or ejaculating prematurely ran through my mind—all connected to the dick-bone—so when I made my

319

move to hump the buxotic after the last show in her Figueroa Street scatter, I felt inadequate. Plain and simple. Fuck, what can I say?

Dave Friedman: Even though he shot the Tempest Storm film, Russ Meyer made the first nudie-cutie in 1959 called *The Immoral Mr. Teas.* It was without a doubt the first nudie-cutie. Absolutely. Prior to that, it was all nudist camp stuff. And I made the second nudie-cutie, called *Lucky Pierre.*

Roger Ebert: The first actual Russ Meyer film was, of course, *The Immoral Mr. Teas,* shot in 1959 at a cost of $24,000 and largely improvised during a four-day shooting schedule. *Teas* was partly bankrolled by a San Francisco burlesque theater owner, and was the first authentic American nudie. Meyers' assignment was to imitate the popular nudist camp films imported from Europe.

Russ Meyer: I invent the plots myself—usually while I'm alone in the car. I have a clipboard and a felt-tip pen and I jot down things that turn me on. I assemble these situations in my mind. I imagine how they develop. Then I bring in a writer to put it into script form. But it's all right here. It's all right here, and it's me.

Roger Ebert: The notion of directing the ultimate nude volleyball game did not much appeal to Russ Meyer. He felt that the success of *Playboy* had prepared the American market for an unabashed, high-quality skin flick. The occupation of his lead character and a great many of his interior locations were suggested when his dentist agreed to let his office be used on a weekend.

As Meyer explained, "The chair was well-lighted."

Dave Friedman: I was trying to sell Rose La Rosa—who owned the Esquire Burlesque Theater in Toledo, Ohio—a film Herschell and I had made called *Living Venus*. And while we're negotiating, Rose said, "Hey, can you guys make some little one-reelers—ten-minute things—with pretty girls in maybe their bra and panties . . . or maybe just their panties . . . or maybe even without the panties if you just showed their fanny?"

I said, "Yeah, why?"

Rose said, "Well, there's still fifty or sixty burlesque houses in the country and they'd pay you a hundred dollars for each."

I did the math and said, "Oh, really?"

So as soon as I got back to Chicago, I said, "Herschell, how much would it cost for us to do some of these one-reelers?"

Herschell said, "We can make 'em for about six hundred dollars a piece."

And it was just at that moment that Russ Meyers' *The Immoral Mr. Teas* opened and I happened to go see it.

Roger Ebert: The premise of *The Immoral Mr. Teas* is simple: Mr. Teas is a harassed city man, cut off from the solace of nature and burdened by the pressures of modern life. He can find no rest, alas, because he has been cursed by a peculiar ability to undress girls mentally. At the most unsettling times—in a soda fountain or dentist's office—women suddenly appear nude.

What's worse, Mr. Teas cannot even control his strange

power; it seems to have been invested naturally in him, and doesn't require the magic sunglasses or secret elixirs employed in such *Teas* imitations as *Bachelor Tom Peeping*.

Bunny Yeager: Russ Meyer's *The Immoral Mr. Teas* is what inspired my husband and I to start making movies. So we took every dollar we had—ten thousand dollars—and made a movie.

It was called *Room Eleven*.

Dave Friedman: I had just seen *The Immoral Mr. Teas*, so while we're in the middle of making these one-reelers, I said to Herschell, "Instead of us making five or six of these little one-reelers, let's make five or six one-reelers with some kind of a continuing thread and we'll put them together and have a feature film when we're done."

And Herschell said, "That's not a bad idea."

Bunny Yeager: *Room Eleven* only had two locations, because my husband said, "The only way to make money is don't have a lot of locations. Don't go here and go there—trying to dress it up."

So half of the movie took place in the lobby—where the people check in—and the other half upstairs in Room Eleven.

And of course, we didn't have any stars. No, you can't make a low-budget picture and have stars, because you try to shoot as cheaply as possible and stars mean money. So I don't know how many couples we had, but the story was about all these different types of people that came to rent Room Eleven.

Dave Friedman: So Herschell and I wrote five or six vignettes—and of course they always had a dirty story to them—and we called this thing, *The Adventures of Lucky Pierre*.

We got a nightclub comic named Billy Fallible from the William Morris Agency who played *Lucky Pierre*. Then we went up to Minneapolis and found a couple of little blond girls and brought 'em back down to Chicago. The rest of the girls we picked up were strippers from around Chicago.

Anyway, when I sold the picture to Dan Sonny, he said, "The girls in your picture look like the grandmothers of the girls in my picture."

I said, "But, Dan, you're out in Hollywood. I mean, they raise 'em out there for these things. But Chicago—it's a different thing."

Bunny Yeager: We shot *Room Eleven* in two days because we knew that we could pay these "actors" to do something and then they might not show up the second day, and we'd be lost, we'd have no movie.

I mean, everybody that wants to work in a movie wants to have lines. They want to be seen with their clothes on. They don't mind taking them off, but boy, if they have lines! So we made them do the nude scenes first, and that's why they all showed up the next day—to do their lines.

Dave Friedman: I took the finished *Lucky Pierre* back to Rose La Rosa and said, "Rose, I took your advice, but we made 'em features."

She said, "That's pretty good."

And I said, "I want you to play it and I want forty percent."

She said, "Are you outta your mind?"

I said, "Rose, I wanna tell you a little secret. There's a new game in town. And it's called film. And every week, I'm gonna send you a couple of cans of film. And the only thing you're gonna have to pay on that is the express charge from Chicago. And you can run those two cans of film fifteen times a day and nobody's gonna argue back with you. Your girls aren't gonna demand more money. You don't have to worry about any stage hands. Those drunken musicians you got down there, you can tell 'em all to get lost."

I could see Rose's eyes lighting up. And I said, "And you won't have any catfights backstage between the girls, and you won't have to put up with them beefing about doing an extra show on Saturday night, because this can of film doesn't talk back."

She said, "Dave Friedman, we're in business."

So that's basically how I took a lot of burlesque theaters in this country and turned them into adult theaters overnight.

Bunny Yeager: *Room Eleven* played mainly at drive-in theaters. You see, once Russ Meyer started making these cute little nudie-cutie movies, well, everybody did—so there were quite a bit of these films at the drive-in theaters.

But the sex was all simulated. In other words, you could not show the man's penis. And the "actors" usually kept everything covered up by being real close together. So basically they'd just be rolling around on the bed.

Just fun nudity, you know? And, yeah, a lot of kissing.

Dave Friedman: Nudie-cuties were very rigid in their construction—you had the boy-girl scene, the girl-girl scene, the orgy scene, and then the kiss-off. They worked just as long as you had those elements in it.

And in the beginning, of course, you didn't dare show pubic hair, because one time an L.A. vice squad cop told me, "If we see pubic hair, then it's pornographic, and that gives us an excuse to pick up the print."

Bunny Yeager: As nudity became more acceptable, nobody wanted to buy my beautiful bikini shots anymore. I mean, even Hefner didn't take any girls from me after the sixties, you know?

But I still tried to shoot pictures. I shot a lot of pictures at that time, but nothing happened. Nobody wanted them. They were too tame.

Dave Friedman: It wasn't until probably 1968 that we began to show pubic hair. And the first nudist camp picture to show "pickles and beaver" was *Raw Ones*.

The heyday of the nudie-cutie was 1967, 1968, 1969, and 1970. Those were the years I was turning out *Brand of Shame, The Head Mistress, Lustful Turk, Trader Horny, Thar She Blows, Starlet* and *The Erotic Adventures of Zorro*—some of the greatest films of the genre. Classics that still live today.

Bunny Yeager: We stopped making our movies because nobody wanted them anymore. All the distributors were calling and saying, "Make it more sexy!"

Of course the distributors wanted them more sexy cause they wanted them to sell. But we weren't in the business to see how far we could go, you know?

We liked making our movies, and I didn't see anything

wrong with nudity—and cute, funny little things. The three movies we made were all comedies—*Room Eleven, Sextet* and *Orgy of Revenge.*

I guess there was just a certain morality that we didn't want to cross. Pornography is a whole different bag; it's a whole other world. There's a reason for pornography, and there's probably a place for it.

I mean, everybody's got a right to do what they wanna do, but I had no reason to get into that world. I didn't need it. I didn't wanna be making it. In stills or movies.

Dave Friedman: Even though nudie-cutie films killed off burlesque—and even though nudie-cutie films killed-off girlie shows at carnivals—the nudie-cutie films were the answer to the showman's prayer. Because he no longer had to worry about live talent, which was always a problem.

Now, of course, all the voyeurs in the audience—instead of staring at some tired old burlesque broad up there, live, on the stage—are suddenly looking at gorgeous, young, blond, tan California girls in all their pristine glory, with their beautiful little breasts and their pert little nipples, and their dimpled little behinds—in Technicolor—on screens forty feet wide and twenty-five feet high. Where would *you* go?

YOUTH VOTE

Danny Goldberg

I t may seem a little ridiculous for someone like me, a guy in the music business, to be criticizing the Democratic party and the American left, but I'm so sick and tired of watching the ideas that I believe in lose political ground.

One problem seems to be that many members of my generation, the generation now in power, feel a basic resentment toward young people. This is a particularly foolish position for people to the left of center, since no progressive change has ever occurred anywhere in the world without the energy and inspiration of young people, who traditionally have provided the shock troops for the left.

Also, liberal snobs and cultural conservatives alike often are what free speech activist Marjorie Heins calls "metaphorically challenged." Educated usually in law, journalism, political science, or sociology, politicians and pundits spend decades viewing human behavior in a linear, literalistic way. Frequently they interpret art and entertainment as if it were devoid of metaphor, humor, irony, or Aristotelian catharsis. Looked at through this lens, neither fairy tales nor Greek tragedies nor Italian opera would pass moral muster.

The same snobbery and insensitivity to young people that drives culture-bashing has created a Democratic party and a

327

public-interest left whose leaders appear unwilling or unable to communicate with the unwashed masses who do not read newspaper op-ed pages or watch public television. This isn't exactly a culture war so much as a disconnect between progressive political leaders and the culture of the people they want to lead.

Conservatives, who control far more media outlets than left-wingers, are clever enough to promote the spokespeople who have "working class," styles—like talk show propagandists Bill O'Reilly and Sean Hannity. The mystery is why so few progressives do the same cultural homework. The obvious exception is Michael Moore, whose populist style has created an enormous audience for his progressive views despite the media bias.

The fact that academics with radical new ideas no longer reached out to a mass audience was lamented as long ago as 1986 by Russell Jacoby in *The Last Intellectuals*. To offer a contrast, he cited Galileo, whose "crime" was not that he had revolutionary thoughts about the solar system, but that he published them in colloquial Italian instead of academic Latin. Most progressives today express themselves in language that might as well be Latin. It's not just Democrats like Al Gore using incomprehensible insider jargon like "social security lockbox."

When I interviewed Gary Hart for *Dispatches from the Culture Wars* he speculated that American politics is less progressive now because more of the public is "less compassionate" than they had been in the 1960s. If this were so, Republicans would have increased their share of eligible voters. Instead, the big increase has been among non-voters, and more recently Nader voters. If Hart were correct, George W. Bush would not have described himself with the poll-tested phrase "compassionate conservative."

The moral lessons of the 1930s and 1960s were ingrained in the majority of the public. There is a consensus against racism and for fairness. The debate that conservatives have cleverly constructed is not about compassionate goals but about whether or not progressive programs actually worked. The failure of progressives has been their inability to explain to average Americans why their particular solutions are better or even how their ideas are different. On the weekend before the 2002 election, the *New York Times* published the results of a poll of Americans in which they asked people about their sense of the vision of each major political party: 42 percent felt that the Republicans "had a clear plan for the country," if they gained control of Congress; only 31 percent felt that the Democrats did.

Jack Newfield asks rhetorically, "How did we get these fucking zombies as our candidates? If you put Mondale, Dukakis, and Gore next to each other, they couldn't utter an interesting sentence between the three of them."

This attitude helped persuade Al Gore to choose culturally conservative moralist Joe Lieberman as his running mate, and to run a shambles of a campaign that reduced the Democratic margin of young voters (ages 18–24) from 19 percent in 1996 to zero in 2000. Martin Luther King, Jr., was a master of media strategy as well as the most compelling orator of the second half of the twentieth century. King knew exactly how Bull Conner's police dogs attacking children in Alabama would play on television and prick the conscience of mainstream

America. At the March on Washington in 1963, King's famous "I Have a Dream" speech followed performances by Mahalia Jackson, Bob Dylan, and Joan Baez.

It is impossible to imagine the civil rights movement, the labor movement, the civil rights movement, the protests against the Vietnam war, the environmental movement, the women's movement, and the struggle for gay and lesbian rights without the powerful catalysts provided by the energy and inspiration of the young and their popular culture. The Democratic party and the left will either heed that message or find themselves doomed to more decades of cultural victories and political defeats.

As I got more involved with Hollywood liberals and pro-gressives in the 1980s, pundits, left-wing activists, and politicians—irked perhaps by the sharp questions some of us posed—would ask me what on earth show business had to do with the serious, complex issues of politics.

I always invoked Ronald Reagan.

For conservatives, Reagan was a galvanizing force, but his ability to get large majorities of Americans behind him had a lot to do with his ability to speak to nonconservatives who liked his accessibility, even if they disagreed with him on such issues as abortion. Reagan's mass appeal was directly related to his back-ground as an actor, and he enthusiastically used all the tools of public relations that more conventional politicians resisted. Reagan shaped perceptions, and gave them concreteness. Millions of working-class whites might already think their per-sonal economic problems were somehow related to the civil rights movement, but Reagan legitimized their worst feelings when he talked about mythical "welfare mothers with Cadillacs."

330

In press conferences, Reagan used humor better than anyone since John F. Kennedy, and unlike any president before or since, Reagan used entertainment-business references to bond with a broad range of Americans. Referring to the Carter administration, Reagan said, "We were being led by a team of people with good intentions and bad ideas, people with all the common sense of Huey, Dewey, and Louie."

Campaigning at the Grand Ole Opry in Nashville, Reagan said: "The other side's promises are a little like Minnie Pearl's hat. They both have big price tags hanging from them." On a college campus, Reagan responded to cheers by saying, "If you ask me, as Robert Palmer has been singing recently, you are simply irresistible." Even on a very serious occasion like his 1986 State of the Union address, Reagan quoted from the film *Back to the Future*: "Where we're going, we don't need roads."

First Lady Nancy Reagan kissed TV star Mr. T on the head at the White House and appeared as herself, preaching against drugs, in an episode of the sitcom *Diff'rent Strokes*. When Ron Reagan, Jr., parodying a scene from the film *Risky Business*, danced in his underwear on *Saturday Night Live,* President Reagan said "Like father, like son." In 1983, President Reagan had posed shirtless and pumping iron for a cover story in *Parade* magazine headlined MOVE OVER JANE FONDA, HERE COMES THE RONALD REAGAN WORKOUT PLAN.

After Gary Hart dropped out of the presidential race, Senator Al Gore started making overtures to Hollywood about his own recently announced candidacy, and one day I got a call from Mike Medavoy cofounder of Orion Pictures and chairman of

Tri-Star Pictures, asking me to meet Gore at his house. "You're both friends of mine," said the avuncular Medevoy, "and you should be friends with each other."

We met in Medavoy's home on Coldwater Canyon Drive, a relatively modest place by mogul standards, but a sunny, comfortable Beverly Hills home with plenty of rooms to get lost in. After making us comfortable and offering drinks, Mike retreated to his study. If things went well, he'd get the credit; if they didn't, he didn't want either of us mad at him. Accompanying Gore was Peter Knight, then Gore's chief of staff, later the campaign chairman for the Clinton-Gore reelection effort in 1996. Mrs. Gore did not attend.

The senator looked uncomfortable. Elected officials do a lot of ass-kissing to get where they are, but it must have been particularly galling for him to be meeting with a mid-level rock manager to deal with his wife's "issue." Presumably, he'd been convinced that meeting with me would make him look like a mensch in the eyes of other possible Hollywood supporters. The strain of the effort showed.

"One thing I wanted to bring up, before we get into the other issues," he began, "is that you had said in an interview that I wasn't really for arms control because I voted for the MX missile." Gore was referring to a remark I made in the *Village Voice* in an article about Tipper. "There was a nuance there that you don't understand," he said in that stiff professorial voice that years later would be fodder for late-night television comedians. "This was a bargaining chip to prevent an even bigger weapons system."

Gore spoke in a pained tone that suggested there were subtleties in government that mere mortals couldn't understand. I shrugged my shoulders. I was certainly not going to start arguing with him about nuclear weapons. Why he would care what a rock manager said about the subject in the *Village Voice* was beyond me.

Gore then addressed the Tipper issue. "She's very sincere about this," he said, "but she's not on some kind of crusade." Gore said he regretted the Senate hearing two years before, and stressed that he envisioned no future hearings. "The point was to create awareness," he said.

We talked for about half an hour, exchanging platitudes, and Gore said he had to go to the airport. He and Knight took me up on my offer to drive them there, and once we were in the car, and the awkwardness of the "meeting" was over, the conversation became more animated. "Come on," I said, "don't you remember being a teenager and laughing at Spiro Agnew when he said the Beatles were causing people to take drugs?" Gore answered, "What about 'I get high with a little help from my friends?'" He drew out the word "high."

I told him that I'd taken a lot of drugs in the sixties, but that I thought of "A Little Help from My Friends" as a song about friendship. Gore laughed skeptically, but I was being serious. I launched into a monologue about the positive value of music and the mysteries of the subconscious as it related to music.

"I believe deeply in God," I said, about to connect the Beatles' song with a positive spirituality.

"You do?" interrupted Gore, sounding amazed. I felt that it was Gore's single unguarded moment with me that afternoon, one that revealed the unvarnished truth of his assumptions about me and my world. It was as if he didn't think that someone in rock and roll, someone who would oppose his wife's noble efforts, could possibly believe in the same God he did. His words hung in the air while we both realized that his revelation of genuine surprise was just too real for a friendly ride to the airport, and we resumed our light banter, staying away from the subject of Tipper Gore.

That spring, a Hollywood forum on the environment was assembled by the Hollywood Women's Political Committee and Show Coalition, the Patricia Medevoy political organization I had been involved with from the beginning. The featured speakers were to be two of the most environmentally active members of the U. S. Senate, Tim Wirth of Colorado and Albert Gore of Tennessee.

Our group didn't really have anything to do with putting the program together. It flashed through my mind that it was weird for Hollywood to legitimize Gore, given his and his wife's attacks on the music business. But Gore was a genuine environmentalist, so I bit my tongue. I joined in the unanimous vote to cosponsor the forum. We agreed to mail invitations to all of our members on our official stationery, which featured my name prominently—for no particular reason, I was at the top of a long list of founders.

Don Henley responded by firing off an irate letter castigating us for hosting Gore. I loved Henley and understood his point of view, but shrugged it off. However, the letter got around.

The event was held at a fabled Beverly Hills mansion built by silent screen comedian Harold Lloyd, now owned by Interscope founder Ted Field. Several hundred people attended. They had to pay close attention to the program after the public address system broke down.

On one of those perfect, clear, and balmy southern California afternoons, Gore was particularly impressive. In the absence of amplification, Gore switched from his pedantic professorial voice to an old-fashioned stump shout, and his heartfelt passion for the environment came through with eloquence and authenticity.

After the speech, I walked over to Gore in one of the many foyers of the mansion and told him I thought he had been great and that it was obvious he had genuine passion for the issue. Gore turned and frowned at me and said, angrily, "I know what you did—how you tried to embarrass me."

Surprised, I snapped back, "Just because Don Henley was complaining about you doesn't mean I had anything to do with that. Everybody in the music business doesn't agree about everything all the time."

"That's bullshit!" Gore screamed at the top of his lungs. "You and your fucking group sent out that letter. You and your fucking group tried to embarrass me."

As Bob Burkett, Ted Field's political advisor, watched in horror, I yelled back, "You don't know what the fuck you're talking about—look at the stationery." I waved a sheet of Show Coalition stationary with my name on top. "I'm one of the people who was attacked by Henley for having you speak." He looked startled by this information, but nonetheless walked away in a huff. I would have preferred that Gore acknowledge his misconception of where the objection to him came from, but I think he was still furious that anyone would have criticized him in the past. I actually appreciated the emotional honesty of his anger, which was a welcome contrast to the insincere affability of most politicians.

Later that year, the rapper Luke Skywalker of 2 Live Crew was arrested after an adults-only performance in Broward County, Florida, that featured songs from the group's controversial new album, *As Nasty as They Wanna Be*. Republican libertarians responded to the arrest with more sensitivity to the First Amendment than did Democrats.

"These are adults," said Republican Congressman Dana Rohrabacher of California. "This is a First Amendment question and the government should not be involved."

And Republican Senator Connie Mack of Florida said, "Freedom is a precious and sometimes delicate issue. I'm sure many people find the lyrics reprehensible. And I agree. But words are words. Our Constitution protects our right to say what we feel. . . . Once we begin selectively defining which words are acceptable, we enter a slippery slope where freedom is compromised. Sometimes the price of freedom is high. But no price is as high as the loss of freedom."

The Democratic Senator from Florida, Bob Graham, avoided the point by generalizing, "No freedom is unlimited. All freedom occurs in the context of freedom for others." He said he had not heard the record nor read its lyrics.

Ronald Reagan, undoubtedly influenced by his background as an actor, had an honest fascination with popular culture that would have helped humanize many policy-wonk Democrats. Nancy Reagan shared some of his qualities. I met the former president and first lady at an event to mark the release of an album to benefit the Pediatric AIDS Foundation, of which the Reagans were honorary cochairs. I accompanied one of my clients, Pat Benatar, who had donated a song, as had Bruce Springsteen, Michael Jackson, and others.

I was introduced to the Reagans shortly before they were to appear at a press conference. Nancy, diminutive and intense, immediately grabbed my hands and said, "I know you." It turned out that she'd seen me as a guest on her son Ron's syn-dicated late-night TV talk show.

"We're changing the show," she told me, never losing eye contact. "The producers have him doing too much serious stuff. People want more humor and entertainment." I nodded silently and agreed wholeheartedly when she said how won-derful her son was. In truth, Ron Reagan was a gracious, self-effacing, and very funny guy.

Only a year or two out of office, President Reagan, through eighty years old, looked extraordinary. With his cheeks as pink as apples, a full head of hair, and a muscular build, he could have easily passed for a man twenty-five years younger.

He raved to his wife about the buffet table, which served Mrs. Fields chocolate chip cookies.

"They're my favorite cookies in the world," Reagan told me, evidently having decided that if I warranted his wife's attention, I should get some of his, too.

"When we were in the White House, I was very excited when they told me Mrs. Fields herself was going to visit. I imagined a matronly, older woman but Mrs. Fields is only in her forties and has young children. Can you believe it? Can you believe that Mrs. Fields is a young woman?" Mrs. Reagan interrupted his reveries and grabbed him by the elbow and snapped, "Come on, Ronnie, lets do the press conference." Once behind a microphone, Reagan spoke eloquently about AIDS, a subject he'd largely ignored as president.

The Southern California ACLU was extremely busy during the years that Los Angeles seethed with racial tension and anger, much of it directed at the Los Angeles Police Department. In April 1991, the brutal beating of Rodney King by four L.A.

policemen horrified millions of Americans when an amateur videotape was shown repeatedly on national TV news. For almost a decade, civil rights groups in Los Angeles and the ACLU had been complaining about the LAPD and in particular about Chief Daryl Gates. Long before the term "racial profiling" entered common usage, activists in Los Angeles charged that people of color were far more likely to be stopped or searched by the LAPD than whites. Several black athletes successfully sued the city of Los Angeles for inappropriate and unwarranted stops, based apparently solely on the color of their skin.

Still, Chief Gates retained the support of the vast majority of the Los Angeles elite. In part, he benefited from the afterglow of the relatively crime-free 1984 L.A. Olympics. It was also rumored that Gates had troublesome personal files on members of the City Council.

The Rodney King tape changed the political reality, with the kind of effect on majority opinion that Bull Connor's police dogs attacking nonviolent civil rights demonstrators had generated a quarter of a century earlier. Years of pent-up resentment of Chief Gates exploded.

Ramona Ripston and the ACLU legal staff had been documenting police abuses for more than a decade, and the ACLU played a pivotal role in the ensuing fight against Gates and abusive cops. Ripston put together a campaign and, within a few weeks, got more than 20,000 signatures on a petition calling for Gates's resignation—"more than we got for Nixon's," she told me. A few weeks after the King beating, actor Wesley Snipes was stopped and detained by the police for no reason while driving through Beverly Hills and he called Ripston fuming with indignation. We organized a press conference for Snipes, Blair Underwood, and several other black actors who had had the same experience.

Not long afterward, we had a public forum at which actor Ed Asner played the role of Daryl Gates, reading actual quotes from the embattled chief, including his notorious statement, "In some blacks, when the choke hold is applied, the veins or arteries do not open up like in normal people."

Mayor Bradley, a former police chief, had refrained from criticizing Gates publicly despite many years of pressure from civil rights groups. Now, Bradley agreed it was time for the chief to go and he appointed Stanley Sheinbaum president of the Police Commission, the five-member body to which the chief officially reported.

Bradley also asked Warren Christopher, the eminent Los Angeles attorney who later would be named Bill Clinton's Secretary of State, to create a bipartisan commission to investigate police practices. The Christopher Commission concluded that the vast majority of the seven thousand Los Angeles police officers were excellent, law-abiding officials, but that there was a group of two hundred to three hundred who regularly were "racist and brutal," and that these officers were responsible for creating a breakdown of trust between the police department and the black community.

It was not until May 1992, when the streets of Los Angeles exploded in a riot after the policemen charged with beating King were acquitted, that Gates finally was pushed out of office. More painful changes in the Los Angeles Police Department were to come over the next decade, as the full extent of the brutality and corruption of a small but powerful group in the department was revealed.

A year before the Rodney King beating set all the changes

in motion, the L.A. group NWA released an album called *Straight Outta Compton*. Considered the first "gangsta rap" album, *Straight Outta Compton* sold two million copies despite getting virtually no play on radio or MTV.

Public Enemy star Chuck D. had called rap music "the CNN of the Ghetto." If the Los Angeles establishment had been tuning in, it might have wondered why an album with so little marketing clout behind it would have sold so extraordinarily well when its best-known song was called "Fuck tha Police."

But no matter who was in the White House, political attacks on popular culture never went away. Booth Gardner, the newly elected Democratic governor of Washington, proudly identified his state as the home of Nirvana in a 1993 address to the legislature. By then, Nirvana had become the most successful and influential rock band in the world. A few months later, the legislature passed a bill making it illegal for kids under eighteen to attend rock shows that included profanity, even when no liquor is allowed.

I called the governor to ask him to veto the bill, which would effectively end rock concerts in the state of Washington, and would also a signal a terrible disrespect to the music scene in Seattle that seemingly he took pride in.

Gardner replied, "I'm going to sign it, but it's unconstitutional so it will never be enacted."

I asked why he was going to sign it if he knew it was unconstitutional.

"I think it sends a message," he responded.

What was that message, I asked—the message he wanted to give Nirvana.

"It sends a message that needs to be sent. I think the

message speaks for itself," the governor concluded, before hastily hanging up.

In the spring of 1995, while we were going through these gut-wrenching changes, Senate Majority Leader Robert Dole, the frontrunner for the Republican presidential nomination in the 1996 election, made a scathing speech about an entertainment culture he described as rife with "nightmares of depravity." According to *The Choice,* Bob Woodward's book about the election, Dole was urged by political advisor Bill Lacy to gain political ground by an "attack [on] Hollywood directly on the grounds of sex and violence in movies and popular music."

The speech, written by Mari Will (wife of conservative columnist George Will), excoriated "a culture business that makes money from 'music' extolling the pleasures of raping, killing, torturing, and mutilating women—from 'songs' about killing policemen and rejecting law."

"The mainstreaming of deviancy must come to an end," Dole proclaimed. "We will name their names and shame them as they deserve to be shamed. One of the companies on the leading edge of coarseness and violence is Time Warner."

Shortly thereafter, Reverend Al Sharpton asked to meet with us. I joined Doug Morris, Elektra Records Chairman Sylvia Rhone, and Ken Sunshine, who had recently been hired by Warner Music as a corporate PR expert, in the Time Warner conference room, where Sharpton urged us not to get rid of rap music.

From his days as a child preacher, the New York civil rights leader had been friends with James Brown. Sharpton had later worked with the Jackson family. He had vivid memories of the fifties and early sixties, when r&b music was banned from pop radio playlists and shunned by many major labels for supposedly moral reasons. After the meeting, he told a battery of news crews he had urged us not to give in to conservative pressure, which he viewed as racist. "When I first was involved with the music business, the record companies were run by real gangsters. Now the records are rapping about gangsters. From where I sit, this is progress."

After losing the 1996 presidential election, the would-be moral leader Bob Dole began appearing on TV and in print ads as a spokesperson for the newly available impotence drug Viagra. With his newfound image as a virile older guy, Dole then appeared in a Pepsi commercial, sitting next to a hound dog watching sexily dressed teenage pop singer Britney Spears dance and gyrate suggestively. As the commercial ends, Dole glances up at the screen, then at his dog, and says, "Down, boy."

In the spring of 2000, another election year, I was asked by the Creative Coalition to attend a meeting with Joseph Lieberman, Republican Senator Sam Brownback of Kansas, and conservative moralist William Bennett, who had been drug czar in the George H. W. Bush administration. Apart from my disagreements with Bennett over pop culture, I have a deep moral aversion to the war on drugs. If today's drug laws had been in force when I was arrested in the late sixties, my life would have been ruined by imprisonment. Millions of poor people who do not have access to good lawyers languish in prisons for nonviolent drug crimes despite ample evidence from other countries that treating of drug abuse as a medical problem, rather than as a criminal problem, creates far less social chaos.

About twenty of us from the entertainment business

packed into a conference room at HBO's New York offices, including NBC's Roz Weinman, venerable film industry spokesman Jack Valenti, TV and film producer Steven Haft (*Dead Poets Society*), and the actor and Creative Coalition president William Baldwin.

I first met Joe Lieberman in 1988, when he was asking for money for a run for the Senate. To my lasting regret, I responded by saying that the Democrats would have a better chance of controlling the Senate if Lieberman defeated Republican Lowell Weicker, and I gave Lieberman $250. Thus, in a tiny way, I was complicit in the defeat of Weicker, who was notably sensitive to civil liberties, and the victory of cultural conservative Lieberman. Beneath his affable demeanor, Lieberman has a self-righteous, intolerant, puritanical streak. "Hollywood is a place that doesn't understand piety," Lieberman once said.

Lieberman led off the meeting at HBO by invoking Columbine and asked, in his scratchy, folksy voice, how we would feel about overall standards for all entertainment, similar to the very strict ones applied in the movie business from the 1930s to the early 1960s. Lieberman expressed his vision, shared by Bennett and Brownback, for the creation of universal ratings for films, television shows, video games, and recordings with a set of standards that all parents could use.

Billy Baldwin asked me to respond first, and I pointed out that music, films, and video games were totally different forms of communication and did not lend themselves to similar types of categorization. As to "standards," people of good will often disagreed about the roles sex and violence play in entertainment. I gave, as an example, Oliver Stone's *Natural Born Killers,* which many social critics had accused of glorifying violence. To me and to many others, it was a black comedy satirizing the news media's infatuation with violence.

I cited *Natural Born Killers* in part because I was sitting next to one of its stars, Juliette Lewis. She reiterated that the film was a satire, and produced research indicating that all of the murderers in eight previous schoolroom shootings, including those at Columbine, had only one thing on common. It was not their taste in entertainment. Each of the young killers had been given prescription psychological drugs such as Ritalin. Lewis pointed out that millions of young children are on such drugs, and cited studies showing that 1 percent of kids taking them could have psychotic reactions. The explosion of violence in schools occured at the same time as the exponential increase in the use of drugs like Ritalin.

Lieberman had received large campaign contributions from pharmaceutical companies. His wife, Hadassah, had formerly worked for Pfizer, which manufactured some of the mood-affecting drugs used to treat kids. He refused to acknowledge Lewis's comment, and acted as if she didn't exist.

None of us agreed with Lieberman, Brownback, and Bennett on universal ratings. "That's off the table," said Haft firmly. But many of the entertainment people said they shared the concern about the state of the culture and welcomed a dialogue.

As the meeting was breaking up, Bennett, who surrealistically has claimed to have dated Janis Joplin, tried to play the part of the affable Washington hipster. He started riffing about the music of Buddy Holly. I quickly left. I couldn't stomach schmoozing with the architect of the war on drugs. I have some standards.

There is a swelling sense that much of our culture has become toxic. That our standards of decency and

civility are being significantly eroded by the entertainment industry's shameless and pervasive promotion of
violence, sex, and vulgarity, and that traditional sources
of values in our society such as faith, family, and school
are in a life-and-death struggle with the darker forces
of immorality."—Senator Joseph Lieberman, *In Praise
of Public Life,* published in September 2000

In the spring of 2000, Ralph Nader asked for my support in
his run for the presidency. I had long admired him for his
public interest work, and there was no question that he was
willing to speak about the environment, economic justice,
and other issues that would otherwise be slighted or absent in
the national campaign. On the other hand, Nader's self-
righteousness in recent years began to grate on me. He
seemed to feel that his approach to any problem was the only
possible choice for any moral person.

Famously out of touch with culture, he had said in a recent
interview in *The Nation:* "Television-watching teaches children that violence is the preferred solution to life's problems.
They are taught to value cheap sensuality in everything from
sex to self-image to food and they become addicted to entertainment that shortens their attention span." When I complained about this outburst, Nader, who has no children of his
own, told me he thought kids would grow up better "if they
performed their own versions of Eugene O'Neill plays or
Romeo and Juliet instead of watching movies or TV."

"Ralph," I responded in frustration, "I've seen two O'Neill
plays in the last year and they were filled with alcoholics and
depressing monologues. *Romeo and Juliet* ends with a murder
and suicide. Frankly, I'm much happier that my kids have

345

memorized large sections of *Austin Powers*." It was obvious from the dead silence on the other end of the phone that Nader had no idea what *Austin Powers* was.

When Nader again parroted the conventional wisdom about violence and popular culture, I got angry and yelled, "You don't know what you are talking about, and you're needlessly alienating millions of young people who might support you."

"I do know what I'm talking about," Nader yelled back, and hung up. Lieberman turned off other voters with his incessant references to his orthodox Jewish faith, which grew so extreme that even the Anti-Defamation League, which was formed to fight anti-Semitism, criticized him for making religion a litmus test of political virtue. Many civil libertarians felt like feminist Ellen Willis, who wrote in Salon.com that she was supporting Ralph Nader specifically because she was so turned off by Lieberman's excessive religiosity. "He's a Christian rightist in Jewish drag," she wrote, and slammed both Lieberman and Gore for "pandering to religious and moral conservatives."

After Al Gore announced that Lieberman was going to be his running mate, Nader called me again. He gleefully asked, "How do you feel now that Gore has picked the arch-critic of entertainment as his running mate?" I told Nader I agreed with him about many issues but I was worried about his effect on the outcome of the election.

"How can you change anything if you don't understand TV?" Michael Moore regularly admonished the left. His TV show *The Awful Truth* and his films *Roger and Me* and *The Big One* had given more mass exposure to progressive ideas than the rest of alternative media combined. His very active Web site had helped galvanize public opposition to the impeachment of Bill Clinton, earning the thanks of both Clinton and Gore. Like me, Moore had decided to support Nader's campaign as a way of broadening the national debate.

"I figured Gore would win by ten points," Moore said to me in wonder as Election Day grew near, and the pollsters declared the race too close to call. "The economy is terrific, the public opposed impeachment, Gore was supposed to be this great debater, facing an idiot. I never thought Gore would lose all of the debates and that it would be this close."

Moore is a charismatic speaker who often appeared with Nader at rallies, but he refused to campaign with him in swing states. He tried unsuccessfully to get Nader to stop it, and called everyone he knew in the Gore campaign, trying to find a way to bridge the gap.

Moore told readers of his Web site that he could understand why Nader supporters would vote for Gore in swing states. Nader supporter Ani Di Franco urged young people in swing states to vote for Gore.

"Maybe Gore could say that he'd be in favor of Ralph being included in debates for the next election," Moore suggested as Election Day drew near. Instead, Gore chose to completely ignore Nader and never referred to him, nor to the millions of people who followed him and voted for him.

Steve Earle, who records for Artemis, tried to encourage his fans to at least not vote for Bush. A longtime and active opponent of the death penalty, Earle and director Amos Poe made a music video of "Jonathan's Song," a farewell to a condemned man Earle had gotten to know in Texas. While the lament played in the background, the video showed the faces of the more than 300 people executed in Texas while George W. Bush was governor.

347

The Sunday before the election, Barbra Streisand called me, explaining earnestly in her New York accent, the real policy differences between Gore and Bush. I agreed with her. So did many people who'd been attracted by Nader at the beginning. The problem wasn't the middle-aged left, or the old left. The problem was young voters who didn't watch C-Span or read the editorial pages, people for whom the *Saturday Night Live* caricatures of Bush and Gore rang true.

I asked her to support Moore's efforts to get Gore to acknowledge Nader, but she said she no longer had any influence with to Gore's campaign. I told Barbra that Lieberman and Gore's attacks on popular culture hadn't exactly helped with young people. Barbra asked me plaintively, "Aren't they doing things on college campuses?"

The answer was, too little too late.

A major reason Gore lost in 2000 was a very severe case of liberal snobbery. With his unwillingness or inability to communicate in ordinary language his shrill attacks on popular culture, his selection of a running mate even more sanctimonious and elitist than he, and his obsessive need to distance himself from President Clinton, Gore turned off millions of voters he could have attracted.

Conservative Democrats and some pundits implausibly blamed what they called Gore's "populist" message for driving away swing voters. This theory totally ignores the voters who swung between Nader and Gore. Even if Gore occasionally said something that could be taken for populism, his style and affect remained hopelessly elitist. Gore had none of the common touch of true populists such as Ross Perot or Jesse Ventura. On the contrary, he always seemed like a lecturing professor, while Bush was able to portray himself as the solid voice of common sense next door.

Gore's dramatic drop in support among younger voters alone cost him the election. The statistics are clear. In 1996, among voters aged 18 to 24, Clinton defeated Bob Dole, the arch-enemy of popular culture, by 19 percent. In 2000, Gore and Bush (the latter who was not identified with attacks on youth culture) essentially split nine million voters in the same age category. If Gore had retained the Democratic margin among young voters from the previous election, he would have added almost two million votes to his national margin. This would have tipped the balance in his favor in several swing states (including, of course, Florida), and he would have won the electoral college, and thus the election, decisively. Although I think Ralph Nader was too cavalier about his effect on the outcome, blaming Nader misses the point. Most people who voted for Nader had made up their mind that they didn't want to vote for Gore *or* Bush.

RIFF ON RIO

Douglas Daly

Rio de Janeiro. No, it's not what you're thinking, not REE-oh-day-zha-NAY-roh, the place whose charm is wedged in the crack of a perfectly round ass, and whose aura is crowned with slum-hills. That place is disturbingly attractive to Southern Californians, and disturbingly familiar to New Yorkers of the 1980s. The spent bullets that emanate like moans from the *morros* haven't yet made it over the high-walled villas of those who own the political way but lack the political will.

I'm talking about HEE-oo-djan-NAY-roo, capital of Brazil, at least until someone had the idea of building Brasília, an ersatz Los Angeles at the country's hydrological vertex and shifting the power and associated cash way inland. Rio had been the true capital, to a large extent the intellectual and cultural as well as political capital of Brazil, its center of music, arts, and letters. Machado de Assis was writing experimental novels half a century before Borges. Hector Villa-Lobos studied for a time in Paris but he took the medium of early twentieth-century classical music and gave it South American roots—and wings. In the 1930s, Jacob do Bandolim won respect via sheer virtuosity for the vagabond street music called *chorinho,* music that had already inspired Villa-Lobos.

351

The center of Rio recalls a long heyday. Some spots are pre-served, like the Bar Luiz, with its white tiles, swaybacked wooden chairs, and long-aproned waiters, and others are recovered, like Scenarium, sagging on a block of former brothels, where jazz or *sambinha* is played on a small stage in the middle of an atrium for an audience that lounges on two floors of eclectic old furnture, all of it for sale.

Rio has changed, but it continues to be a place where my friend Zilmar, a penniless seamstress, can go to a different cul-tural event seven nights a week and spend little more than the bus fares to reach them. Another friend, Alexandre, is from São Paulo, bigger and badder than New York, and for decades the economic and academic powerhouse of Brazil. Still, at the end of his first real visit to Rio a few years ago, he concluded, "Now I understand this so-called rivalry between São Paulo and Rio de Janeiro: it's simple fucking envy."

So it was that in March a group of us made an excursion in sheets of rain to the center of Rio, not far from the Scenarium. The old district seemed deserted, something not helped by the rain hopping off the cobblestones like hot oil. We stopped opposite the entrance to the almost intimate Praáa do Real Gabinete, empty and glistening darkly in floodlights.

Clearly we had come to the wrong place, judging by the steel-shuttered ground-floor doorways, but squinting up into the torrent we could see a long bank of palladium windows, backed by tall wooden doors, peeling in varying dull shades of red, each with its small wrought-iron balcony. A heavy, contented man sat on a stool just inside the one open doorway at street level. He took the tiny cover charge and we climbed a steep, creaky stair-case to the Centro Cultural Carioca, pausing halfway up to leave a coin in the candlelit sconce with the statue of São Jorge.

Outside, flashes of lightning put the churchlike Real Gabi-nete library in sharp relief every so often, but the effect inside was dulled by the curtain of water on both open sides. Sur-rounding a score of little bistro tables, the walls were of bare, battered brick, and along the longer side hung a series of enormous caricatures by the revered octogenarian cartoonist Lā, each including his alter ego, an impish little man with a handlebar moustache—something like a cheerful Toulouse-Lautrec—playing up to a much larger and oblivious *mulata* samba queen with an opulent body. Looking up at the opulent twenty-foot ceiling, I sensed something looming that night.

Tira Poeira. Five young people whom you wouldn't place in the same room but whose instruments converse, whose music is oblique and improvisational and comes impossibly full-circle in the best traditions of jazz, but is applied most magi-cally to the compositions of Jacob do Bandolim, Cartola, Waldir de Azevedo, an endemic tradition for which the word "popular" fails to convey its complexity and subtlety.

Mandolin. At times he ground his hips, at times he marched. His playing could be furious; his phrases slithered and punched. He yanked octaves across the breaks like barbed wire.

Reeds. A handsome guy from the more square-head part of Brazil, who said "I'm from Florian¢polis" by way of explaining his bewilderment at finding himself among such kooks. His often sweet winds rounded the edges of the man-dolin, and he would cross over to meet the *mando* at the center to play impossible organismal unisons.

Classical guitar. Seated and solemn, darkly *barbudo* (bearded), constantly laying down a walking or running bass with his nimble right thumb. He did a flamenco strut during

353

an intermission, but then went back to laying cornerstones on coasters.

Electric. How do you finger-pick a Fender? And that fast? Skinny, and tall, he had an aquiline nose, he had long talons; on his left hand he had eight of them, traveling along the neck like a spider on amphetamines.

Pandeiro. Dressed like a hospital intern but gyrating like a rocker, and doing contortions around his instrument, a glorified tambourine. A tambourine, but outfitted with a microphone taped to the inside, and as each of his taped fingers was doing something different on one or another part of its topography, he was four percussionists—or maybe Elvin Jones.

Their music is playful but seriously ecstatic—like a baby placed in a warm mud puddle. Early on, they had the audience intone the lyrics to a classic song by Francis Hyme, with a line that captured their attitude toward the tradition, and ours toward their transfusion of it: "Que coisa linda, que coisa boa": "What a lovely thing, what a good thing."

Tira Poeira: "Kick up the dust!"

THE RUBAIYAT OF ALFRED J. PRUFROCK, MBA

Ian Williams

This ancient manuscript was found floating in New York Harbor in an empty (but expensive) wine bottle off Battery Park near Wall Street. We know it is old, because it was a French wine bottle, and as we all know, Wall Street no longer drinks French wine since the Iraq war. It could have drifted up the Gulf Stream from some offshore tax haven.

The Rubaiyat of Alfred J. Prufrock, MBA.

Awake! for moaning in the Bowl of Night
Has drop't the tip that put the stocks to Flight:
And Lo! the punter of the East has caught
The Nikkei's index in a Noose of Blight
Dreaming Murdoch's TV was in the Sky
I heard a Voice within the Exchange cry,
"Awake, O my suckers, and buy the stock
Before all these IPO bargains fly."

And, as CNN crews, who stood before
The Exchange shouted—"Open then the Door!
"You know how little cash you have to buy,
And, once departèd, may return no more."

355

Come, buy the shares, and in the Fire of Spring
The net proceeds of your investments fling:
The Bird of Time has but a little way
To fly—and Lo! the Bird is on the Wing.

"How sweet are yearly dividends!"—think some:
Others—"How blest the stock options that come!"
Ah, take the Cash in hand and waive the Rest;
Oh, the brave Music of a distant Drum!
Myself when young did eagerly frequent
Broker and an'lyst, heard great Argument
About puts and on sells: but evermore
Left, broke, by the same Door as in I went.
The sharp broker's pen writes; and, having writ,
Moves on: nor all thy street savvy nor Wit
Shall lure it back to cancel half a buy,
Nor all thy Tears wash out a cent of it.
Lo! some we bought, of the hottest and best
That Time and Fate of all their picks imprest,
Have peakèd and troughèd ofttimes before,
But one by one, disastrously gone West.
Ah Love! could thou and I with fate conspire
To grasp this Enron Scheme of Things entire,
Would not we cash in our Options and run
To spend our net worth on our Heart's Desire!
Ah, Moon of my Delight who Know'st no wane
The SEC are after us again:
How oft hereafter rising shall they look
Through this same Office after me—in vain!
Now the bull Mart reviving old Desires,
The thoughtful Soul to Bermuda retires,

Where the penny Stocks flutter on the Bough
And the splashing of Cash offshore inspires.

Here with a stock report beneath the Bough,
A Flask of wine, a new laptop, and Thou
Beside me singing on the sandy beaches—
And bankruptcy is Paradise enow.

Ah, make the most of what we yet may spend,
Before we too into the dock descend;
Bust after Bust, and in disguise, to flee,
Sans Wine, sans PC, and sans dividend!

DUST RADIO

Greg Tate

The girl from Mars just pencilled herself in.

These Martian girls, who do they think they are?

The kind who think they got it like that, that's who.

Pencilling me in was her way of saying she cared but not so much, really.

Her way of being subtle and blunt, of promising me the world, knowing she intended to deliver nothing. Pencilling herself in signified neither the casual brush-off nor the cold stare of detachment.

Pencilling in allowed her to express sexual boredom and her desire to patronize me as well. If I was lucky, I might become her "special friend"; given time I might even make doormat.

The girl from Mars had been nothing but firm in making her appointment with my associate, Leo. A felt-tip pen was probably her indelible weapon of choice for that little rendezvous. Leo had been told exactly when she'd be coming down to earth, what time to expect her driver, what time they'd get him back home. (Did I mention that our girl from Mars comes from money? She's got it like *that*, too.) Like all Martian girls she seemed human enough: half woman, half machine, more trouble than any good man needed. She was minx and

Sphinx enough, too, had that whole femme fatale mystery-woman thing going on. She came flexing it all: the unanswerable riddle, the insoluble puzzle, the unknowable Feminine. All those allures, all that artillery, all that whole mind-fucking trip. Unfortunately, she was also clueless about what made earth guys tick. She couldn't predict what problems were about to arise from her choosing Leo's company over mine. I mean, here she was, a highly evolved, extremely enlightened, privileged, and entitled Martian woman—*that* nigga—the kind who could see through space and time but could not see all the bad blood her ludicrous fling with Leo was about to stir up in our camp. Or the negative effect she was already having on our trinity with The Anima. Did she even care, you ask? Yeah, *whatever*. But I digress. The pencil-packing girl from Mars was leading Leo, already a class-A fuck-up, into the biggest fuck-up of his young and fucked-up little life. I was supposed to just stand by and watch that happen but I don't think so. Even Leo deserves better. Please don't get me wrong about good brother Leo. I'll be the first to admit Leo has his charms. He's a shady nigga, yes, but shady can be charming, and disarming, and with the right crowd, even seem dangerous. But when it came to dealing with a woman like our little Martian trick Leo was way out of his league. The proverbial child playing with matches. The kind of guy who would go about the task like a squirrel busting a nut. The kind of guy she could easily make believe all his heaving and hoing was going to break her down, bend her to his will. It was that nutcracker logic. Sent up a Martian canal with nothing but a horny paddle. Leo could never break the mind of a woman like that with his brain-dead little prick. There was more to her than the tart redness of her hair, the flaming, undulating dusky meadow that was her elongated torso, the steaming crimson tide always threatening to burst from her luscious bubble lips. There was also her ravenous need to consume an earthman's soul. It was easy enough to see. It practically came bounding out of her eyes. There was more going on behind those eyes than the likes of Leo would ever understand. This Martian girl was an alien succubus, a demi-urge incarnate. You couldn't just fuck her, you had to worship her every stroke of the way. You had to pry her secrets loose with prayer and supplication. Couldn't tell that to Leo, though. To Leo she was just another mark, another resumé builder, another piece of ass to be skinned alive and stuffed Polaroid face-down in his wallet. He was being set up for a heartbreak or worse and I was supposed to just let that happen. I was supposed to sit back and watch him make such a fool of himself. Make a fool of me even, and of really, all earthmen in the bargain. I wasn't about to let that happen. The Anima be damned.

To be fair, the girl from Mars wasn't coming to earth only to have her way with Leo. She was also coming to rant about NASA at the UN, harangue them about what was being done to the remains of her family members. These would be the ones still in the space agency's possession after far too many years. About those remains, several dozen bags of bones and dust, our Martian girl, via a *New York Times* editorial, let all know they should be considered "the sacred property of my remaining people and not some space museum exhibit." No more than she herself, she half-jokingly added, should be considered such.

This was all fine on her end but I did not believe The Anima and Leo and I needed to get caught up in her business. It had nothing to do with our own sacred mission. Yet and still The

Anima wanted us march with her and her followers to the UN, show her we were down with her struggle against the government, too. I knew this was a mistake but I was the only one who was still thinking straight after our first encounter with the girl. I saw the manipulation coming from a mile away. Can't tell The Anima nothing about that, though. Right now the very thought of us marching with Miss Mars and of Leo boinking her later, has The Anima more giddy than a pig in shit. This is how it's supposed to be going down: Three days from now the girl from Mars will send her driver to come knocking on Leo's door. Ostensibly to make good on her promise to take him out on a date. Ostensibly to make good on her promise to fuck him. No, excuse me—to fuck him again, and for the second time in less *than a month*.

"Coming here to jump my bones, Mister Ivy. Twice in two weeks time, nigga, twice."

A taunt to which he added, "Can you stand it, nigga?" because he knew I could not.

Three more days of lust and anticipation were all Leo had to endure. Three more days that were equally certain to bring more quiet exhilaration to the face of our den mother, The Anima. Three more days just as certain to do nothing but build up more rage, envy, and bedevilment within me, the Unchosen One. Three more humiliating days sure to provide one more bitter reminder of how superfly a nigga named Cyril Sirone Ivy used to be.

Other than that, things could not have been going better. Discount all of the above and everything was going as The Anima said it should. Everything, according to her, was just hunky-dory. Everything, to hear her tell it, was right on schedule, going according to The Plan. What The Plan was remained a riddle wrapped in an enigma stuffed inside a puzzle box for the peons like Leo and myself.

All Leo and I knew about The Plan was what The Anima (in the high-handed manner of higher-ups everywhere) told us we needed to know on a need-to-know basis. From the beginning of our relationship with The Anima, Leo and I had been given very circumscribed roles to play: mine was to snoop on my Harlem friends and neighbors, his was to shag exotic, extraterrestial women like our girl from Mars.

I hope you're starting to catch on. I hope you're starting to see the unfairness in the way things are run around here. Call it my eunuch period. Call it the high price one pays for motherly and sisterly love these days. Call it a fair exchange for peace of mind, a purpose in life, and a reason to get up in the morning.

All the things a nigga used to have back when he had a life and a mind that rarely found itself being winked at by the abyss.

Five years ago I trashed my passport to the good life, lost it all, and good riddance, too. Two years later an ex-lover calls out of the blue and invites me over to her house for a holiday soiree. Once I'm there she makes an urgent point of introducing me to The Anima. The occasion was my ex's annual Christmas party, held for the first time at her immaculate brownstone. Once upon a time the place was just a shell; I'd overseen its gutting and renovation into something resembling a Moroccan palace. The overall design had been modeled after my ex's favorite hotel in Fez. The same hotel I'll confess to having designed when I was something of a hotshot in the profession. My ex's party was the kind of Xmas shindig I had once got invited to by the dozen when I was a respectable professional man. Now it was the kind of affair that after a rather noisy, rage-filled and deliberate fall from grace, I would only have been invited to by an ex with a heart of gold and a quality of mercy that was anything but strained. If you'd done a quick scan of who was who there that night you'd have seen many a pampered, inebriated, and quasi-legendary professional Harlem Negro—all inexplicably full of Christmas cheer and holiday spirits just blithely chatting away. You'd also have seen me right there, in that far corner, sober as a judge, way off to the side, away from the action, withdrawn, detached, alone, trapped on a loveseat, looking for all the world like fair game. So much like fair game it seems that my bighearted ex suddenly bounds across her living room to introduce me to a new arrival, that formidable prescence I know now as The Anima and only The Anima, as if she'd gotten there by comic book. At the sight of this impending introduction I thought, "Oh no, bitch, just you watch, this one over here has still got some teeth." Because in taking stock of The Anima's age and girth I had already taken our inexorable arranged meeting as an insult. I swallowed my pride, took her hand, tried not to wince when she squeezed in beside me on the small couch. I also demoted my ex to that brain-deficient status one consigns friends who dare intro-duce us to their busted idea of someone they know would be "perfect" for us.

Don't get me wrong about The Anima because while not a petite woman nor a particularly young one, she is still very beautiful in an Aretha Franklin–Mona Lisa sort of way. Her face is actually that cherubic, beatific, and bewitching. And she is a natural woman whose only bow to cosmetic adornment are the two thinly appliquéd streaks of deep purple lipstick she keeps lined on her generous valentine of a mouth. Her long, thick and extremely well-sculpted crown of salt and pepper dreadlocks are equally sensual even when she keeps them coiled into a stylish bun just behind the top of her head. Bountiful swaths of silken African fabric not only drape but shimmy and slink around her equally bountiful and rhythmically alive body. She is, in other words, just the sort of hip, extra-large, queen-mother Africa type my ex knows has never been my type. I had no choice but to read this forced encounter as my ex's way of showing me how much she viewed me as a fallen man with no romantic prospects in her usual crowd. I knew that, too, and still had the nerve to be offended. I therefore made plans to be as stank towards to this The Anima person as I could muster. A funny thing happened on the way to stankonia though. As we got to talking, The Anima and I, I found myself incapable of being mean to her. I realized I have far too much anger toward the known world to suddenly attack an unknown target. There was also something special going on in The Anima's hand-shake—firm, soothing—and her hug—full bodied and oven-fresh. Both made me almost mystically recall what unconditional love (and not just provisional pity) felt like for the first time in months, perhaps even years. I almost started weeping when she held me but I maintained my kool.

So that somewhere in between helping The Anima dress my ex's Christmas tree and slice guests portions of her crab-stuffed turkey, we discussed many serious, meaningful things. These included her profession (ethnobotanical therapist for a major pharmaceutical corporation specializing in genomic medicine), her kooky, superheroic name (bestowed on her by a Jungian-leaning colleague because of their mutual love for Jung and for the hip hop band De La Soul—go figure). We also listened to me softly rant and rave through clenched teeth about the other guests. She was made to hear my ongoing complaint about the unconscienable apathy displayed by niggas today. She cocked an eager ear when I displayed my derision for the ugly state of black male despair and depression in our time. Raised an intrigued eyebrow when I hysterically swept away the happy-Negro contingent in the room with a royally dismissive hand, leaned in close when I argued that clearly there weren't enough black men suffering from "the noonday demon" of depression these days. For damn sure there weren't enough to suit me since "plague proportions" formed my idea of appropriate num-bers."Instead of going down, down, down to the lower depths as we deserve to and need to , we absurdly contrive to 'stay up'. Bringing us exactly what you see here—all the fake frivolity, unenlightened self-interest and delusional, fiddling-Nero levels of denial served up by a bunch of stiff upper-lipped Ubangis who pray the pursuit of profits and consumption will push back all of their real pain, fear and emptiness." "Too much gain, not enough pain," is also something I may have invented on that occasion. The Anima's prompt, even, response to my bitter, splenetic giving of holy hell to my fellow brothermen was to inquire as to whether I prayed, meditated, or practiced any sort of spiritual discipline.

I mumbled some half-sincere, half-baked hogwash about my general belief in "a God but not the devil," throwing out that if I had any patience for that sort of thing it would be "Buddhism, but the kind of Buddhism where you sit in the mountains, turn away from the world for years on end, paint intricate murals and mandalas with colored sand only to sweep them into oblivion upon completion."

She then took it upon herself to ask how would I feel

about joining a counseling group she and some women friends had formed out of their special concern for African-American men like myself. Once upon a time I might have curtly responded with "Oh yeah, and what sort of African-American men are these, these ones I'm supposed to be like?" But I knew exactly what kind of African-American men she meant. Knowing myself to be one of them, I felt no need to be coy. Because at this point I proudly count myself among that small, overly sensitive contingent of Negro men who'd deliberately set themselves further and further adrift and apart from mainstream black America after "The Great Disappearance." For the uninitiated, The Great Disappearance is the bland euphemism commonly used whenever decent people dare bring up that extravagantly genocidal "event." The "event" had been engineered by the one and only Camelot Drexel, the man *Ebony* magazine had once proudly described as our "Black Apollo of Science" before he began playing dice with the African genome. Drexel was many things rolled into one: a billionaire synaptic software designer, an old-fashioned race man supreme, an African supremacist, a nigga with a god complex. He had, one fateful day in August five years ago, made five million African-American men march into the Nevada desert with him and then collectively vanish from the world's collective sight while cameras were rolling. After he disappeared them, I and others of my ilk had decided the only honorable thing to do was to take leave of our senses and climb down the evolutionary ladder of black bourgeois society. We could no longer pretend to be happy little campers.

A VIEW FROM THE BRIDGE

Terry Bisson

The following is a NY.com interview with Liam E. Suzuki, founder and CEO of Extreme Disasters Unltd.

NY.Com: NY.com is here on the bridge of what is surely the most controversial ship in New York Harbor, hoping to have a few words with—

Here he comes now!

Mr. Suzuki, surely you know that a lot of people disapprove of your company's practices and policies, and particularly this latest enterprise.

Suzuki: It's Captain Suzuki, mate. But seriously, you can just call me Liam. And of course I know we're controversial. Extreme sports, adventure travel, risk-taking in general have always been controversial. Ever since the first primate tried to see how far he could crawl out on a limb before it broke. It's a love-hate thing with danger.

NY.Com: But don't you think this is going a little too far?

Suzuki: That's a familiar refrain, too. Look, extreme means extreme. The first BASE jumpers were considered crazy.

Hell, maybe they were. That's what I liked about them, anyway.

NY.Com: BASE jumping? Is that how you got started?

Suzuki: No, I worked up to it. I started back in high school in Orange County. We used to crash cars to set off the air bags. It sort of grew. We figured if you packed enough kids into a Volvo with front and side air bags nobody could get seriously hurt. We were wrong about that, but still, we had fun.

NY.Com: No outdoor sports?

Suzuki: That came later. I got a bungee jump for a graduation present. I started sky diving after that. Did a little knife-edge snowboarding, avalanche racing, stuff like that. Then I met my wife Darlene—she turned me on to BASE jumping. We were part of the crowd that rollerbladed off Century Tower in downtown L.A. last New Year's.

NY.Com: That one had a pretty grim casualty rate.

Suzuki: Well, it was midnight. And the drinking, you know. Which reminds me . . . *[Here Suzuki made a quick cell phone call to make sure the champagne had been loaded onto the ship.]* But we learned from that. We learned that a few fatalities could add to, rather than detract from, an event.

NY.Com: So you went from Adventure to Disaster.

Suzuki: Not right away. It was a process. You might say it began when Darlene and I BASE jumped off a twenty-story housing project just as it was being brought down with explosive charges. That gave us the idea of staying in the building to see if we could survive.

NY.Com: And you did. Survive, I mean.

Suzuki: Pretty much. I lost these two fingers. Darlene lost a leg. We were in the news after that, and people started contacting us. It was a short step to taking groups, packaging the tour as an earthquake-survival experience. We called it Rocking Richter. That led straight into Towering Inferno.

NY.Com: So it became a business.

Suzuki: We weren't incorporated yet but, yes somebody had to handle the permits, the logistics. Darlene and I started hiring staff, mostly thrill hounds like ourselves. Towering Inferno was an awesome money maker. We ran six in the first two years. Booked solid, months in advance.

NY.Com: Thrill hounds, as you call them.

Suzuki: Not strictly. Corporations, too. Corporate accounts were our bread and butter. Enron, Microsoft, WorldCom. They used it for team building. I guess you learn a lot about your coworkers when you are trapped on the top floor of a burning building.

NY.Com: If you make it.

Suzuki: Oh, you mostly make it. In fact, we guaranteed a casualty rate of not less than one or more than five, out of a group of twenty-five.

NY.Com: So what made you decide to go historical?

Suzuki: It was Darlene's idea. She's a sort of a history buff, loves famous disasters. We did the Shackleton Trek (only we lost a couple) and then the Medusa Disaster, based on the ninteenth-century French shipwreck. A hundred naked people adrift on a raft. No food, no water.

NY.Com: That's when Extreme Disasters became controversial.

Suzuki: You're talking about the cannibalism. But you have to understand, controversy draws as many people as it repels. We don't do the Medusa anymore but we do a Donner Pass every winter. We have to turn people away. The Medusa was our only flop.

NY.Com: What about the Hindenburg?

Suzuki: All right, that, too. It's hard to get people on a disaster tour with *no* survivors. But the Hindenburg did push us into aviation. As a matter of fact, our most popular event today is Flight 13.

NY.Com: How can you make that one affordable?

Suzuki: Well, for one thing, you don't need a new plane. We build in a failure but it's always different. Engine, hydraulic, cabin pressure, you name it. Sometimes it's ten minutes into the flight, sometimes an hour or so. The first year we used an off-lease DC-9. Now we use a 747 twice a year, and we're booked at 100-percent capacity.

NY.Com: You don't have to be athletic for that one.

Suzuki: That's right! That's one key to its popularity. Plus since there's a survival rate of almost seventy percent, people can bring kids. It's great for bonding. Say the power goes out at 39,000 feet—it can be a good ten-to-twelve minutes before you ditch. You can get real close to your wife, your kids, and yourself in that time. It's an unforgettable experience. Have you ever tried it?

NY.Com: No. My fiancée tried the Amtrak Experience once.

Suzuki: How'd she do?

NY.Com: Fine. A scar on her chin she likes to show off.

Suzuki: See! That's what we provide—bragging rights. A little excitement. Something for everybody—in this case a controlled derailment on a dirt embankment, with no fire. That keeps fatalities way down. In fact, they say it's safer than regular Amtrak. But that's a whole other story.

NY.Com: How about outdoor disasters? That's more our readers' speed.

Suzuki: They should check out our Andean Avalanche, or

Mexican Mudslide. Those are both very athletic. As a matter of fact, we lost Darlene in last fall's mudslide tour.

NY.Com: Oh, I'm sorry.

Suzuki: That's OK. Darlene died doing what she loved, which was trying to stay alive. We don't allow wheelchairs in that one anymore. So you learn from your mistakes.

NY.Com: You mentioned kids. Does Extreme Disasters have anything for seniors?

Suzuki: You bet. We have two that come with with AARP discounts—the Casino Bus Crash and the Nursing Home Fire. We're working out a deal with Elderhostel for an in-school shooting thing, sort of a geriatric Columbine. And of course we have lots of seniors aboard on this trip.

NY.Com: What about this trip? I have several questions, beginning with the name.

Suzuki: The "Gigantic"? It's an approximation. We couldn't use the original name. Too many permissions problems, what with the movie and all. But people know what it is. We were booked solid the first week we announced the cruise in the catalog.

NY.Com: Is "Gigantic" a one-timer?

Suzuki: We hope to do it every year. We'll see how it goes. It's our most expensive event so far, but look what you get for your money: great food, fine wine, even ballroom dancing—ending in an unforgettable adventure which you have a pretty good chance of surviving.

NY.Com: No steerage passengers? Without steerage, how can it be authentic?

Suzuki: We're not about total authenticity. We're about bringing you the spirit of the thing. We only have 1,800 passengers and crew, but the lifeboat-to-passenger ratio is exactly the same as the original. So it should be quite a scramble, those last few hours.

NY.Com: Any idea how long it will take?

Suzuki: Four to six days tops. We'll steam north for three days, and then start looking for an iceberg. There's the ten-minute whistle right now.

NY.Com: I'd better get ashore.

Suzuki: Care to join us? Always glad to have NY.Com aboard. I'll comp you, as a crew member. You get a uniform and a little revolver—but no life jacket!

NY.Com: It's tempting, but I have a thing about cold water.

Suzuki: I can dig it. Maybe you'll be our guest in Honolulu in December for our first international U.S./Japanese coproduction. Live ammo, and the water will be warmer for sure.

NY.Com: I'll keep it in mind. Good luck, Captain Suzuki; or bad luck, since that's what turns you on, it seems. And thanks for sharing the secrets of Extreme Disasters Unltd. with our readers.

CAUGHT UP IN THE MIX: SOME ADVENTURES IN MARXISM

Marshall Berman

Once a theatregoer buttonholed [Arthur] Miller and put the question to him: "What's he selling? You never say what he's selling." Miller quipped, "Well, himself. That's what's in the valise."
—*John Lahr, "Making Willy Loman"*

Marxism has been part of me for all my life. Late in my fifties, I'm still learning and sorting out how. Until now, I think I've had only one real adventure in Marxism. Still, that one was formidable. It helped me grow up and figure out who I was going to be in the world. And it makes a good story. My father also had a Marxist adventure, one more tragic than mine. It's only by working through his life that I'll be in a position to take hold of my own. Life studies is one of the big things Marxism is for.

My father, Murray Berman, died of a heart attack in 1955, when he was just short of forty-eight, and when I wasn't quite fifteen. He grew up on New York's Lower East Side and in the Bronx, left school at twelve, and was thrown into "the business world"—that's what he and my mother called it—pushing a truck in the garment center to help support his parents and nine kids in one room. He called it "the rack," and often said he was still on it. But the garment center's friendly malevolence felt like home to him, and we would never leave that home.

Over the years, he graduated from outdoor *schlepper* to indoor *schlepper* (I guess it would be called stock clerk today) and then to various clerical and sales jobs. He was on the road a lot before I was born and when I was very young. For several years he worked, as both reporter and an advertising salesman, for *Women's Wear Daily*. All those years are vague to me. But I know that in 1948, he and a friend from the Bronx made a great leap: they founded a magazine. Its theme, announced on the masthead, was "The garment industry meets the world." Its central idea, so he said just before he died, was "SPORTSWEAR WILL CONQUER THE WORLD." My father and his friend Dave had little education and less capital but lots of foresight—the Yiddish word is *sachel*. Globalization in the garment center was an idea whose time was coming, and for two years the magazine thrived, selling ever more advertising space (my father's specialty), which, in capitalist economies is what keeps newspapers and magazines alive.

But then, suddenly, in the spring in 1950, there was no money to meet the payroll, and just as suddenly his friend Dave disappeared. My father took me to the Natural History Museum one Saturday morning; Saturday afternoon, we walked around the Upper East Side, searching for Dave. In his favorite Third Avenue bars, no one had seen him for two days. His doorman said the same but he directed us to Dave's floor and said we would hear his dog barking if he was around. We didn't, and he wasn't, and while my father cursed and worked on a note to slip under his door, I looked into a half-open door in the hall and saw an open elevator shaft. As I looked down, curious, my father grabbed me and threw me against the wall—it was one of the two times he ever touched me violently. We didn't talk much as we took the subway back to the Bronx. The magazine went bankrupt overnight. The next month my father had a heart attack that nearly killed him.

We never saw Dave again, but the police tracked him down. It turned out he had a mistress on Park Avenue, another in Miami, and a gambling addiction. He had emptied the magazine's account, but when they found him there was little left, and nothing for us. My father said the whole story was such a garment center cliché (that was how I learned the meaning of the word *cliché*), he just couldn't believe his friend could do it to him. Several years later, out of the blue, Dave called again, with a new name—another garment center cliché—and a new proposition. I answered the phone, then put my mother on. She said he had ruined my father's life once, and wasn't that enough? Dave urged her to be a good sport.

My father gradually got his strength back, and my parents were now the "Betmar Tag and Label Company." They lived in the garment center's interstices as brokers or jobbers, middlemen between garment manufacturers and label-makers. This company had no capital; its only assets were my father's aptitude for *schmoozing* and my mother's for figuring things out. They knew their position was precarious, but they performed a real function, and they thought they had enough local knowledge to stay afloat. For a few years, it was a living. But in September 1955 my father had another heart attack, and from this one he died.

Who killed him? This question haunted me for years. "It's

the wrong question," my first shrink said fifteen years later. "He had a bad heart. His system wore out." That was true; the army saw it and rejected him for service during World War II. But I couldn't forget his last summer, when all at once he lost several big accounts. The managers and purchasing agents were all his old friends: they had played stickball on Suffolk Street, worked together and dealt with each other for years; these guys had drunk to his health at my *bar mitzvah,* just two years back. Now, all of a sudden, they wouldn't return his calls. He had said he could tell he'd been outbid by somebody; he just wanted a chance to make a bid and to be told what was what. All this was explained to us at the funeral (a big funeral; he was well liked) and during *shiva* week just after. Our accounts, and dozens of others, had been grabbed by a Japanese syndicate, which was doing business both on a scale and in a style new to Seventh Avenue. The syndicate had made spectacular payoffs to its American contacts. (Of course they didn't call them payoffs.) But it had imposed two conditions: it must not be identified, and there must be no counterbidding. We pressed his friends: Why couldn't you tell Daddy—even tell him there was something you couldn't tell him? They all said they hadn't wanted to make him feel bad. Crocodile tears, I thought, yet I could see their tears were real. Much later, I thought that here was one of the first waves of the global market that Dad foresaw and understood. I think he could have lived with that better than he could live with his old friends not calling him back.

My mother carried the company on briefly, but her heart wasn't in it. She folded it and went to work as a bookkeeper. Together, one night in the summer of 1956, near the end of our year of mourning, my mother, my sister and I threw enormous reams of paper from the lost accounts down our incinerator in the Bronx. But my mother held on to the manila folders that they had used for those accounts. ("We can still get plenty of use out of *them*," she said.) Forty years later, I'm still using those folders, containers of long-vanished entities—Puritan Sportswear, Fountain Modes, Girl Talk, Youngland—where are they now? Does it mean that, in some way, I've stayed in my father's business? (Happy Loman, at the very end of *Death of a Salesman*: "I'm staying right in this city, and I'm gonna beat this racket!") What racket? What business? My wife defined the relationship in a way I like: I've gone into my father's *unfinished* business.

"The only thing you got in this world is what you can sell." Another line from *Death of a Salesman*. It was my father's favorite play. My parents saw *Salesman* at least twice on stage, starring Lee J. Cobb, and again in film form starring Fredric March. It became a primary source of material in the endless affectionate and ironic repartee they carried on till he died. I didn't know that till I got to see the movie, just a few months before his death; then all at once the meaning of years of banter became clear. I joined in the crosstalk, tried it at the dinner table, and got all smiles, though the lines were tragic, and were about to become more tragic still. One hot day in the summer of 1955 he came home drained from the garment center and said, "They don't know me any more." I said, "Dad . . . Willy Loman?" He was happy that I knew he was quoting, but he also wanted me to know it was not only a quote but the truth. I got him a beer, which I knew he liked in the summer heat; he hugged me and said it gave him peace to know I was going to be freer than he was, I was going to have a life of my own.

Soon after he died, scholarships and good luck propelled me to Columbia. There I could talk and read and write all night and then walk to the Hudson to see the sun at dawn. I felt like a prospector who had made a strike, discovering sources of fresh energy I never knew I had. And some of my teachers had even told me that living for ideas could be a way for me to make a living! I was happier than I had ever been, steeped in a life that really felt like *my life*. Then I realized this was exactly what my father had wanted for me. For the first time since his death, I started thinking about him. I thought about how he had struggled and lost, and my grief turned to rage. *So they don't know you!* I thought. *Let me at those bastards, I'll get them for you. They don't remember? I'll remind them.* But which bastards? Who were "they"? How could I get them? Where would I start? I made a date with Jacob Taubes, my beloved professor of religion. I said I wanted to talk about my father and Karl Marx.

Jacob and I sat in his office in Butler Library and talked and talked. He said that he sympathized with all radical desire, but revenge was a sterile form of fulfillment. Didn't Nietzsche write the book on that? Hadn't I read it in his class? He said that in the part of Europe where he came from (b. Vienna 1927), the politics of revenge had succeeded far beyond anything Americans could imagine. He told me a joke: "Capitalism is the exploitation of man by man. *Communism is the opposite.*" I had heard that joke before, maybe even from my father; it had gone round many times, for good reasons. But it was a dark joke and it hurt to laugh at it, because what followed seemed to be a total human impasse: the system is intolerable, and so is the only alternative to the system. *Oy!* So what then, I asked, we all put ourselves to sleep? No, no, said Jacob, he didn't mean to immobilize me. In fact, there was this book he had meant to tell me about: Marx wrote it "when he was still a kid, before he became Karl Marx"; it was wild, and I would like it. The Columbia Bookstore ("those fools") didn't have it, but I could get it at Barnes & Noble downtown. The book had "been kept secret for a century"—that was Jacob's primal romance, the secret book, the *Kabbalah*—but now at last it had been released. He said some people thought it offered "an alternative vision of how man should live." Wouldn't that be better than revenge? And I could get there on the subway.

So, one lovely Saturday in November, I took the #1 train downtown, turned south at the Flatiron Building, and headed down Fifth to Barnes & Noble. B&N then was far from its 1990s monopoly incarnation, "Barnes Ignoble," scourge of small bookshops; it was only one store, just off Union Square, and it traced itself back to Abe Lincoln and Walt Whitman and "The Battle Hymn of the Republic." But before I could get there, I passed another place that I had always walked on by: the Four Continents Book Store, official distributor for all Soviet publications. Would my Marx be there? If it really was "really wild," would the USSR be bringing it out? I remembered the Soviet tanks in Budapest, killing kids on the streets. Still, the USSR in 1959 was supposed to be opening up ("the thaw," they called it), and there was a possibility. I had to see.

The Four Continents was like a rainforest inside, walls painted deep green, giant posters of bears, pines, icebergs and icebreakers, shelves stretching back toward a vast horizon, lighting that evoked a tree cover more than a modern room. My first thought was, How can anyone read in this light? (In retrospect, I realize it resembled the lighting in certain 1950s furniture stores and romantic comedies. It was the light scheme in the bachelor flat where the hero brought home Doris Day.) The staff knew just what book I wanted: *Marx's Economic and Philosophical Manuscripts of 1844*, translated by Martin Milligan, and published in 1956 by the Foreign Languages Publishing House in Moscow. It was a collection of three youthful notebooks, divided into short essays. The titles didn't seem to emanate from Marx himself; they appeared to be provided by twentieth-century editors in Moscow or Berlin. It was midnight blue, nice and compact, a perfect fit for a side pocket in a 1950s sports jacket. I opened it at random, here, there, somewhere else—and suddenly I was in a sweat, melting, shedding clothes and tears, flashing hot and cold. I rushed to the front: "I've got to have this book!" The white-haired clerk was calm. "Fifty cents, please." When I expressed amazement, he said, "We"—I guess he meant the USSR—"don't publish books for profit." He said the *Manuscripts* had become one of their bestsellers, though he himself couldn't see why, since Lenin was so much clearer.

Right there my adventure began. I realized I was carrying more than thirty dollars, mostly wages from the college library; it was probably as much as I'd ever carried in my life. I felt another flash. "Fifty cents? So for ten bucks I can get twenty?" The clerk said that, after sales taxes, twenty copies would cost about $11. I ran back to the rear, grabbed the books, and said, "You've just solved my Hanukkah problem." As I *schlepped* the books on the subway up to the Bronx (Four Continents tied them up in a nice parcel), I felt I was walking on air. For the next several days I walked around with a stack of books, thrilled to be giving them away to all the people in my life: my mother and sister, my girlfriend, her parents, several old and new friends, a couple of my teachers, the man from the stationery store, a union leader (the past summer, I'd worked for District 65), a doctor, a rabbi. I'd never given so many gifts before (and never did again). Nobody refused the book, but I got some weird looks from people when I breathlessly delivered my *spiel*. "Take this!" I said, shoving the book in their faces. "It'll knock you out. It's by Karl Marx, but before he became Karl Marx. It'll show you how our whole life's wrong, but it'll make you happy, too. If you don't get it, just call me anytime, and I'll explain it all. Soon everybody will be talking about it, and you'll be the first to know." And I was out the door, to face more puzzled people. I stopped at Jacob's office with my stack of books, told him the story, went through the *spiel*. We beamed at each other. "See, now," he said, "isn't this better than revenge?" I improvised a comeback: "No, it's the best revenge."

I try to imagine myself at that magic moment: *Too much, man! Was I for real?* (Those are things we used to say to each other in 1959.) How did I get to be so sure of myself? (Never again!) My intellectual impulse-buying; my neo-*potlatch* great giveaway of a book I hadn't even properly read; the exuberance with which I pressed myself on all those people; my certainty that I had something special, something that would both rip up their lives and make them happy; my promises of lifetime personal service; above all, my love for my great new product that would change the world: Willy Loman, meet Karl Marx. We entered the Sixties together.

What was it in Marx, all those years ago, that shot me up like a rocket? Not long ago, I went through that old midnight blue Four Continents book. It was a haunting experience, with the Soviet Union dead; but Marx himself moved and lived. The book was hard to read because I'd underlined, circled and asterisked virtually *everything*. But I know the ideas that caught me forty years ago are still part of me today, and it will help this book hold together if I can block out at least some of those ideas in a way that is brief but clear.

The thing I found so striking in Marx's 1844 essays, and which I did not expect to find at all, was his feeling for the individual. Those early essays articulate the conflict between *Bildung* and alienated labor. *Bildung* is the core human value in liberal romanticism. It is a hard word to put in English, but it embraces a family of ideas like "subjectivity," "finding yourself," "growing up," "identity," "self-development," and "becoming who you are." Marx situates this ideal in modern history and gives it a social theory. He identifies with the Enlightenment and with the great revolutions that formed its climax when he asserts the universal right of man to be "freely active," to "affirm himself," to enjoy "spontaneous activity," to pursue "the free development of his physical and mental energy" (74–5). But he also denounces the market society nourished by those revolutions, because "Money is the overturning of all individualities" (105), and because "You must make all that is yours *For Sale* . . ." (96; Marx's emphasis). He shows how modern capitalism arranges work in such a way that the worker is "alienated from his own activity," as well as from other workers and from nature. The worker "mortifies his body and ruins his mind"; he "feels himself only outside his work, and in his work . . . feels outside himself"; he "is at home only when he is not working, and when he is working he is not at home. His labor therefore is not free, but coerced; it is forced labor" (74). Marx salutes the labor unions that, in the 1840s, are just beginning to emerge. But even if the unions achieve their immediate aims—even if workers get widespread union recognition and raise wages by force of class struggle—it will still be "nothing but salary for a slave," unless modern society comes to recognize "the meaning and dignity of work and of the worker" (80). Capitalism is terrible because it promotes human energy, spontaneous feeling, human development, only to crush them, except in the few winners at the very top. From the very start of his career as an intellectual, Marx is a fighter for democracy. But he sees that democracy in itself won't cure the structural misery he sees. So long as work is organized in hierarchies and mechanical routines and oriented to the demands of the world market, most people, even in the freest societies, will still be enslaved—will still be, like my father, on the rack. Marx is part of a great cultural tradition, a comrade of modern masters like Keats, Dickens, George Eliot, Dostoevsky, James Joyce, Franz Kafka, D. H. Lawrence (readers are free to fill in their personal favorites) in his feeling for the suffering modern man on the rack. But Marx is unique in his grasp of what that rack is made of. It's there in all his work. But in the *Communist Manifesto* and *Capital,* you have to look for it. In the *1844 Manuscripts,* it's in your face.

Marx wrote most of these essays in the midst of one of his great adventures, his honeymoon in Paris with Jenny von Westphalen. The year I had my Marxian adventure, I had just fallen in love, first love, and this made me very curious whether he would have anything to say about love and sex. The Marxists I had met through the years seemed to have a collective attitude that didn't exactly hate sex and love, but regarded them with impatience, as if these feelings were to be tolerated as necessary evils, but not one iota of extra time or energy should be wasted on them, and nothing could be more foolish than to think they had human meaning or value in themselves. After I had heard that for years, to hear young Marx in his own voice was a breath of fresh air. "From this relationship, one can judge man's whole level of development" (82). He was saying just what I felt: that sexual love was the most important thing there was.

Hanging around the Left Bank in Paris, Marx seems to have met radicals who promoted sexual promiscuity as an act of liberation from bourgeois constraints. Marx agreed with them that modern love could become a problem if it drove lovers to possess their loved ones as "exclusive private property" (82). And indeed, "Private property has made us so stupid that an object is only *ours* when we have it" (91; Marx's emphasis). But their only alternative to marriage seems to have been an arrangement that made everybody the sexual property of everybody else, and Marx disparaged this as nothing but "universal prostitution."

We don't know who these "crude, mindless communists" were, but Marx's critique of them is fascinating. He uses their sexual grossness as a symbol of everything that he thinks is wrong with the left. Their view of the world "negates the personality of man in every sphere." It entails "the abstract negation of the whole world of culture and civilization"; their idea of happiness is "leveling down proceeding from a preconceived minimum." Moreover, they embody "general *envy* constituting itself as a power" and "the disguise in which *avarice* re-establishes itself and satisfies itself, only in another way." They promote "regression to the unnatural simplicity of the undemanding man who has not only failed to go beyond private property, but has not even yet attained to it" (82–3). Marx is focusing on the human qualities of greed and crudity that makes some liberals despise and fear the left. He would say it is stupid prejudice to think that *all* leftists are like that, but it is right to think that *some* leftists are like that—though not him or anyone close to his heart. Here Marx is not only reaching out to the Tocqueville tradition but trying to envelop it.

When Marx calls the bad communists "thoughtless," he is suggesting not just that their ideas are stupid, but that they are unconscious of what their real motives are; they think they are performing noble actions, but they are really engaged in vindictive, neurotic acting out. Marx's analysis here is stretching toward Nietzsche and Freud. But it also highlights his roots in the Enlightenment: the communism he wants must include *self-awareness*. This nightmare vision of "crude, thoughtless communism" is one of the strongest things in early Marx. Were there real-life models in the Paris of the 1840s? No biographer has come up with convincing candidates; maybe he simply imagined them himself, the way novelists create their characters. But once we have read Marx, it is hard to forget them, these vivid nightmares of all the ways the Left could go wrong.

There is another striking way in which young Marx worries about sex and conceives it as a symbol of something bigger. When workers are alienated from their own activity in their work, their sexual lives become an obsessive form of compensation. They then try to realize themselves through desperate "eating, drinking, procreating," along with "dwelling and dressing up." But desperation makes carnal pleasures less joyful than they could be, because it places more psychic weight on them than they can bear (74).

389

The essay "Private Property and Communism" takes a longer view and strikes a more upbeat note: "The forming of the five senses is a labor of the whole history of the world, down to the present" (89). Maybe the joy of a honeymoon enables Marx to imagine new people coming over the horizon, people less possessive and greedy, more in tune with their sensuality and vitality, inwardly better equipped to make love a vital part of human development.

Who are these "new people" who would have the power at once to represent and to liberate humanity? The answer that made Marx both famous and infamous is proclaimed to the world in the *Manifesto*: "the proletariat, the modern working class" (479). But this answer itself raises overwhelming questions. We can divide them roughly in two, the first line of questions about the membership of the working class, the second about its mission. Who are these guys, heirs and heiresses of all the ages? And, given the extent and depth of their suffering, which Marx describes so well, where are they going to get the positive energy they will need not merely to gain power, but to change the whole world? Marx's 1844 *Manuscripts* don't address the "membership" questions, but he has some fascinating things to say about the mission. He says that even as modern society brutalizes and maims the self, it also brings forth, dialectically, "the rich human being [*der reiche Mensch*] and rich human need" (89).

"The rich human being": Where have we seen him before? Readers of Goethe and Schiller will recognize the imagery of classical German humanism here. But those humanists believed that only a very few men and women could be capable of the inner depth that they could imagine; the vast majority of people, as seen from Weimar and Jena, were consumed by trivialities and had no soul. Marx inherited Goethe's and Schiller's and Humboldt's values, but he fused them with a radical and democratic social philosophy inspired by Rousseau. Rousseau's 1755 *Discourse on the Origins of Inequality* laid out the paradox that even as modern civilization alienates people from themselves, it develops and deepens those alienated selves and gives them the capacity to form a social contract and create a radically new society. A century later, after one great wave of revolutions and just before another, Marx sees modern society in a similarly dialectical way. His idea is that even as bourgeois society enervates and impoverishes its workers, it spiritually enriches and inspires them. "The rich human being" is a man or woman for whom "self-realization [*seine eigne Verwirklichung*] exists as an inner necessity, a need"; he or she is "a human being in need of a totality of human activities" (91). Marx sees bourgeois society as a system that, in an infinite number of ways, stretches workers out on a rack. Here his dialectical imagination starts to work: the very social system that tortures them also teaches and transforms them, so that while they suffer, they also begin to overflow with energy and ideas. Bourgeois society treats its workers as objects, yet develops their subjectivity. Marx has a brief passage on French workers who are just (of course illegally) starting to organize: they come together instrumentally, as a means to economic and political ends; but "as a result of this association, they acquire a new need—the need for society— and what [begins] as a means becomes an end" (99). Workers may not set out to be "rich human beings," and certainly no one else wants them to be, but their development is their fate, it turns their powers of desire into a world-historical force.

"Let me get this straight," my mother said, as she took her book. "It's Marx, but not Communism, right? So what is it?" Marx in 1844 had imagined two very different Communisms. One, which he wanted, was "a genuine resolution of the conflict between man and nature, and between man and man" (84); the other, which he dreaded, "has not only failed to go beyond private property, it hasn't yet attained to it" (83). Our twentieth century had produced a great surplus of the second model, but not much of the first. The problem, in short, has been that the second model, the one Marx dreaded, has had tanks, and the first, the one he dreamed of, has not. My mother and I had seen those tanks on TV in Budapest, killing kids. We agreed, not Communism. But if not that, then what? I felt like a panelist on a TV quiz show, with time running out. I reached for a phrase I had seen in the *New York Times*, in a story about French existentialists—Sartre, de Beauvoir, Henri Lefebvre, André Gorz, and their friends—who were trying to merge their thought with Marxism and create a radical perspective that would transcend the dualisms of the Cold War. I said, "Call it *Marxist humanism*." "Oh!" my mother said, "Marxist humanism, that sounds nice." Zap! My adventure in Marxism had crystallized; in an instant I had focused my identity for the next forty years.

And what happened then? I lived another forty years. I went to Oxford, then Harvard. Then I got a steady job in the public sector, as a teacher of political theory and urbanism at the ever-assailed City University of New York. I've worked mostly in Harlem, but Downtown as well. I've been lucky to grow old as a citizen of New York, and to bring up my kids in the fervid freedom of the city. I was part of the New Left thirty years ago, and I'm part of the Used Left today. (My generation shouldn't be embarrassed by the name. Anyone old enough to know the market's ups and downs knows that used goods often beat new models.) I don't think I've grown old yet, but I've been through plenty, and through it all I've worked to keep Marxist humanism alive.

As the twentieth century comes to an end, Marxist humanism is almost half a century old. It's never swept the country, not in any country, but it has found a place. One way to place it might be to see it as a synthesis of the culture of the Fifties with that of the Sixties: a feeling for complexity, irony and paradox, combined with a desire for breakthrough and ecstasy; a fusion of "Seven Types of Ambiguity" with "We Want the World and We Want It Now." It deserves a place of honor in more recent history, in 1989 and after, in the midst of the changes that their protagonists called the Velvet Revolution.

Mikhail Gorbachev hoped to give it a place in his part of the world. He imagined a Communism that could enlarge personal freedom, not crush it. But he came too late. To people who had lived their lives within the Soviet horizon, the vision didn't scan; they just couldn't see it. The Soviet people had been burned so badly for so long, they didn't know him; he called, and they didn't return his calls. But we can see Gorbachev as a Willy Loman of politics—a failure as a salesman, but a tragic hero.

Some people think Marxist humanism got its whole meaning as an alternative to Stalinism, and that it died with the crumbling of the USSR. My own view is that its real dynamic force is as an alternative to the nihilistic, market-driven capitalism that envelops the whole world today. That means it will have plenty of work to do for a long time to come.

CAUGHT UP IN THE MIX

There is a wonderful image that emerged early in the 1990s—at least that is when I first heard it, at my school, CCNY—from the street life of America's black ghettos, and particularly from today's hip hop music scene, where music becomes itself not by being harmonized, but by being mixed. Here's the image: *caught up in the mix.* "She's all caught up in the mix"; "I got myself caught up in the mix." This image has caught on because it captures so much of so many people's lives. *My father was caught up in the mix. So were the friends who betrayed him.* I think Marx understood better than anybody else how modern life is a mix; how, although there are immense variations in it, deep down it's *one* mix—"the mix"; how we are all caught up in it; and how easy, how normal it is for the mix to go awry. He also showed how, once we grasped the way we were thrown together, we could fight for the power to remix.

Marxist humanism can help people feel at home in history, even a history that hurts them. It can show them how even those who are broken by power can have the power to fight the power; how even survivors of tragedy can make history. It can help people discover themselves as "rich human beings" with "rich human needs" (*MER*, 89–91), and can show them there is more to them than they thought. It can help new generations to imagine new adventures, and arouse their powers of desire to change the world, so that they not only will be part of the mix, they will get to do part of the mixing.

FROM RFK: A MEMOIR

Jack Newfield

R obert Kennedy sat down on the floor, in a corner, to watch television and light up a small victory cigar. He seemed to savor every puff. Writer Budd Schulberg, intense and bearded, came in and began to talk to Kennedy, who wanted Schulberg's ideas for his victory statement.

"Well, of course, you know who won this election for you," Schulberg began.

"You're going to give me that speech about 85 or 90 percent black vote, and the Chicanos' practically 100 percent."

"Bob, you're the only white man in the country they trust."

"Is Cesar Chavez downstairs?" Kennedy asked. "I was hoping he would be on the platform with me." And then Kennedy began to talk to Schulberg about his projects—the Watts Writers' Workshop and the Douglas House Theatre. "I think you've touched a nerve. We need so many new ideas. I had one, about the private sector joining with the public to encourage business enterprise in the ghettos. . . . I have a feeling of what they need, and must have. But we need so many ideas. I've learned a lot since you and I first talked about civil rights. I think that workshop idea of yours is a kind of throwback to the Federal Theatre and Writers Project of the New Deal. We have to encourage not just mechanical skills

395

and jobs in those areas, but creative talent. I saw it in Watts, at the Douglas House—so much talent to be channeled, strong self-expression. I'd like to see it on a national scale, with Federal help, I'll do everything I can. . . ."

At that point Speaker Unruh came over to tell Kennedy it was almost time to go down to the ballroom to claim his comeback triumph.

For a few minutes Kennedy disappeared into the bathroom with Ted Sorensen for a private talk. When he came out it was almost the stroke of midnight. He looked down at Ethel who was stretched out, resting on the bed.

"Ready?" he asked softly, and Ethel bounced up.

"Do you think we should take Freckles down?" Kennedy asked puckishly. "You know McCarthy said I needed a dog and an astronaut to win."

Then they left the suite: the Kennedys, Unruh, Fred Dutton, Rafer Johnson, and Bill Barry, to take the honorable adventure's next step. I started to move toward the elevator with them, and asked Kennedy, "What are you going to do for an encore?"

"Try to talk sense to your sick liberal friends in Manhattan," he replied. There was a crush at the elevator, everyone pushing and shoving, and I fell back. "See you at The Factory," Kennedy waved, disappearing into the overcrowded elevator. With Robert Scheer of *Ramparts*, I went back to room 516 to watch Kennedy's victory statement in comfort, on television, and pour another victory drink.

There were about twenty of us, grouped in a happy semicircle around the television screen as Kennedy, looking out over a jungle of microphones, and flanked by his wife and brother-in-law, began his exuberant victory speech.

"I want to express my high regard to Don Drysdale, who pitched his sixth straight shutout tonight, and I hope that we have as good fortune in our campaign."

And then the list of thank-yous. Jesse Unruh. Steve Smith, "who was ruthless, but has been effective." And to his sisters, Jean and Pat, "and to my mother, and all those other Kennedys.

"I want to express my gratitude to my dog Freckles. . . . I'm not doing this in any order of importance, but I also want to thank my wife Ethel. Her patience during this whole effort was fantastic." The crowd was loving it, and the laughter and cheering mingled into the special sound of celebration. And Kennedy continued in a bantering way to thank people.

"All of the students who worked across the state [cheers]. I want to thank Cesar Chavez [great cheering] who was here a little earlier. And Bert Carona, who also worked with him, and all those Mexican-Americans who were supporters of mine [more cheering]. And Doris Huerta, who is an old friend of mine, and has worked with the union. . . . I want to also thank my friends in the black community [cheers] who made such an effort in this campaign. With such a high percentage voting today, I think it really made a major difference for me. I want to express my appreciation to them.

"To my old friend, if I may, Rafer Johnson, who is here. And to Rosey Grier, who said that he'd take care of anybody who didn't vote for me [laughter]. In a kind way, because that's the way we are [laughter].

"And if I may take just a moment more of your time to express my appreciation to Paul Schrade, from the UAW, who worked so hard . . ."

At that point Carol Welch, Kennedy's campaign secretary, who used to work in the Johnson White House with Bill

Moyers, came over to me and said, "Jack, the Senator is going to leave for The Factory right from his press conference in the Colonial Room. You ought to go down now, so that you don't miss him."

Robert Scheer and I took the elevator down, and pushed our way into the rear of the sweltering Embassy Ballroom as Kennedy was concluding his remarks.

"So I thank all of you who made all this possible. All of the effort that you made, and all of the people whose names I haven't mentioned, but who did all the work at the precinct level, who got out the vote. I was a campaign manager eight years ago. I know what a difference that kind of effort, and that kind of commitment made. I thank all of you.

"Mayor Yorty has just sent me a message that we've been here too long already. So my thanks to all of you, and on to Chicago, and let's win there." And he flashed a V-for-victory sign, and the students in the crowd signaled it right back to him. His hand flicked nervously at his hair, and he turned to leave. The crowd again began to chant, "We want Kennedy. We want Kennedy."

Scheer and I were about to walk over to the Colonial Room for the press conference when something seemed to be happening near the podium. There was an awful sound that rolled across the packed ballroom that was like a moan. Then a few people started running, and a girl in a red party dress, sobbing uncontrollably, came by me, screaming, "No, God, no. It's happened again." And the moan became a wail until the ballroom sounded like a hospital that has been bombed; the sound was somehow the sound of the twice wounded.

Other people were now running and crying, and one of them screamed, "They've shot Steve Smith!" But somehow I knew it was Kennedy, and said it to Scheer. Numbed, I tried to find a television set, and wandered into another ballroom, where the victory celebration for Max Rafferty, who had won the Republican Senate primary, was going on. There were no panic and no tears here. Older people, all of them white, were blowing noisemakers, cheering and dancing. Steve Smith suddenly appeared on the television to ask very calmly for a doctor. Kennedy was clearly shot, but the Rafferty party went right on as if nothing had happened.

I ran back into the hysteria of the Embassy Ballroom. Girls in red and blue campaign ribbons, and RFK plastic boaters, were on their knees praying and weeping. A big Negro was pounding the wall in animal rage, shouting out of control, "Why, God, why? Why again? Why another Kennedy?" A college kid with an RFK peace button was screaming, "Fuck this country, fuck this country!" I found Scheer, and in silence we went back up to the Kennedy suite on the fifth floor.

Upstairs the victory party had turned into a vigil. I walked into Kennedy's bedroom, and Ted Sorensen was sitting on the bed, trying to comfort the wife of John Bartlow Martin. I thought how controlled Sorensen was, but perhaps it wasn't so terrible the second time.

In room 516, the people who had come to share the joy of winning with Robert Kennedy were united in sorrow around the television set, waiting for more details. There was something close to acceptance in many of the dazed faces, as if they all had a fatalistic premonition that he would end this way.

George Plimpton, who had helped capture the assassin, rushed in, his eyeballs the size of marbles, wanting the latest news. How bad was it? Was he still alive?

The television stations began to play and replay the tapes of Kennedy's zestful victory statement, and the longest night began to pass very slowly in the Kennedy suite. Stan Tretick sat on the couch in the corner, hugging his wife. John Lewis sat on the floor, shaking his head, and asking himself, "Why, why, why? Why him?" John Bartlow Martin, his gaunt face the color of chalk, said to no one in particular, "Bomb America. Make the Coca-Cola someplace else."

The phones began to ring, and Scheer and I, to keep our minds busy, began to help Carol Welch answer them. Did we need a surgeon? Could I give blood? One call came from London, another, barely coherent, from Edith Green in Oregon. A McCarthy worker, weeping, promised she would switch to Bobby "if he lives."

Slowly, the time passed. We finished all the liquor, but no one could get drunk. The television showed Frank Mankiewicz outside the Hospital of the Good Samaritan, saying the operation was still going on, longer than anyone thought. A bad omen. A woman moaned in another room, and I began to pace the hall. There were police everywhere now. I went into Kennedy's empty bedroom again, and a local television station was showing the tape of an old speech. Poverty was unacceptable. Starvation in Mississippi and suicides on Indian reservations were unacceptable. I began to cry for the first time. As I wept, two crew-cut employees of the Los Angeles telephone company came into the room and mechanically began to remove the special telephone lines that had been installed for the evening, direct lines to South Dakota and to the ballroom. They worked very professionally, pulling all the wires out of the wall and coiling them around the phones, while Kennedy's image preached, and I twitched to hold back the tears.

At about 5:30 A.M. somebody asked Scheer and me to take a campaign car and pick up Ed Guthman at the hospital. Outside the Ambassador Hotel, on the steps, sat Charles Evers alone, watching the gray sunless dawn come up. He embraced me, and croaked, "God, they kill our leaders and they kill our friends."

The streets were silent and empty until we got to the hospital. There a crowd of about five hundred, mostly press, milled gently behind a police barricade.

Out of the crowd in front of the hospital came a face I hadn't seen for three years, D. Gorton. D. was a poor white boy from Mississippi who had joined the old anarchist SNCC in 1963, and later worked with SDS in Chicago. He had two cameras with him, and it is his picture of Kennedy that appears on the cover of this book, RFK: A Memoir.

"I knew it was against my politics," D. said, "but I loved Bobby Kennedy. The way the Chicanos and blacks trusted him moved me so much that I supported him." I realized D. was talking about Kennedy in the past tense.

Guthman, his strong face a ruin, came out finally, and we began to drive back to the Ambassador in silence, through the now awakening city. After a long while Guthman said, "You know, there were a hundred people in that hotel who would have gladly taken that bullet for Bob."

I went back up to the fifth floor, and saw Fred Dutton sag into his room alone, shut the door, and soon his sobbing filled the hallway. I knew then that Kennedy would not live.

I went back to my room—it was now about 8 A.M.—and fell asleep in a chair with my clothes and the television both on. I woke up two hours later, Mayor Yorty's burlesque comic's face on the screen, saying something about Communists. "You helped kill him, you fuck," I thought, or maybe I said it out loud to myself.

I shaved and showered, and returned to the Embassy Ballroom. Scavengers were there, stealing banners, posters, and hats from the floor as souvenirs. I found Robert Scheer again, and, like drugged men, we went to the exact place in the serving pantry where Robert Kennedy had fallen. There was one red rose now on the dirty floor to mark the spot. On the wall above the rose was a neatly lettered cardboard sign that read "The Once and Future King." A kitchen employee explained to us that the sign had been up there for a few weeks.

Yorty, Disneyland, Nathanael West, Joe Pyne, Sirhan Sirhan. I had to flee Los Angeles. I left at 5 P.M., on a nearly empty TWA flight, with Kennedy still clawing to the edge of life.

The plane took off and quickly the stained city grew smaller, and vanished under a permanent shroud of haze. The flight, I thought, would retrace—West to East—America's geography of assassination. Los Angeles. Dallas. Memphis. New York. Kennedy. Kennedy. King. And Malcolm X. I imagined a bloody, crescent-shaped scar on the face of the land, linking the four killer cities.

I tried to read the Los Angeles papers, filled with sidebar stories about violence in America. Sociologists, politicians, and religious leaders blaming movies, comic strips, and television. No one seemed to think that Vietnam, or poverty, or lynchings, or our genocide against the Indians had anything to do with it. Just popular culture like *Bonnie and Clyde*, never political institutions, or our own tortured history.

I got home about 2 A.M. New York time, and put on the television to see a tape of President Johnson announcing a new commission to study the causes of violence in America. One of the members of the commission, he said, would be Roman Hruska, the Republican Senator from Nebraska who was the major Congressional spokesman for the National Rifle Association. I could imagine Bobby wincing as he heard the absurd news.

I unpacked, and then, with the lights out, I sat in a chair and tried to adjust to the reality of Robert Kennedy dying. Why did it happen? What did it mean? What did I think about violence? My thoughts were not clear: they were not strong enough to support my feelings. I finally wrote down just three words on a lined yellow pad. "He is irreplaceable." A little before 5 A.M. the phone rang, and it was Ronnie Eldridge. "He's gone," she said, her voice cracking. "They're bringing Bobby home tonight. Don't feel sad. Just think how privileged we were to have known him, even if it was so short."

Then I went to sleep, remembering he was only forty-two years old.

At 1 A.M. on Friday, June 7, one thousand people already stood on line along East 51st Street, outside the great Gothic cathedral where Robert Kennedy's body lay. Some Kennedy would have recognized as "my people"—a few shaggy students, a Negro man in a wheelchair, several young Puerto Ricans. Police and television cameras, gawkers and mourners. All casting their shadows. At the fringes were the *Day of the Locust* people, the lost lonely souls whose daily lives are so empty they must associate themselves with a historical event in order to feel alive.

St. Patrick's would open at 5:30 that morning to the glare of television lights over the light mahogany coffin on its black steel frame. But now it was night and William Haddad was in the church with Ronnie Eldridge, improvising an honor vigil around the casket. Haddad beckoned to me and led me and my friends, Tom Hayden, Paul Gorman, and Geoff Cowan, a McCarthy worker in Connecticut, inside past heavy security.

As I waited my turn to stand vigil, I noticed Tom Hayden walk away from us and slump back in the shadows. Sitting alone in an empty pew, tears began to form in his eyes. Tom Hayden, a revolutionary, an apostate Catholic, a green cap from Havana sticking out of his pants pocket, weeping for Robert Kennedy.

I stood between actor Robert Vaughn and radio personality Barry Gray. In that moment I learned again just how much historical space Robert Kennedy occupied. Hayden, the per-sonification of the New Left, was crying somewhere behind me, Barry Gray was holding back his tears and Irish Joe Crangle, the Democratic leader of Erie County, was off mourning alone. Paul Gorman, a McCarthy man, was weeping now too, lighting a candle for Bobby. And me. And the curious, bereft people waiting out on 51st Street all night long. And I thought again of the quotation from Pascal that Camus invokes at the start of *Resistance, Rebellion and Death*: "A man does not show his greatness by being at one extremity, but rather by touching both at once."

I stood there in tears while a priest intoned a prayer in Latin. I stood there where Robert Kennedy's raw hands should be, reaching out for black hands, making a pleading fist to 19,000 roaring students in Kansas, trembling behind a lectern while he says violence and hate are unacceptable.

Now I realized what makes our generation unique, what defines us apart from those who came before the hopeful winter of 1961, and those who came after the murderous spring of 1968. We are the first generation that learned from experience, in our innocent twenties, that things were not really getting better, that we shall *not* overcome. We felt, by the time we reached thirty, that we had already glimpsed the most compassionate leaders our nation could produce, and they had all been assassinated. And from this time forward, things would get worse: our best political leaders were part of memory now, not hope.

The stone was at the bottom of the hill and we were alone.

CONTRIBUTORS

Steve Earle, renowned singer/songwriter/revolutionary/bard and author of *Doghouse Roses,* twice flew in from Nashville just to read at the KGB. Attaway, Stevc!

Marcelle Clements is the author of *The Dog is Us* and *The Improvised Woman,* as well as the novels *Rock Me and Midsummer.* Her always discerning journalism has appeared in many of the best venues including, the *New York Times, Vanity Fair,* and *Rolling Stone.*

Ivan Solotaroff is a journalist and impassioned commentator who has been published in *Esquire, Village Voice, Philadelphia* magazine, and many others. He is the author of *The Last Face You'll Ever See* (i.e. the man who executes you), and a collection of essays, *No Success Like Failure.*

Teddy Atlas, known to sports fans everywhere for his commentary on ESPN's *Friday Night Fights,* is the former trainer of two heavyweight champions, Michael Moorer and Mike Tyson, who was known to actually listen when Teddy talked.

Vanessa Grigoriadis is the always pithy journalist whose work has appeared in a variety of publications including the *New York Times.* She is currently a contributing editor at *New York* magazine.

Michael Taussig, the esteemed professor of anthropology at

Columbia University, is the author of numerous books including *Shamanism, Colonialism, and The Wildman, The Magic of the State*, and *My Cocaine Museum*.

Patrick Symmes is a contributing editor at *Harper's* and *Outside* magazines. His work has been selected for *Best American Travel Writing* and he is the author of *Chasing Che: A Motorcycle Journey in Search of the Guevara Legend*.

Lucius Shepard, famous the world over for such remarkable sci-fi and fantasy collections as *The Jaguar Hunter and The Ends of the Earth*, will publish his long-awaited novel *A Handbook of American Prayer* in the fall of 2004.

Bart Plantenga, novelist, journalist, and worldwide intellectual raconteur, has made a career of knowing about things that others don't, but should. He has contributed to many musical and pop culture journals, including the *American Music Research Center Journal*. He lives in Amsterdam.

Fred Brathwaite aka Fab 5 Freddy, is a fimmaker, writer, and cultural luminary known globally for having been the original host of *Yo! MTV Raps* and producing and starring in hip hop's first feature film, *Wild Style*.

Peter Schjeldahl, noted poet, is the art critic for *The New Yorker*.

Mark Zwonitzer has produced and directed numerous documentary films, including *The Pilgrimmage of Jesse Jackson* and *Joe DiMaggio: A Hero's Life*. His book on the Carter Family,

Will You Miss Me When I'm Gone?, was a finalist for the National Book Critics Circle Award.

Darius James, always a font of the arcane yet indispensable, is the esteemed author *Negrophobia* and *That's Blaxpliotation*. He lives in Berlin, a place which suits his classic expatriate proclivities.

Matthew Shipp, both as a fixture in the David S. Ware Quartet and leading his own numerous groups, has gained recognition as one the truly great jazz piano players working today. He lives on the Lower East Side of Manhattan.

Jon Langford, a great American, especially for a Welshman, is the renaissance man/magick prankster guitarist and song-writer for the great Mekons as well as The Waco Brothers as well as half a dozen other bands. He is also a painter of no small repute who owes me a picture of Tupac Shakur.

Ada Calhoun is a writer and editor living in New York City. Currently a bigwig at Nerve.com, she hopes everyone may someday experience the pleasure of reading a story about vaginal probes to a room full of drunk, famous journalists.

J. Hoberman, son of Queens, NY, and the best American film critic for what seems eons, has somehow maintained his unerring sense of excellence through the screening of a million bad movies. His most recent book is *The Dream Life: Movies, Media, and the Mythology of the Sixties.*

Chris Smith, the never daunted journalistic jack-of-all-trades, never met a story he couldn't make something out of. He is contributing editor at *New York* magazine.

Michael Daly is a columnist for the *New York Daily News*, where his ever incisive hardnosed/big-hearted writing appears twice a week, or more, if something big is happening. He is the author of the novel *Under Ground*.

Steve Fishman's extensive journalistic oeuvre has appeared in *Details*, the *New York Times*, *New York*, and many other venues. His recent *Karaoke Nation—Or, How I Spent a Year in Search of Glamour, Fulfillment, and a Million Dollars* did not quite make him a million dollars, but he vows to keep trying.

Mark Jacobson, editor of the current volume, has been a staff writer at the *Village Voice*, contributing editor at *Esquire*, *New York*, *Rolling Stone*, and *Natural History*. His latest book, written with his daughter Rae Jacobson, is *12,000 Miles in the Nick of Time*.

Daniel Jeffrey Ricciato, a young lit-stud with that lean and hungry Cassius look in his eye, is currently in the employ of the Grove/Atlantic publishing house.

Luc Sante, nonpareil cultural decoder and archivist, is the author of the acclaimed *Low Life*, *The Factory of Facts*, and *Evidence*. He lives in Ulster County, New York.

Bruce Stutz is the former editor in chief of *Natural History* magazine. Someone who actually cares whether Earth continues to spin on its axis, his large-spirited books include

Natural Lives, Modern Times: People and Places of the Delaware River and the forthcoming *Chasing Spring*.

Mike Wallace is the director of the Gotham Center for New York City History. He is the coauthor of *Gotham*, which won the Pulitzer Prize in 1999.

Budd Schulberg, a bona fide national treasure, is the author of, among other books, *What Makes Sammy Run?* His screenplay *On The Waterfront* won an Academy Award. Recently celebrating his ninetieth birthday, Budd still sees, hears, thinks, and throws back vodka tonics better than almost anyone.

Neil de Grasse Tyson is an astrophysicist at the American Museum of Natural History and the director of the Hyden Planetarium. He is the author of *The Sky is Not the Limit, One Universe: At Home in the Cosmos*, and *Just Visiting This Planet*.

Legs McNeil, the original "Resident Punk" of *Punk* magazine, is the author of the best-selling *Please Kill Me*. He continues his assiduous delve into the American nether side with his forthcoming *The Other Hollywood: The Uncensored Oral History of the Porn Film Industry*.

Danny Goldberg, a hero for putting his money where his mouth is, currently serves as chairman of Artemis Records and is the author of *Dispatches From the Culture Wars: How the Left Lost Teen Spirit*.

Douglas Daly is an Amazonian botanist (by profession), hack musician, and natural history writer who spends a lot of time in Brazil and Ireland, which are more similar than you might think.

Ian Williams, always introduced at KGB as "the dean of UN correspondents," covers that august body for *The Nation*. A veritable writing machine in the best British tradition, he is most currently the author of *Deserter: Bush's War on Military Families, Veterans, and His Past*.

Greg Tate has long been a long-time staff writer for the *Village Voice*, where many of his classic "Ironman" pieces appeared. He has a night job as the leader/composer of the Burnt Sugar Orchestra, a persona that seamlessly merges the Atom Dog with Toscanini.

Terry Bisson, the original cofounder of the KGB nonfiction series, is the author of several books including *The Pickup Artist* and *On a Move: The Story of Mumia Abu-Jamal*, as well as being a prince of a man.

Marshall Berman is Distinguished Professor at CUNY/Council, is working on *One Hundred Years of Spectacle: Metamorphoses of Times Square*.

Jack Newfield, whose famous motto, "an eye and an ear for an eye" has long been the guiding spirit of his groundbreaking, muckraking career, is the author of nine books including *RFK: A Memoir* and *The Full Rudy*. He won an Emmy Award for his documentary on arch-scalawag Don King.

PERMISSIONS

413